# Connected Health

## Improving Care, Safety, and Efficiency with Wearables and IoT Solution

# Connected Health

## Improving Care, Safety, and Efficiency with Wearables and IoT Solution

Rick Krohn, MA, MAS
David Metcalf, PhD
Patricia Salber, MD

CRC Press
Taylor & Francis Group
Boca Raton  London  New York

CRC Press is an imprint of the
Taylor & Francis Group, an **informa** business

A PRODUCTIVITY PRESS BOOK

CRC Press
Taylor & Francis Group
6000 Broken Sound Parkway NW, Suite 300
Boca Raton, FL 33487-2742

**Visit the Taylor & Francis Web site at**
**http://www.taylorandfrancis.com**

**and the CRC Press Web site at**
**http://www.crcpress.com**

# Contents

# Welcome

**Movie 1: Welcome to Connected Health**
https://vimeo.com/156566151

So why the title "Connected Health"? We really wanted to play off the idea of not just mHealth, as we've written about in several past books, but also the idea of eHealth and the whole digitization and series of tools that are available.

Of course, from our subtitle, you would know that this is particularly inclusive of wearable technology, but not entirely exclusive. Part of what we wanted to do is to look at how this is pervading every aspect of what we traditionally think about mHealth care with, of course, hospitals, clinics, and practices, but also a broader position in a home office community, or city, or regional level with wellness prevention as well as healthcare.

The idea of innovations and the Internet of Things being pervasive throughout all these environments for the benefit of health, is where we get the idea of Connected Health. We felt that Connected Health encompassed this broad focus while tying into wearables and the Internet of Things for health in a meaningful way. We hope you agree and we will see this theme carried out throughout the chapters, thought pieces, and case studies that make up the sections of this book.

Connected Health: Improving Care, Safety, and Efficiency with Wearables and IoT explores the current state and future prospects for wearables as tools of healthcare management, the role of wearable technology in the growth of the "healthcare citizen", the intersection of wearables and the IoT, and the wellspring of technology innovation that is not only disrupting traditional medicine – it's replacing it.

To conduct this examination of Wearables and the IoT, co-editors Rick Krohn, David Metcalf and Dr. Patricia Salber have identified several key areas of discussion beginning in Part One with an assessment of the wearables market, followed by key issues and best practices for wearable market adoption. The discussion further provides to the reader a solid understanding of the wearables market, in terms of form and function, applications in the consumer and clinical environments, customer bases, and the issues that will define market maturity. In these chapters and throughout the eBook, we have inserted cases drawn from a panel of thought leaders, mHealth executives, clinicians and mHealth entrepreneurs. Each case compliments the preceding topical content with real world evidence.

In Part Two, the discussion shifts to an examination of the Internet of Things (IoT) – what it is, how it can be leveraged in healthcare, and how knowledge gained via Wearable technologies are being integrated into consumer, provider and enterprise systems via IoT and Machine2Machine (M2M) architectures. We also take a closer look at two of the IoT in healthcare's rising stars—Big Data and analytics.

In the final content chapter of Connected Health: Improving Care, Safety, and Efficiency with Wearables and IoT , we look ahead at the rapidly evolving Wearables market including a focused examination of implantable technologies.

We close our discussion with a video roundtable discussion of Wearables featuring a world class panel of experts including Daniel Kraft of the Aspen Institute, Robert Wachter, M.D., Dept. of medicine, UCSF, and Eric Topol, Professor of Genomics at The Scripps Research Institute.

With perspectives from the editors, contributors and leading digital health luminaries, and with evidence-based use cases, in the following pages we will peer ahead at "always there, always on" healthcare. We invite our readers to share their stories of wearable and IoT success as we embark on our journey into connected health and the era of the Internet of Things.

— *Rick Krohn, David Metcalf, Patricia Salber*

Go Mobile! Go Healthy!

# Rick Krohn, MA, MAS

An expert in corporate strategy and strategic marketing, business development, corporate communications, technology development and commercialization. Since 1998, Rick Krohn has served as President of HealthSense, an IT and digital transformation consultancy serving the healthcare, telecom and education industries. His prior industry experience was gained in the health plan, hospital, physician practice and vendor spaces. He has published over 100 articles on a wide range of health care subjects and written three mHealth texts published by HIMSS. In addition to writing, Rick is a frequent speaker at national health care conferences sponsored by VHA, Premier, AMGA, ACHE, MGMA, HIMSS, mHIMSS, CTIA, AIC and others about strategic, business, technology, and operations issues. Rick has earned degrees from Towson University, American University and Johns Hopkins University. Further information about Rick can be found at www.healthsen.com.

# David Metcalf, PhD

As a research faculty member, Dr. Metcalf is responsible for inspiring innovation in the field of learning, performance and well-being. Dr. Metcalf brings partnerships and existing research and development relationships to the world-class Institute. Dr. Metcalf provides advisory services and develops new innovations in mobile technology for healthcare and other industries. The Mixed Emerging Technology Integration Lab that he leads has provided strategy and solutions for Johnson & Johnson, Google, Microsoft, Tufts, Univ of Miami, US Army, Joint Forces among others. He is a frequent author and presenter in the learning and healthcare fields. Notable works include mLearning (2006) and mHealth (2012).

# Patricia Salber, MD

Patricia Salber MD, MBA is a physician executive and serial entrepreneur. Her company, The Doctor Weighs In, is a multimedia company with the mission of helping healthcare innovators tell their stories to the world. She uses video, radio, social media, and her very popular blog, The Doctor Weighs In, to reach a global audience of hundreds of thousands of people with her stories.

In the past, Dr. Salber has worked in almost every aspect of healthcare starting as a double-boarded Emergency Physician at Kaiser Permanente, years as a physicians Executive for Kaiser's corporate headquarters, and various leadership roles with employers, such as GM and health plans, such as Blue Shield of California.

She serves as an advisor to a number of early stage companies and not-for-profit organizations. She was the founder and President of Physicians for a Violence-free Society.

She has published widely in both peer-reviewed journals, trade press, and popular press. Her book, The Physicians Guide to Violence Prevention was the first book for physicians on the topic.

For fun, she likes to hike and travel the world. Her most recent trip was to Madagascar to cavort with the lemurs.

# Part One:

# Wearables for

# Healthcare

# Chapter 1

# Wearables and the IoT for Healthcare

# Introduction

As an industry, healthcare is notoriously resistant to change, and in the realm of clinical information, this limitation is felt most acutely. Traditionally, enterprise information has been sequestered in silos, and distributed among a carefully controlled circle of stakeholders. This failure to leverage the power of shared information has had consequences that can be directly traced to excess cost and uneven quality. It's been the Achilles heel of the industry - but today real foundational change is taking place in the application of healthcare information. It's a vast, sweeping tide of innovation – medical product and clinical process innovation, finance and delivery model innovation, and stakeholder participation innovation – all based on information liquidity.

There are seminal moments in the evolution of healthcare – think the invention of the stethoscope, the discovery of penicillin, cracking the genetic code. We're in such a moment today, and the organizing principle of this current wave is data driven, digital transformation. Through technology, healthcare information is becoming more granular, more liquid, more relevant, and is being employed with greater efficiency and effectiveness.

We're entering the third wave of digital healthcare. The First wave, dating back to the mid 90's, was about the Internet and connectivity. The Second, more recent wave of the 00's has been dominated by mobility. And the Third wave, currently underway, is about personalizing healthcare. It's about trends like the quantified self and the increasing awareness of the consumer that they are the stewards of their own health.

It's also about software, mobile platforms and the power of data to not only intervene earlier but to intuit health issues before they occur. For providers, it's about employing technology solutions to close the gaps in care delivery,  about extracting greater value from data, and delivering real results against healthcare's triple aim — improving the experience of care, improving the health of populations, and reducing per capita costs of health care.

# Evolution of Healthcare
New technologies support real-time, continuous, self-care/monitoring

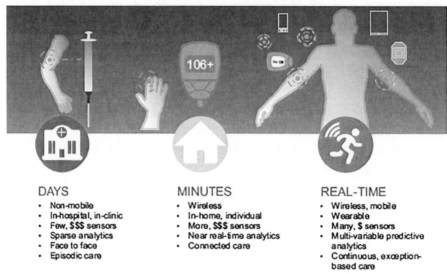

| DAYS | MINUTES | REAL-TIME |
|---|---|---|
| • Non-mobile | • Wireless | • Wireless, mobile |
| • In-hospital, in-clinic | • In-home, individual | • Wearable |
| • Few, $$$ sensors | • More, $$$ sensors | • Many, $ sensors |
| • Sparse analytics | • Near real-time analytics | • Multi-variable predictive |
| • Face to face | • Connected care | analytics |
| • Episodic care | | • Continuous, exception-based care |

*Illustration Based on Source: Tectonic Shifts in Healthcare, James R. Mault MD, FACS, VP & Chief Medical Officer QUALCOMM*

Wearable and nearable technologies are integral to this third wave of digital medicine. Wearables – the Wristbands, monitors, and an ever widening assortment of purpose built wearable devices like the smart contact lens and the smart bra (no, not a misprint…), are recalibrating where and how healthcare occurs. They remove the complexities and inefficiencies of facility based care and replace traditional, hidebound delivery processes and venues with on-demand, self-directed diagnostics and personalized therapeutics. And nearables – small, wireless devices equipped with sensors that work as transmitters of data – are incubating healthcare's Internet of Things.

Communicative biomedical sensors/biosensors and wearable integrated systems are major disruptors to traditional care. And at the cutting edge of these sensor technologies are implantables. These devices – often micro devices – are going to change our relationship with technology. With the introduction of implantables, we're traversing a path from isolated content to connected experiences ranging from patient wellness to diagnosis, monitoring and adherence. Persistent, intuitive, and invisible, these devices are personal health coaches, diagnostic monitors and treatment managers. They mitigate the human element that is at the heart of noncompliance (which according to the CDC costs the U.S. $300 Billion annually), and they integrate with mobile devices and provider systems, delivering ever-granular insights into our daily health. They promote a collaborative provider-patient dialogue and preempt expensive, invasive treatments. Implantables are being developed to address a host of health conditions - Smart pills that monitor and wirelessly transmit biomedical data to providers and alerts patients to take their meds, a dime-sized chip that allows your doctor to continually monitor your vitals, a "bionic eye" that allows the blind to see, a cardioverter-defibrillator that treats sudden heart attacks, "hearables" - the list keeps growing. The promise of implantables is this: healthcare technology will become increasingly commoditized, connected, minimally invasive, and creates new treatments, changes behaviors, and introduces an immersive provider-patient relationship.

Collectively, wearables, nearables and implantables are sourcing a quantum leap forward in healthcare's personalization and efficiency. New research indicates that digital health solutions will save the American healthcare system more than $100 billion over the next four years, and FDA-approved health solutions (33 in 2014, over 100 by 2018) are changing the patient-provider dynamic, raising consumer awareness, accountability, and engagement.

Wearables represent a huge proportion of that growth. According to an IDC report, consumers and businesses will buy nearly 112 million wearable computer devices by 2018, a 78.4% growth rate from 2014's predicted sales of about 19 million units – and most of these gadgets fall in the realm of health-related devices. [ http://www.fool.com/investing/general/2014/07/09/who-stands-to-benefit-when-healthcarewearables-ar.aspx?source=iaasitlnk0000003]

But is this upsurge in wearable adoption really new? Many people have been living with pacemakers, cochlear implants, implanted biochips, and other medical devices for many years.  What's new is a consumer trend that allows healthy individuals to take personal responsibility for their health coupled with more powerful, cheaper devices. Wearable technologies provide new insights into the lives of their users. They activate consumer self-awareness, and promote "actionable" conversations with a care circle – providers, family and friends. And now wearable technologies are growing beyond personal wellness to become more clinically focused – for chronic disease monitoring and for data integration with enterprise systems.

There is also a subtle but influential human factor in play: the culture of healthcare delivery is changing as providers and patients become comfortable with personalized devices, with an electronic dialogue and

**Movie 2: Has the IoT and wearables changed the way you do your work?**
**by Eric Topol**
https://vimeo.com/156567446

with the efficiency and convenience of virtual medicine in an already stretched industry. But this cultural shift is not principally defined by access - wearables provide a foundation for "always on, all about me" stakeholder partnerships that promote accountable, preventive care. Collectively, these trends are reordering the structure of the provider-patient relationship and increasingly positioning the consumer as their primary health manager.

Whether worn on the wrist, head, foot, or body as a garment, or inside the body, wearable devices are being designed in every conceivable form factor, with convenience and utility in mind. Using sensors to measure various aspects of a patient's health, wearable devices now offer richer, actionable data that extend beyond body diagnostics – they now can educate, alert and anticipate health issues. But wearables are not strictly a product play – these technologies are increasingly being integrated within a larger catalogue of mobile and Cloud platforms; enterprise systems, clinical workflows and consumer health solutions. With guidance from NIST, FDA and others we're seeing an increase in device integration with the EHR, PHR, office systems and patient portals. Its' here that wearables meet the Internet of Things ("IoT"). Apps that capture and interpret data, integrated enterprise and cloud data repositories, and the networks of these devices form the underlayment of Healthcare's IoT. Enterprise systems offer some –

but not enough information about a patient's health indications, and certainly not persistently. This is where wearables and the IoT fill a huge gap in care. Wearable technologies offer a huge opportunity to deliver actionable insights at the point of care, to monitor and intervene in patient health issues in real time, to circumvent the lack of interoperability imbedded into vendor systems, to improve diagnostic accuracy and promote patient engagement. Via the IoT, data generated from wearables can be streamed seamlessly to provider and enterprise systems and the Cloud, to paint a more complete picture of the patient's condition, and prompt intervention. The Cloud is a key component of the IoT: it introduces a common platform to store and retrieve information and to network devices and systems; it is endlessly scalable; and it reduces – greatly reduces the barriers to entry for smaller enterprises.

To date, the wearable space has been a largely retail market, fueled by fitness and health related devices. But that market dynamic is changing, as new products appear and new payers enter. Gartner predicts that by 2018 through 2020, 25% of fitness monitors will be sold through non-retail channels—including gyms, wellness providers, insurance companies, employers, and weight loss clinics—at subsidized or no cost. http://www.informationweek.com/ healthcare/mobile-and-wireless/wearables-carve-new-path-tohealth-in-2015/d/d-id/1318279

But beyond the fitness crowd, there is a shift in healthcare spending underway, revealing some interesting demographic trends. Millennials are becoming health "hackers" and fueling wearable diversification due partly to their skepticism about traditional medicine and their bias towards wellness. Seniors are becoming more activated in managing their health issues, and find wearable devices comfortable, convenient, affordable and effective. The increasing sophistication of wearable devices – sensors, trackers, monitors, and now implantables, are drawing a widening customer base– including the chronically ill, the caregiver and the aging in place among others.

Payers are also entering the fray. A shift to value-based reimbursement and incentives are creating a fertile ground for adoption of new business models and clinical approaches incorporating wearable solutions. In the thrust towards value based care and risk based contracting models like the Provider Sponsored Plan, Payers are beginning to covver member costs for wearable technologies if they are deemed medically necessary. The payback? Patient accountability, patient engagement, and patient (member) satisfaction) – and lest we forget, huge cost savings. Doctors will uncover new methods for the diagnosis and treatment of their patients, which will likely impact doctors' relationships with the insurance companies who can accommodate wearables as well.

FDA-approved devices have already started to disrupt the traditional provider-patient dynamic, introducing shared accountability, earlier intervention, and better outcomes. In 2014, web-enabled medical devices increased treatment adherence and behavior modifications, while simultaneously decreasing urgent episodic medical care and costs totaling $6 billion. We've just scratched the surface of industry potential for the IoT and wearables.

— Rick Krohn

# Chapter 2
---
# Types of Wearables

**Movie 3: Types of Wearables by Aenor Sawyer**
https://vimeo.com/156568010

# Editor's Note

Whether worn on the wrist, head, foot, or body as a garment, wearable devices are being designed in every conceivable form factor, with convenience and utility in mind. Some of them are even beginning to be devised for use inside the body. Using sensors to measure various aspects of a patient's health, wearable devices now offer richer, actionable data that extend beyond body diagnostics – they now can educate, alert and anticipate health issues. Sensors and data links offer possibilities for monitoring a patient's behavior and symptoms in real time and at relatively low cost, allowing physicians to better diagnose disease and prescribe tailored treatment regimens. Patients with chronic illnesses, for example, have been outfitted with sensors so that their conditions can be monitored continuously as they go about their daily activities. Sensor enabled patients can now be monitored remotely and continuously, giving practitioners early warning of conditions that would otherwise lead to unplanned hospitalizations and expensive emergency care. The potential for clinical efficiencies and cost savings are enormous - better management of chronic conditions could reduce hospitalization and treatment costs by a billion dollars annually in the United States.

Wearable health care technology divides into three separate groups:

- Complex accessories (currently the most popular category) operate semi-independently but need a smartphone, tablet, or computer for full functionality. These include Fitbit, Jawbone UP, Nike+ FuelBand.

- Smart accessories are consumer health care products that can work with third-party apps. IDC predicts that this will be the leading category of health care wearables within five years.

- Smart wearables, such as Samsung smartwatches and Google Glass, which operate independently (requiring only an Internet connection) and use third-party health-related apps.

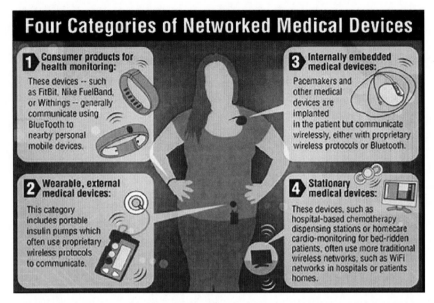

**Four Categories of Networked Medical Devices**

**1** Consumer products for health monitoring:

These devices -- such as FitBit, Nike FuelBand, or Withings -- generally communicate using BlueTooth to nearby personal mobile devices.

**2** Wearable, external medical devices:

This category includes portable insulin pumps which often use proprietary wireless protocols to communicate.

**3** Internally embedded medical devices:

Pacemakers and other medical devices are implanted in the patient but communicate wirelessly, either with proprietary wireless protocols or Bluetooth.

**4** Stationary medical devices:

These devices, such as hospital-based chemotherapy dispensing stations or homecare cardio-monitoring for bed-ridden patients, often use more traditional wireless networks, such as WiFi networks in hospitals or patients homes.

From the outset, consumer wearables have been the engine of growth for this market, and the catalogue of personal fitness and wellness wearables has reached the saturation point. As shown below, there are personal monitors and coaches to address an ever more granular range of health concerns – and the good news for the consumer is that many of these capabilities are being packaged within a single wearable device, at declining price points.

In the clinical setting, the most popular devices are currently heart monitors, but other devices perform a wide range of medical, health, and fitness functions. Some devices monitor sleep or pain so that a doctor can recognize patterns in a patient's health and wellbeing.

Others track data for fitness regimens that both consumers and doctors can use to dictate how the wearer's exercise routines progress. In essence, wearable technology allows doctors to monitor their patients outside of the office while they go about their daily routines. The list keeps growing.

— Rick Krohn

Wearable Activity Devices

Activity Apps

Sleep Apps & Devices

Mood Apps

Food & Calorie Apps

Heart Health Apps & Devices

Connected Scales

Healthy Habit Apps

# Exploring Brain Health: The Inevitable Rise of Brain  Wearables

— TARA SHELTON
  RESEARCH ANALYST, FROST & SULLIVAN

The idea of "brain health" has become popular in recent years as an increasing number of products and services have begun targeting this market. Brain health is loosely categorized as anything that affects thinking, feeling, playing, working, sleeping and remembering. Actions that have been shown to improve brain health include being physically active, eating healthy, being social and challenging personal cognitive abilities. Technologies that address the cognitive aspect include computer and smart phone applications like Lumosity, a company that classifies itself as a "brain training" program. These programs suggest that they help users increase cognitive abilities by playing games that have been developed to stimulate and measure user performance.

Frost & Sullivan has categorized the devices in this market space into two broad segments: brain wearables and brain implants (Figure 1). Brain wearables can be put on and around the head to measure and interpret an individual's Electroencephalogram (EEG) waves. Brain implants are devices placed in or around the head to stimulate or record brain activity.

**FIGURE 1 Market Segmentation. Neural Interface Technologies**

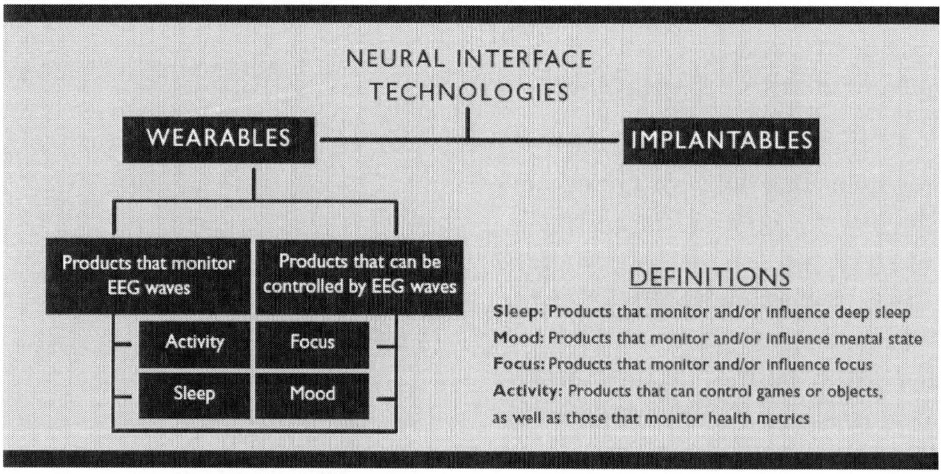

Overall, medical devices that are currently on or coming to the market in the near future are innovative and expanding the current diagnostic paradigm to include brain monitoring.

The brain wearable industry is diverse as various companies can utilize this technology for unique and customizable products. Within this market, one cannot ignore the large video game or "gamer" population. This group can utilize the EEG sensors to alter a game's color, landscape, characters and objects by receiving feedback on the user's mood or activity. On the opposite side of the spectrum, the fashion industry has taken interest with a European designer creating a unique dress fabric that can change colors depending on feedback received on the user's emotions. While these industries are commercial, the segment with the most to gain from this technology is the healthcare industry, wherein preventative healthcare and wellness is taking center stage.

# Healthcare Opportunities

Overburdened with rising costs and a growing aging population, consumers are looking toward new technologies to assist in patient monitoring and care (Figure 2). There are brain wearable products currently on the market that promote the improvement of relaxation and focus with the monitoring of EEG waves.

**FIGURE 2 Brain Wearables Market Opportunity**

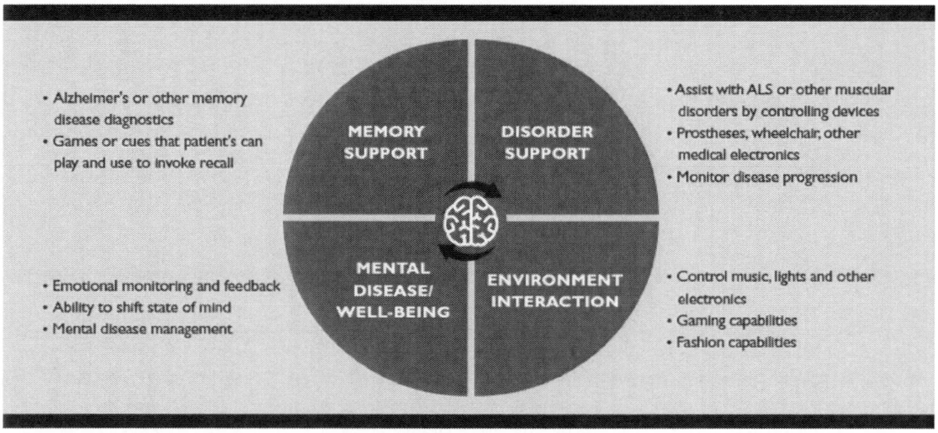

This information can help consumers monitor their environment to better understand their personal mental state and offer them a broader picture of their mental health. Companies hope that with this information, individuals can address their needs of increased focus or clarity by learning when and what they need to relax. Sleep and the crucial REM cycle can also be measured with brain wearables and in greater detail when compared to traditional bracelet wearables. Other companies have found that by monitoring overall EEG characteristics, it is possible to establish a baseline of personal brain health. With this information, health professionals could be able to learn more about cognitive function and eventual decline. Devices that could monitor disease progression or provide other diagnostic measurements could be highly sought after in the medical field. One of the more futuristic areas of brain wearables is the ability to control and move objects based on EEG waves. This could be a great support to the medical device industry as wheelchairs, prostheses and other products could be controlled by thought.

## Areas of Benefit

The benefits of this burgeoning technology include increased awareness and the ability to analyze an individual's personal brain health with the help of EEG waves.

**FIGURE 3 Brain Wearables Products by Use Case**

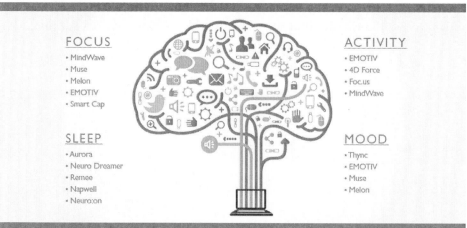

Physicians are not currently promoting these brain wearables as a performance measurement tool, but that could change in the future as providers incorporate more wearable devices into their practice. While physician promotion is ideal for any wearable, the majority of this market is dominated by online sales from company websites. This includes personal purchases as well as the licensing of EEG monitoring technologies to research institutions. Researchers and large corporations are utilizing

EEG technology to complete studies on disease monitoring, management and analytical data points. Brain wearables are portable, user-friendly devices that allow anyone to monitor and track their own progress within the comfort of their home and, more importantly, without medical supervision. Whether it is researchers performing studies or users monitoring their cognitive health, the brain wearable market is continuing to grow.

# Vendor Environment

While the brain wearable market has been around for more than five years, it is finally picking up steam as users become more comfortable with integrating smart devices into all aspects of their lives. The remaining question on investors' minds is if consumers will want to wear devices around their head in public. While Google Glass received initial backlash and clever nicknames for its users, the clamor has briefly receded as physicians and professionals have found this technology useful. The benefit of brain wearables in their ability to track alertness, encourage relaxation or perhaps improve focus could far outweigh the social stigmata associated with current devices. It should be noted that there are few, if any, studies that look at the long-term health risks associated with wearables that are placed around the head. Whether they are different from traditional Bluetooth earpieces that have been around for more than 10 years is not mentioned, but it is important to note nonetheless. While the research community plays catch-up to this late-blooming industry, companies are continuing to expand the market with next-generation products that are more creative, sleek and affordable (Figure 4). The opportunities for brain wearables are infinite as we have yet to scratch the surface of the human brain and its limitless capabilities.

**FIGURE 4** Vendor and Product List

| VENDOR | PRODUCT | WEBSITE |
|---|---|---|
| Wearable Technologies Group | 4D Force | http://4dforce.com/ |
| iWinks LLC | Aurora | https://iwinks.org/ |
| Emotive Inc | EMOTIV | http://emotiv.com/ |
| Focus Labs | Foc.us | http://www.foc.us/ |
| Melon | Melon | http://www.thinkmelon.com/ |
| NeuroSky | MindWave | http://neurosky.com/products-markets/eeg-biosensors/hardware/ |
| Interaxon | Muse | http://www.choosemuse.com/ |
| Napwell | Napwell | http://napwell.com/ |
| Intelclinic LLC | Neuro:on | https://neuroon.com/ |
| Cornfield Electronics, Inc | Neuro Dreamer | http://www.neurodreamer.com/ |
| EdanSafe Pty Ltd | SmartCap | http://smartcap.com.au/smartcap-overview/ |
| Thync | Thync | http://www.thync.com/ |

*This list is not exhaustive

# *Case Study:* Precise RTLS in Healthcare Can Yield New Understanding and Unexpected Benefits

— WILLIAM D. KEARNS, PHD

In 2010 Traumatic Brain Injury (TBI) accounted for 2.5M emergency room visits, hospitalizations or deaths1. It can result from a fall in the shower, a sports injury, an automobile accident, or from a battlefield injury from an improvised explosive device or IED. Charting recovery of function in TBI can be very challenging because the injuries can be very specific to a single area of the brain (as the result of a glancing gunshot wound), or very diffuse (as in the case of an injury from an explosive). In a recent publication in the Journal of Head Trauma Rehabilitation2 , we report successful use of a Ubisense Real-Time Location System (RTLS) to track the functional recovery of veterans who had suffered a TBI. We used the location data generated by veterans to study how they moved about in a rehabilitation facility over durations of as long as one-year.

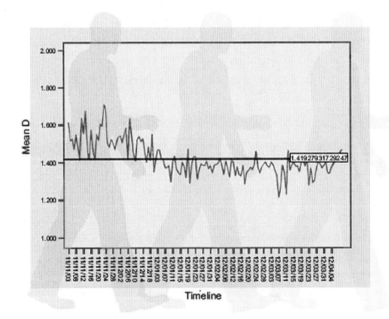

We found that the straightness of the paths they walked was directly related to their clinical prognosis. Those veterans with very erratic walking patterns (High Mean Fractal D) did more poorly than those whose patterns became more normal during their residential treatment. Below is an example of a veteran who's walking became less erratic over time and who had a better prognosis. (Higher D is more erratic)

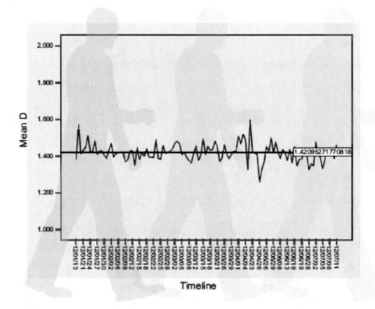

**Lesson learned:** High precision real-time location systems can produce unexpected benefits for health care when the data is subjected to nnovative analytical procedures. These low hanging fruit can inform and change clinical practice thereby improving health outcomes for persons suffering traumatic brain injury.

# References

1.   Centers for Disease Control and Prevention. Traumatic Brain Injury in the United States: Fact Sheet [Internet]. CDC.gov.Atlanta (GA): CDC; [updated 2015 Jan 12].Available from: http://www.cdc.gov/traumaticbraininjury/get_the_facts.html
2.   Kearns, W., Scott, S., Jozard, J.L., Dillahunt-Aspillaga, C. & Jasiewicz, J. Decreased movement path tortuosity is associated with improved functional status in patients with traumatic brain injury. Journal of Head Trauma Rehabilitation. (In press) 2.3

# *Case Study*: **Smart Rehabilitation for the 21st century**

— THE TAMPA SMART HOME FOR VETERANS WITH TBI

"Using an ultra-wide band wireless tracking system, the James A. Haley Veterans Hospital's Polytrauma Transitional Rehabilitation Program Smart Home enhances patient safety while providing a cognitive prosthetic. The system provides: an interactive facility map; a check-in/check-out kiosk; a scheduling and medication management system; and a behavior tracking application that supports timely prompting for necessary activities." Steven Scott O.D., Chief, Physical Medicine and Rehabilitation and Director, Patient Transitional Residential Program, J.A. Haley Medical Center, Tampa, Florida.

The James A. Haley Veterans Hospital Polytrauma Transitional Rehabilitation Program (PTRP) Smart Home facility in Tampa, Florida addresses 1) patient safety and 2) inconsistent timing and repetition of prompts intended to overcome TBI-related cognitive deficits. Smart homes pervasively support cognitive rehabilitation of patients with traumatic brain injury (TBI)[1]. At the core of the Tampa PTRP Smart Home is a tracking system that locates a patient within 15cm and permits customized medication prompts and appointments to be presented through interactive multimedia wall displays. A customized smart watch generates vibratory, visual and auditory prompting signals based on inferred behaviors, identity, place and time[2] and may be used in conjunction with wall-mounted displays. The location data also provides a continuous estimate of fall risk derived from everyday ambulation related to walking during the course of treatment in the PTRP as well as in assisted living facilities.

TBI resulting from polytrauma is the most serious and common injury. The variable emotional, cognitive and behavioral consequences of TBI determine rehabilitation strategy. The smart house sensor technology monitors a person's behavior sequences, and applies decision rules to detect crucial but omitted behavior sequences, then prompts the resumption of the behavior at the point where it ended. The Smart Home enhances overall safety and help patients reacquire behaviors lost due to TBI; the three implemented applications include location assistance, scheduled reminders, and interactive prompts.

The Smart Home provides PTRP staff the means locate patients to enhance overall safety by reducing unattended exiting or AWOL. The Smart Home employs two touch screens in the lobby; one for Checking-in Checking-out (CICO) of the facility and the other to prompt the Veteran if they attempt departure at the exit door without logging out via the CICO console. CICO requires the patient to select a destination from a menu and indicate their estimated return time. A Veteran forgetting to check out (or check in upon returning) is reminded to do so.

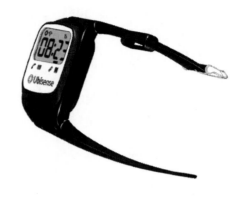

The precise therapeutic information potentially available to the recovering Veteran is a powerful feature of the Tampa Smart Home. Individual level data for every interaction with the interactive displays and clinical and medical staff is recorded continuously and analyzed using state-of-the-art data mining software. This allows visualization of significant behavioral changes to inform treatment plans, and prevent adverse medication effects. It yields information that helps therapists first target problem behaviors, and then allowing automata to ensure therapy is provided consistently.

Tracking movement variability is unique to the Tampa Smart home program which relies on data automatically generated by the location aware technology, including distance and travel rate. The location coordinates are defined relative to a reference system of sensors, e.g., GPS for outdoor or an array of sensors for indoor movements. Most interesting is Fractal Dimension (Fractal D), which calculates vector changes in successive movement episodes as the person ambulates. The lower limit (one) indicates the patient is pursuing a straight path between two locations while greater values indicate an increasingly chaotic path containing more random twists and turns. Higher Fractal D values in assisted living facility (ALF) residents have been linked to cognitive deficits including clinical diagnoses of dementia. In older ALF residents, those with increasingly severe cognitive deficits with or without clinical diagnoses of dementia take progressively more tortuous paths. In middle-aged and elderly persons, abrupt increases in Fractal D during the 7 days preceding a movement related fall distinguish fallers from vvcontrols. Current evidence indicates that decreases in Fractal D over the course of treatment corresponds with improvements in clinical assessments of functioning used as criteria for discharge from the program. Fractal D has been observed to be greater in community dwelling Veterans with a history of TBI than in Veterans with no such history.

The Smart Home employs Ubisense Real Time Location System (RTLS) to track an active Radio Frequency Identification (RFID) tag using wall mounted sensors in the 2.4 24 PTRP. Sensors are grouped into cells, each covering a segment of the PTRP. The tags broadcast their ID on a 6-8GHz ultra-wideband channel at an adjustable rate (up to 40Hz) determined by tag location and velocity. The sensor group tracks a tag using time-delay-of-arrival and angle-ofarrival methods to determine tag position in 3 dimensions to within 16cm. The position information informs each of six applications: the scheduling application, the prompt generator, the real-time fractal path analysis tool, the behavior tracking system, logs to a MySQL database for post hoc analysis of patient behaviors and interactions, and a .NET web service which wraps portions of the Ubisense API to provide access for iOS and Android devices.

The Windows client systems run on the desktop and wall mounted LCD to administer tracked objects, approved locations for patient access (checkin/ check-out system), behavioral prompting configuration, and task scheduling. An interactive facility map displays all tracked objects on the desktop computers and the wall mounted LCD panels. The displays respond to tag presence and a dashboard gives access to the map, scheduler and user settings based on least privileged access determined by tag id.    The iOS client systems are designed for PTRP staff and duplicate desktop administration client and map applications on the iOS devices by developing a .NET web service to wrap the necessary elements of the Ubisense API, allowing the creation of new applications to send and receive data from the Ubisense core services using the open standard HTTP REST methods (GET, POST, PUT, & URL Query Strings). The current iOS applications are written using the Unity engine, which will allow us to use the same applications on Mac OS, iOS, Android, and Windows based devices.

# References

1. Jasiewicz J, Kearns W, Craighead J, Fozard JL, McCarthy J Jr, Scott DO. Smart rehabilitation for the 21st century: The Tampa Smart Home for veterans with traumatic brain injury. Journal of Rehabilitation Research and Development. 2011 Nov; 48(8):vii-xviii.
2. Kearns WD, Jasiewicz J, Fozard JL, Scott S, Craighead J, McCarthy J Jr, Webster P, Bowen ME. Temporal- spatial prompting for persons with cognitive impairment using a smart wrist-worn interface. Journal of Rehabilitation Research and Development, 2013 in press.

This article is courtesy of Jasiewicz J, Kearns W, Craighead J, Fozard JL, Scott S, McCarthy J. (2011) Smart rehabilitation for the 21st century: The Tampa Smart Home for veterans with traumatic brain injury. Journal of Rehabilitation Research & Development; 48(8): vii-viii. DOI:10.1682/ JRRD. 2011.07.0129

# Chapter 3
# Wearables for Professionals

**Movie 4: Wearables for Professionals by Daniel Kraft**
https://vimeo.com/156580470

As Dr. Kraft explains in his video interview for this book, physicians like Drs. Szotek, Prevel, and Megha are exploring the leading edge of wearable technology in clinical settings and surgical suites.

— David Metcalf

# Introduction

The emergence of wearable technology in the consumer and enterprise sectors has presented healthcare professionals with a unique opportunity to improve patient care quality, patient access and reduce health care costs. The media industry and technology corporate research efforts have focused on leveraging real time audio and video streaming in a variety of healthcare sectors (Table 1 A). Such applications utilize a wearable upper body camera to send real-time first person point of view (FPPOV) images to other remote healthcare providers. These real-time images enhance efficiency and coordination of care between different medical teams during virtual patient consultations. This technology creates the ability to provide on-demand specialty consultations to remote locations, reducing the time todefinitive care with improve outcomes at lower costs.

In addition, this technology can provide unique live educational mentoring opportunities for healthcare professionals as well as a tool for quality improvement and specialty recertification. Newer wearable devices (Table 1 B) expand on this functionality with multifunctional augmented reality applications allowing the incorporation of text, picture, video, radiologic images, vital signs, and other personal health information. Healthcare professionals and big data can utilize this continuous data stream for both focused and broad view decision making.

## Definitions

Prior to any discussion of the use of Wearable Devices to facilitate surgical procedures, a brief discussion of Virtual Reality and Augmented Reality is useful.

> "Virtual reality (VR) is an artificial environment created with software and presented to the user in such a way that the user suspends belief and accepts it as a real environment. In a digital environment, VR is primarily experienced through two of the five senses: sight and sound."
>
> (http://whatis.techtarget.com/definition/virtual-reality)

"Augmented reality (AR) is the integration of digital information with the live video of the user's environment in real time. AR takes an existing visual digital feed and blends new information to create an augmented environment."
(http://whatis.techtarget.com/definition/augmented-reality-AR)

"While VR aims at immersing the user into a computergenerated virtual world, AR (Augmented Reality) takes a different approach, in which virtual computer generated objects are added to the real physical space." Wesarg et al 2004

"Medical AR takes its main motivation from the need of visualizing medical data and the patient within the same physical space." Sielhost et al. 2008

"AR is VR plus real life."
Scott Stein, CNET, January 21, 2015 (http://www.cnet.com/news/microsoft-hololens-not-a-hologram-exactly-but-anotherentry-in-an-augmented-reality-turf-war/)

In addition, the physics of Real 3D versus Real Holographic require clarification.

Real 3D displays an image in three dimensions. This is a significant difference from stereoscopic displays, which display only two offset images and use the observer's head and eye movement to "fill in" for the more limited amount of data present.

Real Holographic displays have the ability to provide all four mechanisms: binocular disparity, motion parallax, accommodation and convergence. In addition, 3D objects can be viewed without wearing special glasses and no visual fatigue will result following use.

AR superimposes computer-generated images on a user's perception of the real world rendering a composite view. AR is often referred to as Soft AR or Hard AR and the two differ in their abilities to mask the real world. Computer generated images that overlay the physical world and can be interacted with while not masking the physical world are referred to as Soft AR. Conversely, when the images overly the complete field of vision to mask the physical world they generate true Virtual Reality (defined as a three-dimensional image or environment that can be interacted with in a physical way) and are referred to as Hard AR (previously referred to as VR)

# Identification of Need

## *Work-Flow*

Many physicians view wearable devices as a unifying technology that can serve as a platform to symbiotically merge multiple EMRs for referencing patient information while maintaining focus on the patient. If this vision proves correct, wearables will be one of the first new technologies to restore the doctor-patient relationship.

## *Education*

The modern era of healthcare education has undergone a seismic shift that has affected both the preparation of healthcare professionals during formal training as well as their continuing medical education throughout their careers. The reduction of work hours, operative volumes, and clinical exposure for trainees, combined with the exponential growth f medical information has presented a challenge that prior generations of physicians have not faced. Many graduating residents report they are under prepared for practice when they finish formal training.

Unlike many other technically challenging professions that require integration of knowledge and technical skills to perform a specific function (e.g. airplane pilots and professional sports athletes), medicine is one of the few professions that does not use continuous video based performance review to improve outcomes and reduce costs of care. Currently, few surgeons assess their own performance on a monthly or quarterly basis. To some degree, this can be attributed to the absence of a HIPPA compliant data analysis system. As a result, wearable technology may serve as a conduit to reduce the time-to-proficiency of training through FPPOV telementoring with real time interaction between experts and trainees. In addition, the FPPOV provides the ability for budding and veteran surgeons to "watch film" and improve performance at all levels at the time of decision making, enhancing the overall process. Initiation of telementoring and recording as a standard mainstream activity will likely result in a model of continuous performance improvement similar to other professions and ultimately result in enhance outcomes/quality for our patients.

As devices evolve, the future will likely be driven by augmented reality simulation and possibly augmented reality directed surgical procedures as a type of guidance system in the operating room. Imagine, a second year medical student enters the lecture hall and the professor tells the students to put on their hard AR devices. Suddenly the students are transported into a virtual operating room. Within the scenario, the student must establish the diagnosis, propose a treatment plan, and carry out the operation. Afterward a virtual quiz, the students are transported from the hard augmented reality, back to reality, and soft augmented reality ensues, and posts the quiz results for the class on the board. The professor has real-time feedback on his student's weaknesses and can in real time, provide additional information to fill in the gaps.

Finally, Wearable AR Devices will also likely play a role in board certification, credentialing, and maintenance of certification to improve the validity of these processes, which currently have no component of case, based technical skill assessment.

# Modern Wearable Operating Room Technology

### Point of View Cameras

In the operating room, surgeons are used to wearing eye protective shields, magnification loupes, headlamps, and head mounted cameras to record their surgeries for educational purposes. Basic Point of View cameras available today for use are the Designs for Visions NanoCam, LoupeCam, and the GoPro. These devices have the ability to provide images that can be recorded and even possibly live streamed to outside audiences to watch and listen. These devices also produce footage that can be utilized in standardized testing as mentioned above. However, these first person POV devices have a major disadvantage when compared to smart wearables due to their inability to provide real time audio feedback, telestration, text, or content feedback to the surgeon. There is also the absence of a platform for integration with other smart devices or EMRs that will likely be a part of the smart operating room of the future.

### Head Mounted Wearable Computers

The introduction of the head mounted wearable computer Google Glass (2013, Figure 2) generated enthusiasm from healthcare providers due to the promise of seamlessly integration of data without the interruption of work flow (Figure 1). In addition to Google Glass, several other basic head mounted computer devices (See Table 1B) are also available that can be divided into either Soft AR or Hard AR.

**FIGURE 1 Soft AR with Google Glass**

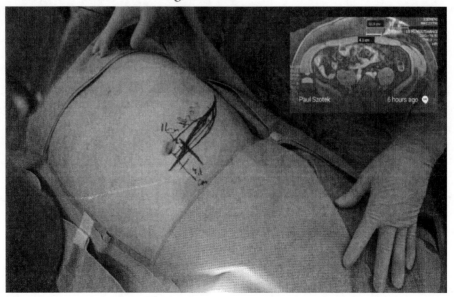

Paul Szotek, MD performs the first surgery using GoogleGlass in the operating room taking advantage of the soft AR capabilities of the device to view the MRI of the patient fordirect correlation in real time with the patients anterior abdominal wall.

The current available applications involve simple telementoring with telestration and two-way audio communication (Third Eye Health, Pristine, and CrowdOptics). These platforms provide data collection in the FPPOV and surgeons may review them for process improvement in real time. In the future, FDA regulation is on the horizon, as these devices evolve to provide a clinical function (Soft AR).

# Wearable Operating Room Technology in the Future

The emergence of wearable technology uses in healthcare today will likely provide the foundation for training at all levels and evolve into enhanced patient safety. In the near future, binocular augmented reality devices will have the capability of producing immersive simulation for training, overlay content in the visual field during procedure performance, real time access

**TABLE 1** Healthcare Sectors Testing POV Streaming Applications & Devices

| A. SECTORS | B. DEVICES |
|---|---|
| First Responders (Police, Fire, EMS) | Google Glass |
| Emergency Department (ER Dr., Nurse, etc.) | Vuzix |
| Neurology (Telestroke) | Sony |
| Teletrauma (Primary Survey, Resuscitation & FAST) | Atheer |
| Operating Rooms | Microsoft Hololens |
| Interventional Radiology | Magic Leap |
| Cardiologists | Pivot Head, GoPro, LoupeCam, Designs for Vision NanoCam |

to patient specific data, on-demand reference content delivery and on-demand mentoring such as Atheer One and Microsoft Hololens (Figure 2). These devices and others will have the capability to provide a visual dashboard for the surgeon and physician of the future to combine all sources of data into an on-demand visual experience that can be accessed while performing tasks hands free.

**FIGURE 2** Augmented Reality Wearable Devices

**Microsoft Hololens**     **Atheer One**

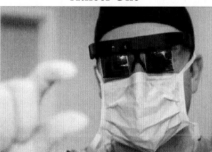

**Google Glass**

For example, a surgeon can parallel process hands free in the OR by referencing a CT scan, an anatomic database or consult a surgical colleague in another time zone (Figure 3 and Supplemental Video 1). As the ability of AR technology advances and imaging modalities improve 3D rendering of patient specific imaging, one day it may be possible to overlay a virtual road map of the anatomy in front of the surgeon (Figure 4 and Supplemental Video 2). Imaging techniques that allow the visualization of blood vessels, ureters and bile ducts and may ultimately be integrated into the operative experience so that vital structures can be highlighted using AR wearable devices. Unfortunately, none of these devices are ready for these types of uses as of today but they hold the key to the future of the augmented operating room, augmented training, enhanced patient safety, improved efficiency, improved operating coordination of care, enhanced preparation for operations, and improved patient care.

Finally, the latest disruptive technology in the AR environment is Microsoft Hololens. It is the first stand-alone wearable technology device that does not require pairing with another device. The stand-alone feat is achieved with the use of three different processors consisting of a central processing unit, a graphics-processing unit, and unique holographic processing unit.

Its holographic processing unit functions like the thalamus of our brain as it relays sensory input from the environmental detectors of the Hololens to the CPU and GPU, then back here it generates the hologram that is being interacted with by the user.

In conclusion, the ability to live stream footage from the healthcare environment provides physicians, from across the globe, the venue to learn new techniques offered by the leading physicians in their specialty. As with all new medical IT devices, hospital and governmental regulations will slow the adoption of this technology due to requirement of a HIPPA compliant virtual environment. However, as this technology improves and governmental regulations evolve, Wearable AR Devices will become a disruptive force in health care education, training and certification.

**FIGURE 3** Augmented Reality Surgeon Dashboard

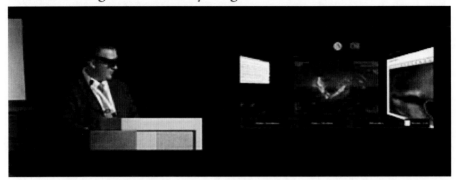

Atheer One surgeon soft AR Dashboard demonstrating telementoring (upper left panel), Crowdsourcing (upper right panel), radiology viewing (lower right panel and main window on right), and fully interactive 3D model reference (left lower panel – heart).

**Supplemental Video 1**
https://youtu.be/e9Tiz1BQAac?list=PL99QOSJoaLfgqfBIL3ip1PGV8V4Vh-Chca

**FIGURE 4** Augmented Reality Training Module

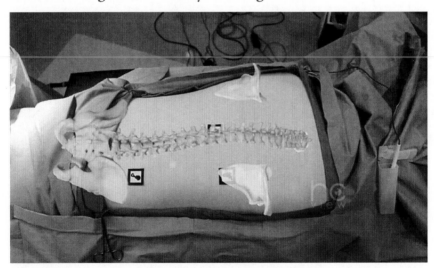

Soft AR onlay of 3D reconstruction of spine in aminectomy training module provided by Hodei Technology.

**Supplemental Video 2**
https://youtu.be/yTkk4-BkTGo?list=PL99QOSJoaLfgqfBIL3ip1PGV8V4Vh-Chca

*Paul Szotek, MD*
Assistant Professor of Clinical Surgery
Indiana University Health
Indianapolis, Indiana 46202
Office: 317-963-1436
pszotek@iuhealth.org

*Christopher D Prevel, MD, FACS, FAAPS*
Acting Chief of Surgery – Surgical Service – Orlando VA Medical Center
Clinical Associate Professor of Plastic Surgery – UCF College of Medicine
Research Associate & Strategic Advisor: Surgical Simulation – UCF IST
Plastic Surgery Consultant – National VA SimLEARN Center
Clinical Educator – VA Southeastern Center of Innovations
Christopher.Prevel@va.gov

*Rishi Megha, MD*
General Surgery Resident
St. John Providence Hospital
16001 W. 9 Mile Road
Southfield, MI 48075
rishimegha@gmail.com

# Wearables - Implantables and Invisibles

-Rick Krohn

As an industry, healthcare is notoriously resistant to change, and in the application of clinical information, this limitation is felt most acutely. It's been the Achilles heel of the industry - but today real foundational change is taking place in the application of healthcare information. It's a vast, sweeping tide of innovation - medical product and clinical process innovation, finance and delivery model innovation, and stakeholder participation innovation – all based on information liquidity.

At the forefront of this pivot towards clinical knowledge sharing are mobile tools -  communicative biosensors, wearable and nearables. Whether worn on the wrist, head, foot, or body as a garment, these devices are being designed in every conceivable form factor, with convenience and utility in mind. Using sensors to measure various aspects of a patient's health, wearable devices now offer richer, actionable data that extend beyond body diagnostics – they now can educate, alert and anticipate health issues. Sensors and data links offer possibilities for monitoring a patient's behavior and symptoms in real time and at relatively low cost, allowing physicians to better diagnose disease and prescribe tailored treatment regimens

As a class of clinical solutions, biosensors are major disruptors to traditional care, and at the cutting edge of these sensors are implantables. Embedded under the skin, these invisible - often micro devices seamlessly integrate into our lives, removing the "friction" between people and technology. Persistent, intuitive, and invisible, these devices are personal health coaches, diagnostic monitors and treatment managers. They mitigate the human element that is at the heart of non-compliance (which according to the CDC costs the U.S.  $300 Billion annually), and they integrate with mobile devices and provider systems, delivering ever-granular insights into our daily health. They promote a collaborative provider-patient dialogue and preempt expensive, invasive treatments.

And with the introduction of implantables, we're traversing a path from isolated content to connected experiences ranging from patient wellness to diagnosis, monitoring and adherence.

Implantables are being customized to address specific health issues, and can tremendously improve patient compliance.  Some examples -  Smart pills that monitor and wirelessly transmit biomedical data to providers and alerts to patients to take their meds, a dime-sized chip that allows doctors to continually monitor patient vitals, a "bionic eye" that allows the blind to see, a cardioverter-defibrillator that treats sudden heart attacks - the list keeps growing

But are implantable solutions really new? Many people have been living with pacemakers, cochlear implants, implanted biochips, and other medical devices for years. What's new is the trend toward healthcare consumerism that allows individuals to more actively manage their conditions, coupled with more powerful, functional, less invasive, cheaper devices. Implantables activate consumer self-awareness, improve treatment compliance, and promote "actionable" conversations with a care circle – providers, family and friends. And increasingly, these devices are becoming integrated with enterprise systems.

We're still at the forefront of implantable technologies, and hurdles remain. FDA approval can take years, and any device inserted into the body must be biocompatible – probably for years. There is the concern of accidental malfunctions and malicious cyber interference with implantable devices. Those obstacles aren't new to Health IT, and as in the past, they will be addressed in the implantables sphere.

The potential for clinical efficiencies and cost savings are enormous - better management of chronic conditions could reduce hospitalization and treatment costs by a billion dollars annually in the United States. Looking ahead, the promise of consumer facing solutions like implantables is this: healthcare technology will become increasingly commoditized, connected, and minimally invasive. For the patient, they will create new treatments, change behaviors, and introduce an immersive provider-patient relationship.

# Virtual Reality Gets Personal in Healthcare

-Rick Krohn

Virtual Reality - the term conjures up a number of images. For the millennial, it's gaming; for those of a certain age, it's 3D glasses; and for all of us, it's an ever-expanding template for immersive entertainment. "VR" is rapidly evolving however, and today serves as an umbrella for related technologies including augmented reality ("AR") and 3D. These collective components of VR can be described as: a) VR- an artificial environment created with software and presented to the user in such a way that the user suspends belief and accepts it as a real environment; b) AR- the integration of digital information with the live video of the user's environment in real time (AR takes an existing visual digital feed and blends new information to create an augmented environment); and c) 3D – which displays an image in three dimensions. The VR/AR distinction: while VR aims at immersing the user into a computer generated virtual world, in AR virtual computer generated objects are added to the real physical space.

"VR" technology is actually almost a century old, and until recently has been most recognizably a feature of mass market entertainment. But today, with the release of head mounted displays like Facebook's Oculus and Samsung's Gear, VR technology has advanced to the point where consumer facing, immersive VR experiences are accessible at reasonable price points. VR is now personal and highly interactive – we can now enter a computer-generated simulation of a three-dimensional world, using helmets, gloves and other sensors to interact with this virtual environment.

Virtual Reality is a century–old idea …

.... that has evolved from a mass market entertainment medium to a personalized, immersive class of technologies.

SAMSUNG GEAR VR

Piper Jaffray analyst Gene Munster has dubbed VR and AR "the next technology megatrend" with "the potential to make every computer and entertainment interface disappear." Until recently, healthcare was not a headliner for VR investment, mainly due to the expense and lack of demonstrated scalability of VR solutions aimed at a patient base. But as healthcare pivots towards a retail marketplace, that economic calculus changes. According to Goldman Sachs, healthcare VR applications are forecast to top $5.1 billion in sales by 2025, with 3.4 million active users, including 1.5 million medical professionals.

To date, VR has gotten traction in healthcare mainly as a training and education device. Unlike a textbook or a classroom demonstration, VR in healthcare education introduces a visual, participatory experience featuring accurate and realistic simulations. In medical training VR can take the risk out of complex medical procedures, bringing students close to the procedure while still leaving the actual work in the hands of the expert guide. Not surprisingly then, VR is getting its greatest traction in the healthcare enterprise.

In other healthcare verticals however, it's still early days for VR. In the physician office, in biopharma, and in the consumer (retail) space, VR development is still largely in the pilot and boutique solution stage. That said, Industry-wide, it's a green field for innovation. Some opportunities:

VR in the Physician Office
Behavior change
Virtual diagnosis
Education and Prevention

VR in Pharma
PTSD
Rehabilitation
Pain management
Drug efficacy

VR/AR applications for patients and consumers
Immersive health/wellness
Gamification
Brain injuries
Behavioral health (ex. anxiety, body image, phobia)
Chronic disease management


Early days, but even today there are some VR footholds in healthcare – among the leaders are the VA and DoD, who are leading development of VR and AR healthcare apps to address field medicine, PTSD, rehabilitation, pain management and behavioral health. On the commercial side institutions like Cleveland Clinic have developed VR to treat Parkinson's Disease, and St. Jude's Children's Research Hospital has developed a virtual experience to treat cancer patients. Payers like Cigna have created an innovative 3D meditative experience and Florida BCBS teamed with Disney to produce Habit Heroes, an immersive healthy lifestyle experience aimed at kids.

We've only scratched the surface of VR's potential to disrupt healthcare delivery. New revenue, cost savings and quality gains can be captured across multiple verticals – health system, provider, pharma, payer and the consumer. VR not only leverages market trends like population health, consumerization, value metrics, risk management and personalized care, it introduces opportunities to create retail solutions, to drive patient and consumer engagement strategies, to support patient enrollment and member retention, and as a tool to promote sales, alliances and networks. Clinical opportunities include provider and patient education, best practices, wellness and prevention, behavioral health, chronic disease management, rehabilitation and drug therapy.

There are of course hurdles to VR 's broadcast adoption in healthcare. First, new technology aversion – VR is a young technology not easily deployed in enterprise environments due to infrastructure, integration and equipment costs. Next, there is pushback from physicians unaccustomed to retail solutions, many of which have a short or nonexistent catalog of success. And since VR is largely a retail play, it's still unclear that VR can deliver a truly engaging augmented reality experience in a practical, affordable, consumer-ready device. Finally, there are the ever-present issues of privacy, security, and validation.

To achieve scale in healthcare, VR developers must act strategically. VR can leverage proven techniques to weave itself into the fabric of healthcare delivery through gamification, social media, narrative, visioning, goal setting and rewards.  It can score early wins by addressing population health issues such as childhood obesity, replacement drug therapy, and smoking cessation. But VR solution developers must know the customer - younger gens and millennials will be more receptive and comfortable with virtual worlds. They must architect VR technologies to immersive experience and delivery capabilities (i.e. mobile). They must mitigate cost, development and adoption through partnerships and affordable-device enablement.  And they must recognize that from clinical education to marketing, technology isn't the centerpiece of the VR solution – the message or the story is.

# *Case Study*: Secure Smartphones Optimize Care Collaboration and Coordination

TREY LAUDERDALE • SALLY REEVES, VOALTE

## The Challenge

Frisbie Memorial Hospital is an 88-bed, acute-care community hospital in Rochester, New Hampshire. In 2008, the hospital completed a successful $30 million expansion and renovation, adding a new tower and building and doubling the campus footprint. As a result of the expansion, the hospital faced an unexpected challenge. Trips for supplies and transport added about a third more time and distance that staff had to travel. The distance covered by staff responsible for blood draws and dietary almost doubled.

In an effort to address the larger floor space, hospital planners had placed nursing substations throughout the units, rather than relying on a central nurse's station. Even with the distributed arrangement, challenges abounded.

The regular communication and unit cohesion that once easily occurred around the central nursing desk diminished significantly. Sally Gallot-Reeves, MSM, CPM, CCM, RN, Healthcare Project Director, Frisbie Memorial Hospital, said, "From an operational standpoint, the expansion separated nursing stations from each other more than we had anticipated— not so much geographically as from the standpoint of having access to each other and availability."

Nursing managers quickly realized that the existing communication solution of pagers, legacy phones and overhead paging was inadequate.

# The Solution

Within every challenge lies opportunity. Frisbie leadership moved quickly to create and implement a three-step strategic plan that involved researching proven clinical communication products and solutions including mobile technology. They explored active solutions at other hospitals and conducted site visits to observe products being used. They scheduled onsite product demonstrations and reviewed the functionality —voice, text, and administrative functions—of each solution.

After carefully considering various alternatives, Frisbie Memorial Hospital decided that what they really needed was to abandon legacy devices (including chargeable phones and pagers) completely and make the switch to enterprise wide smartphone-based communications to optimize care collaboration and coordination. They wanted a secure, efficient and HIPAA-compliant way for shift workers to communicate with each other inside the hospital as well as a way for caregivers to securely communicate with doctors outside the hospital, in their homes or clinics.

The technology they ultimately deployed is a mobile communications platform from Voalte, a Sarasota, Floridabased company that began adapting smartphone technology for use in hospital communications systems in 2008 and was the first to introduce healthcare to the dedicated use of smartphones. Voalte was chosen for the strength of their platform solution which has the ability to integrate future needs and technologies. For example, many hospitals start with inside hospital use (caregivers can communicate with each other using a hospital's secure Wi-fi) and later can expand it for outside use (allowing physicians to securely communicate via cellular data in BYOD initiatives). The solution aligned with Frisbie's strategy to leverage smartphone technology not simply for communication at the point of care but as a care coordination tool, which required process and workflow enhancements.

# Implementation

In late 2010, Frisbie launched the mobile communications platform from Voalte, secured through the hospital's WiFi system. The platform utilizes the smartphones provided and stored inside the hospital; a software solution that includes a directory, messaging by group, unit or individual employee; and an individualized text library.

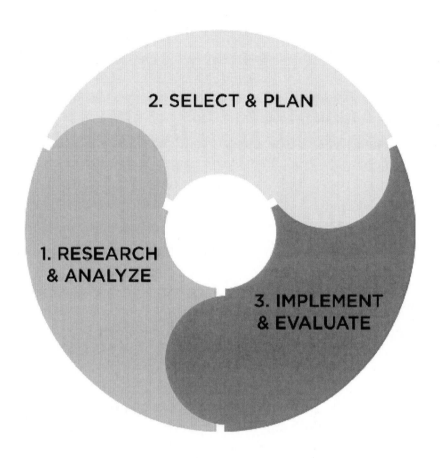

**Frisbie Memorial's Three Step Plan**

To ensure a smooth implementation, the hospital's nursing and IT leadership worked hand in hand with Voalte to carefully manage the integration process and guide the project through a variety of steps, including Wi-Fi assessment, PBX integration, clinical unit observation, workflow observation and workflow assessment, iPhone/network security review and configuration, clinical training, and go-live support.

Says Gallot-Reeves, "When we were presented with Voalte, light bulbs went off in our heads. It opened a world of possibilities with the ways we could use smartphones for voice, alarm and text capabilities to bring people closer together and optimize workflow."

## Key Learnings

- Complete a facility-wide assessment of wireless coverage creating a plan to address Wi-Fi weaknesses before implementing any devices
- Be open to products that meet your goals even if they require process and workflow changes
- Choose a vendor that supports your implementation needs, staff engagement, system maintenance and future technological growth
- Create a Change Management plan to facilitate process and workflow changes
- Develop Policies and Guidelines for staff to follow regarding privacy, security, use of battery packs and inventory control

## Results

Frisbie Memorial Hospital timed how long various communication transactions between a nurse and physician took using traditional pagers, telephones or cell phones. Results ranged from six minutes as the most efficient, to as long as 28 minutes. By using mobile smartphones, powered by a robust mobile healthcare communication platform, Frisbie replaced these sometimes lengthy communication processes with instant, direct and highly secure messaging between care members.

Frisbie Memorial Hospital
**Post-Mobile Device** Time Study

| STEP 1 **Nurse Contacts Physician** | STEP 2 **Physician Contacts Nurse** |
|---|---|
| 1. Nurse texts or calls physician on Voalte smartphone............... 10 seconds | 2. Physician texts or calls nurse on Voalte smartphone............... 10 seconds |
| Average response time ................... <5 minutes | Average response time ................... <5 minutes |
| Total Voalte communication time ............. 10 seconds - 5 minutes | Total Voalte communication time ............. 10 seconds - 5 minutes |

| **Total communication time** | **20 seconds - 5 minutes** |

To say this has made a difference is a significant understatement. Communication transactions between caregivers is now typically between 20 seconds and five minutes, which has had the cumulative effect of reducing all communication time between caregivers by 82 percent. Using shared smartphones, caregivers connect inside the hospital and access electronic medical records and barcode scanners, all on one device.

Amy Murphy, RN, of the Women's & Children's Unit, cites an example: "I was with a mom in hard labor and I needed Respiratory to do a cord gas. Instead of having to leave the room, page a Respiratory Therapist, and then wait for a call back, I just text messaged them and never left the mother. I got a response quickly, and later got a message back when the results were in. I never left the room."

Surveys showed an increase in staff satisfaction as a result of the new smartphones. Patients are happier, too. "We saw a 6 percent increase in HCAHPS scores relating to patients getting help as soon as they wanted it, after pressing the nurse-call button," says Gallot-Reeves.

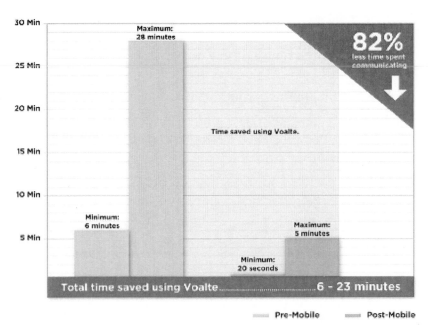

The hospital also noticed that the mobile solution was actually helpful in rebuilding unit cohesion, which had suffered as a result of the distributed floor plan. Denise Thomas, ICU Unit Coordinator, states, "Relationship building is happening in new and unexpected ways because of the visual directory, which lists users not only by name, but also title, department and photo. We have people walking down the hall now, stopping and saying, 'I didn't know that was you!' It's bringing people together and impacting the morale and attitude that our people have for each other."

As communication improved between departments, the hospital saw additional efficiencies. Surgical Services staff are now able to manage patient flow proactively because of the ease with which they could communicate with the Anesthesia department. Diane O'Connell, Assistant Director of Surgical Services, says, "Our care teams are engaged in proactive planning of processes and care—as opposed to being forced to wait for specific times (huddles, after rounds, and so on). They know daily what things come up regularly and are able to plan accordingly."

## Results

- HCAHPS scores relating to how quickly patients received help after pressing the nurse call button rose 6%.
- Total communication time between nurses and physicians dropped by 82% with a savings of 6-23 minutes per person per call.
- Workflow was streamlined resulting in significant patient throughput improvements.
- Phone calls dropped precipitously from 1,200 a month to 300 and overhead paging was almost eliminated.
- Other ongoing positive outcomes include: better care coordination because the technology facilitates communication among multi-disciplinary teams and quicker patient response time that enhances satisfaction among both patients and nurses.

## Expansion

In phase one, Frisbie deployed 90 iPhones and 21 Voalte Messenger clients, spanning 21 departments. In phase two, the hospital added 50 smartphones, expanding to Support Services and the hospital's ambulances. Caregivers currently exchange more than 120,000 text messages per month.

Frisbie has experienced such success with the Voalte platform that plans are in place to incorporate barcode scanning of patients and medications using the MC40-HC Android device. This will reduce or even eliminate much of the current manual work required to verify patient identification, medication administration and other routine but essential patient care tasks. Frisbie also plans to extend the messaging solution to providers and managers' personal smartphones with Voalte Me. This will enable two-way communication with caregivers inside the hospital on Voalte One and providers outside the hospital walls on Voalte Me.

Given that Frisbie has already made substantial reductions in communication time—a full 82 percent decrease— expectations are high that these new features will likewise enhance collaboration and coordination between caregivers dedicated to swiftly meeting patient needs.

"Communication transactions between caregivers is now typically between 20 seconds and five minutes, which has had the cumulative effect of reducing all communication time between caregivers by 82 percent."

"We saw a 6 percent increase in HCAHPS scores relating to patients getting help as soon as they wanted it, after pressing the nurse-call button," says Sally Gallot-Reeves.

# Resources

1. HIMSS. Five Steps to Improve Clinical Communication Using Enterprise Smartphone Solution. PatientSafe Solutions, Inc. San Diego, 2014. Hancock, Geoffrey. "Smartphone Security: The First Link in
2. the Healthcare Value Chain." HIMSS. August 8, 2012.
3. Bambot, Farida. "Bring Your Own Device (BYOD) to Work -Should We Even Go There?" HIMSS. February 3, 2012.
4. Mobility in Nursing: An Ongoing Evolution http://www.healthcare-informatics.com/article/mobility-nursingongoing-evolution
5. How can we be sure that mobile healthcare isn't just technology-driven hype?http://www.pwc.com/gx/en/healthcare/mhealth/#&panel1-1
6. Global mobile health market to grow to $49B by 2020 http://mobihealthnews.com/30616/global-mobile-healthmarket-to-grow-to-49b-by-2020/
7. Are smartphones hitting their stride? http://www.mhealthnews.com/news/are-smartphones-hittingtheir-stride-healthcare

———

# Chapter 4

# Wearables in the Healthcare Enterprise

**Movie 5: Wearables in Healthcare by Steven Chan**
https://vimeo.com/156569155

# Editor's Note

Wearables are not strictly a product play – these technologies are increasingly being integrated within a larger catalogue of mobile and Cloud platforms; enterprise systems, clinical workflows and consumer health solutions. With guidance from NIST, FDA and others we're seeing an increase in device integration with the EHR, PHR, office systems and patient portals. Its' here that healthcare meets the Internet of Things. To be discussed in greater detail in later chapters, the IoT in healthcare is a heterogeneous computing, wirelessly communicating system of apps and devices that connects patients and health providers to diagnose, monitor, track and store vital statistics and medical information – within the enterprise and beyond.

> *"The aging population and cost pressures on in-hospital care is driving a need for health-related IT scenarios that include remote patient monitoring, self-diagnosing kiosks in pharmacies, and other mobile healthcare apps that will drive next-generation services, consequently the healthcare sector could experience explosive IoT growth." IDC*

Enterprise systems offer some – but not enough about a patient's health indications, and certainly not persistently. This is where wearables and the IoT fill a huge gap in care. Wearable technologies offer a huge opportunity to deliver actionable insights at the point of care, to circumvent the lack of interoperability imbedded into vendor systems, to improve diagnostic accuracy and promote patient engagement. Via the IoT, data generated from wearables can be streamed seamlessly to provider and enterprise systems and the Cloud, to paint a more complete picture of the patient's condition, and prompt earlier, informed intervention.

—Rick Krohn

# Wearables in the Healthcare Enterprise

—SATISH RAVOOR, M.B.A, M.S, PMP HFHS CORP IT
HENRY FORD HEALTH SYSTEM

**Movie 6: Wearables in Healthcare by Robert Wachter**
https://vimeo.com/156569347

## Abstract

With the advent of wearable technologies, Health care organizations have been seeking creative ways of leveraging the technologies to improve patient care in the preventive and proactive medical practices within the enterprise.

This chapter focuses on how wearables can be used in a healthcare enterprise and optimize areas of TIMWOOD. The methodology to identify 7 wastes of Lean six sigma practice is TIMWOOD (Transport, Inventory, Motion, Waiting, Over-processing, Over Allocation, Defects). Each area will be used to explore opportunities, use cases and how effectively the work flow can be managed by wearable technologies.

**Transportation** - Wearables can go a long way to enable efficient routes for patient transportation.

**Inventory** - Surplus ordering shortage of medical supplies can be avoided

**Motion** - A care team can be more efficient in areas where a patient motion is a critical factor.

**Waiting** - Wait time of patients in a healthcare setup can be minimized

**Over-Processing** - Redundant collecting and storing of the patient information can be optimized

**Over Allocation of time** - Effective use of Physicians or specialist time can be optimized by using wearables along with Telemedicine strategies.

**Defects** - Erroneous collection of vitals can be minimized by the use of wearables

# Transportation

Finding the way inside and outside of a Healthcare enterprise can be at times traumatic. Devising efficient, quickest path for patient transportation can be a challenge for transporters. Although smart wearable glass technologies have not been fully matured for healthcare usage, several use cases already exist to benefit in units like Emergency Medical Services. Some applications include a catalogue of medical libraries and other searchable recommendations that have the potential to display such data on a smart glass hence resolving significant challenges in patient triage.

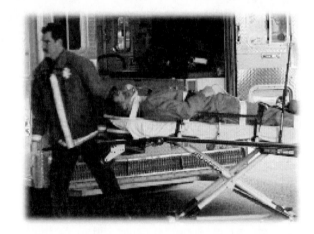

Apps for smartphones already exist to help responders locate the address of a call from dispatch. A smart Glass can incorporate the capabilities to display the information at eye-level through a mapping software so the personal does not have to look down as they are driving. A connected ambulance may someday wirelessly stream vehicle speed, Global Positioning Systems coordinates and more rational data on a wearable smart

Integrated health systems can stream live images of a patient's medical condition to specialists. Wearable smart watches potentially include the ability to pull up patient medical data to better determine course of care, display patient vitals and quickly search for medical procedure, all hands-free as the care team focusses on the patient being transported into the enterprise.

## Inventory

One of the many hidden challenges in hospital systems is to ensure adequate supplies are readily available and in the right quantities. Notable manpower is invested in Supply chain management so that patients can receive proper care without interruption. An optimized supply system that uses modern technology like wearable smart gear and centralized distribution will help minimize costs and improve patient care. When a patient requires immediate care in the emergency room (ER), the medical staff often uses considerable supplies while attempting to diagnose the issue. The supplies are pulled from cupboards, storage carts, and supply closets nearby. If the required item is not found where expected, there is a room for diminished patient care.

To avoid such a situations, medical staff replenishes supplies in higher quantities, and the additional inventory is "hidden" in certain places throughout the ER by individuals, without the knowledge of others on the team.

Over time, inventory levels increase in these stockpiles, yet the supplies continue to be ordered and stored. Not only are the invisible supplies take up valuable space, the items also may expire or be recalled. At the end of the year, inventory reconciliation reduces this stock to a certain amount, which consequently causes shortages later on, fueling the vicious cycle.

A full-service integrated Wearable technologies for material handling systems can improve fulfillment operations and maximize supply level efficiency. The next generation Inventory management Systems are ready to track and maintain via wearables like Smartwatches. The wearables allow supplies managers to gather critical key performance indicators to better manage their distribution and fulfillment operations from their wrist. With real-time visibility into supplies operations 24/7, managers can better meet the demanding requirements of today's modern healthcare operations in an Enterprise.

# Motion

There are studies to state that moving or turning women who are in labor and on epidurals will speed their labor and potentially could reduce the need for C-sections. There is a huge potential for use of a wireless monitoring wearables technologies that will reduce the length and discomfort of labor and provide expectant mothers with a much easier birth experience.

Healthcare Enterprises can capitalize on the effort to lessen caesarian sections using a wearable to track the movements or turns for mothers who are on epidurals so they can be repositioned every 30 minutes to counter the effects of epidural anesthesia. Nurses or the care team can get the turn alerts on the system when the bed-ridden mothers have been in the same position for 30 or more minutes. Nurses will also be able to see on the monitoring data when mothers are sitting upright, a position that is highly encouraged.

Some higher risk populations, including elderly and bariatric patients can get benefited with a similar wearable technologies. Emergency Departments can use similar patient Monitors, to enable the clinical staff to monitor patients who are being observed. Typically, the ED staff is not required to periodically turn patients, however the standard of care can be enhanced for the prevention of pressure ulcers.

# Wait Time

New wearable technologies are also emerging to transmit the data collected through mobile phones and wearable devices to healthcare professionals directly, allowing them to review and analyze data. This strategy helps them to be more prepared in case of an emergency. Wearable technology is especially beneficial for those who have a risk of heart failure or heart complications. Patients can be monitored right from their homes without having to be admitted to a hospital and hence overcoming the challenge of longer wait times. Not only is this convenient for patients, but it also helps to cut down on long wait times and overcrowding in hospitals, ultimately reducing stress on the healthcare enterprise itself.

Since wearable technology has the ability to monitor patients around the clock, it can often predict and recognize when something is going on before irreparable damage is done. It makes it possible for patients and healthcare providers to act quickly and take necessary steps to prevent health issues from escalating. Waiting for a call from a primary care physician (PCP), or for an ambulance to arrive, can sometimes make a difference in receiving ample care exactly when it is needed.

Wearable devices with the ability to facilitate healthcare monitoring gives care team a major advantage in these scenarios. These devices are not just for those suffering from chronic cases, these devices can also help monitor and treat people suffering from other ailments, many of which are often associated with old age—illnesses such as diabetes, urinary tract infections, and serious breathing problems and  more.

## Over Processing

During multiple instances data collection is deemed to be a redundant process and manifests itself as a key patient satisfier within an enterprise. There are certain key data elements like heart rate monitoring and body temperature which has to be recorded on a timely basis. A care team needs to be along the bedside to physically collect the data.

As an example, Henry Ford Hospital Systems are in the process of integrating Apple health kit to overcome some of the challenges. Health kit originally was released to track 60 data elements and now is up to 72 data points.  The number of KPI's is expected to grow.

- Health Kit application acts as a data aggregator from a multiple sources to provide users with one place to store health-related information.

- Data can come from multiple sources:
    - Other smart phone apps such as health tracking applications where users enter their fluid intake or blood test data
    - Some cell phone apps exist to use blue tooth as a way to connect existing  monitoring devices like scales, blood pressure cuffs, blood sugar monitors, fitness monitoring devices or spirometers

- Not all devices have an app of their own but can have Bluetooth connectivity and can use the GATT data standards (a protocol for sending information in a standard way)
- Once stored in the app, data is available for viewing by the user and it can be made available to other applications  for export.
    - Data is securely  stored within the apple health kit on the phone encrypted) and is not sent to the Apple cloud unless sent out as an encrypted blob of information for back up to which Apple does not have the key)
    - Applications such as Epic's MyChart can be given permission by the user to access the data from Apple Health.  In this fashion the data can be moved into MyChart and from there on into Epic at large.

# Over Allocation of Time

As healthcare organizations and their health IT vendors develop more workflow-friendly ways of harnessing the data from wearable devices, the market for additional tools to analyze and report on patient-generated health data will likely push the remote care market and telemedicine strategies  to even greater heights.

Time to travel from point A to Point B, effective use of Physicians time in terms of Geo agnostic scheduling could be made possible by use of wearable monitors like Blood pressure cuffs and other similar Health data trackers.

While wearables are becoming popular among patients who wish to track their basic health statistics, healthcare providers and technology developers are still investigating meaningful ways to integrate patient-generated health data from wearables into the telemedicine workflow setup.

Wearable devices go hand in hand as hot  ticket item for Telemedicine healthcare team and as a key for remote health monitoring. As  mHealth becomes increasingly important in the fight for chronic disease and reduced preventable readmissions, lower healthcare costs would drive the usage of wearable technologies.

EHR vendors are ever eager to take advantage of growing interest in care coordination wearable technologies that can potentially keep patients healthier at home for longer period and leading the way in a telehealth market and hence invariably minimizing the time on a patient encounter.

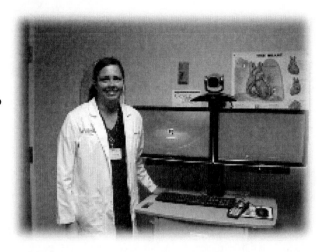

Wearables are becoming a technology of choice for connecting with pa-tients as the shortage of physician's time, especially in rural areas, squeezes healthcare providers into developing alternative service methods.  While reimbursement challenges still make it difficult for some providers to par-ticipate in emerging remote care strategies, leading healthcare vendors are innovating the wearables to overcome some of these challenges.

# Defects

There is an increasing need to collect accurate wellness and health data in a timely manner. Any room for error in the data collection could impede the meaningful use of the collected data.

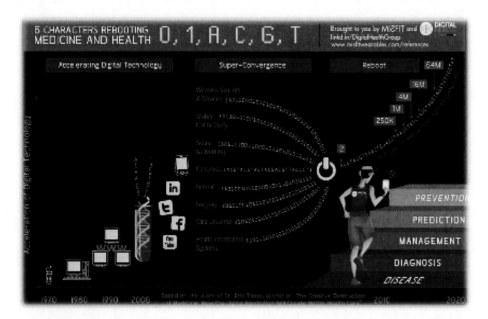

Use of Wearables data can be helpful to overcome such defects. Today's range of wearables are ready to measure and record multiple Key Performance health indicators in both accurate and timely manner. More than just being on the proactive 'early warning system' for serious illnesses, the collected health data could have a major impact on the following areas of the global healthcare industry and research:

- Stride length, distance, step count, cadence and speed (Post surgery care)
- Body temperature (A baseline for any health check)
- Calories burned, distance travelled (Weight loss clinics)
- Sleep quality, sleep patterns (Patients suffering from sleep apnea)
- Back posture: sitting position, chest and shoulders (Acute care)
- Force of impact to the head (used in contact sports)
- Exposure to the sun (UV measurement)
- Bio-mechanical data collected while running (Athletic Medicine)
- Motion parameters including speed and acceleration.

- Heart rate, heart rate variability, heart rate recovery, respiration rate, skin temperature, skin moisture levels, breathing rate, breathing volume, activity intensity ( To treat heart related ailments)
- Repetitions of specific physical activities (e.g. sit ups, dips, press ups).

# Conclusion

The development in the wearable technologies and the use cases are outpacing the level of Healthcare enterprise's adoptability ratio. EHR vendors are opening up the applications to interact with real-time patient data to a greater degree in a way imitating the success of technologies like Smartphone platforms which owe some popularity and utility to their interaction with engaging healthcare applications.

EMR integration of patient data with the tool set that wearable technologies enable Health data to allow care givers access to many devices and applications with one unified goal. This aspect can open up the health system to more innovation in a cost effective manner.

Enterprises must carefully consider changing the future of patient care in a more real time and pre-emptive manner. Wearable technologies that exist today can ideally help setup a hands-on patient monitoring system similar to OnStar technologies that GM had championed for the auto industry. There are some open opportunities that has to be brain stormed on how to store imported data from the wearables and a good approach to the responsibilities of obtaining the data.

Healthcare enterprises must of course cautiously continue to consider the adoption of these new wearable technologies for enhancing patient care thereby enriching overall human wellbeing.

# References

1. "Telemedicine - Google Search." Telemedicine - Google Search. N.p., n.d. Web. 02 Sep. 2015.
2. Wikipedia. Wikimedia Foundation, n.d. Web. 04 Oct. 2015.
3. "Congreso Wearables Big Data Salud 2." Flickr. Yahoo!, n.d. Web. 26 Aug. 2015.
4. Wikipedia. Wikimedia Foundation, n.d. Web. 26 Aug. 2015.

5.  "Am I One of the Cool Kids Now? #iwatch #applewatch." Flickr. Yahoo!, n.d. Web. 26 Aug. 2015.

6.  "Jennifer Witting, Nurse at Aspirus Keweenaw Hospital in Laurium, Michigan." Flickr. Yahoo!, n.d. Web. 26 Aug. 2015.

7.  "Wearables - Google Search." Wearables - Google Search. N.p., n.d. Web. 02 Sep. 2015.

8.  "Telemedicine Consult." Flickr. Yahoo!, n.d. Web. 01 Sept. 2015.

## Special Regards

Brian Day
Chief Technology Officer at Henry Ford Health System

Mary Alice Annecharico
SVP and CIO at Henry Ford Health System

Dr. David Allard
Chief Medical Information Officer - Henry Ford Hospital and Health Network at Henry Ford Health System

# *Case Study*: Seeing New Opportunity - Cardinal Health Inventory Management Solutions Optimize the Supply Chain

## Taking Control of the Future

The Affordable Care Act (ACA) mandates that health systems eliminate waste, and across the country they're responding by pledging to cut billions of dollars in unnecessary costs. A prime target is the medical-surgical supply chain. And for Emory Saint Joseph's Hospital in Atlanta, a key strategy is improving inventory management by automating product tracking and utilization.

"With the rollout of the ACA and changes to reimbursements, it's important that we control expenses more than ever," said Julie Swann, MBA, MHA, BSN, RN, Specialty Director, Cardiology Services/eICU for Emory Saint Joseph's Hospital. "Over the next five years, it will be a mandate for C-Suites everywhere. At Emory Saint Joseph's, we're being careful with supply costs, so we don't have to look at reducing labor to control expenses. The Cardinal Health RFID solution is a solid way to help us do that. Now we have an up to date and live look at inventory— easily seeing expired and missing products in real time and setting par levels." And that's just the beginning.

## Meeting Aggressive Goals

Part of the Emory Healthcare system, Emory Saint Joseph's Hospital was founded by the Sisters of Mercy in 1880 and is Atlanta's oldest hospital. Today, the 410-bed, acutecare facility is recognized as one of the top specialty-referral hospitals in the Southeast.

The Cardinal Health RFID solution is helping Emory Saint Joseph's effectively manage more than $2.5 million in inventory, monitoring over 2,000 SKUs in seven Cardiac Catheterization labs and three Electrophysiology labs.

The approach is improving financial, clinical and operational performance by:

- Saving inventory costs: The Cardinal Health RFID solution reduces and right-sizes on hand inventory, setting accurate par levels based on real-time usage patterns. The approach also optimizes bulk buys to take advantage of cost savings without tying up cash on the shelves with unneeded products. And it eliminates overnight shipping due to stockouts.

- Maximizing revenue: Emory Saint Joseph's captures all patient charges at the point of care—and manages missing items daily to avoid loss charges.

**ROI at a glance**

**Saved**
3 hours in labor every day ordering products.

**Eliminated**
100% of overnight shipping costs due to stockouts.

**Recovered**
$300,000 in chargeable product costs through active alerts.

Improved Electrophysiology Lab (EP) inventory turns by 60%

**Automated**
100% of expiration and recall alerts to meet highest patient safety standards.

**Tracked**
100% of short-dated products to help avoid expiration and maximize utilization.

Reduced aging inventory and maximized throughput with
84% of products less than one year old.

## Tracking Products, Setting Pars

"The problem in the procedure areas was that there was a lot of product in the storerooms," Swann said. "When we first started using the Cardinal Health RFID solution, we were able to do some 'spring cleaning' right away and save $10,000 in inventory holding costs." With that baseline inventory level established, Emory Saint Joseph's was then able to adjust par levels to match utilization.

> *"Now we're tracking actual usage patterns in real time—and automatically setting par levels."*
>
> **Chuck Naylor**
> **Senior Business Manger**
> **Emory Saint Joseph's Hospital**

"Before RFID, our inventory visibility was limited to knowing what we had ordered. Now, we're tracking actual usage patterns in real-time—and automatically setting accurate par levels," said Chuck Naylor, Senior Business Manager at Emory Saint Joseph's Hospital. "There's not enough time in the day to manually set pars. Now, they're preset and can be overridden if necessary—and there's no learning curve to do it."

In the first 18–24 months of using Cardinal Health RFID, Emory Saint Joseph's was steadily shrinking inventory to match utilization. According to Naylor, "Cardinal Health RFID definitely reduces inventory," in a controlled and measured way.

> *"Cardinal Health RFID integrates with our charting and documentation system, which cuts down on manual errors and improves charge capture."*
>
> **Lisa Newton**
> **Unit Director, EP Lab**
> **Emory Saint Joseph's Hospital**

Automated reports also improve inventory management. For example, Emory Saint Joseph's can create prospective reports for products due to expire in the near future. So they can be used or replaced, as needed, before expiration.

> *"The staff said, 'This is all I have to do, and Cardinal Health does the rest?' There was immediate buy-in."*
>
> **Lisa Stepps**
> **Account Manager, RFID-enabled technologies**
> **Cardinal Health**

The Cardinal Health RFID solution improves revenue as well. "Cardinal Health RFID integrates with our charting and documentation system, which cuts down on manual errors and improves charge capture," said Lisa Newton, Unit Director of the Electrophysiology (EP) Lab.

# Launching Success

"Once the RFID infrastructure was set up, the Cardinal Health team came in en masse," Naylor said. "There were plenty of boots on the ground. During the first month of implementation, there was a dedicated Cardinal Health RFID person on-site." Products were tagged over a weekend, and Emory Saint Joseph's was able to identify and pull expired products right away. "It was eye opening. The staff was pleasantly surprised — and it was a win-win from day one," Stepps said. "The staff said, 'This is all I have to do, and Cardinal Health does the rest?' There was immediate buy-in. There was also a lot of confidence from the physicians, who have never been without a product since the implementation of the Cardinal Health RFID solution."

> **Just getting started.**
>
> The more hospitals systems are tasked with reducing costs while improving patient care, the more technology can play a critical role. For Emory Saint Joseph's, the Cardinal Health RFID solution is an important part of the leading hospital's savings and quality strategy. And we're just getting started.

Because of the high product visibility that the system provides, there is ample flexibility to adjust inventory levels based on changes in utilization patterns. "Can I order more or less, based on these patterns—and still save money as I do? Cardinal Health enables Emory Saint Joseph's to do just that," Stepps said.

# Improving Supplier Relations

"Suppliers love the stronger communication and collaboration that Cardinal Health creates," Stepps said. For example, the data generated by the Cardinal Health RFID solution supports the hospital's compliance with their market share agreements. "In fact, many suppliers tag their products for us," Stepps said, further saving staff time at Emory Saint Joseph's.

# *Case Study*: Celebration Health - Florida Hospital Pioneers Use of RTLS and Business Intelligence to Improve Nursing Workflows

— STANLEY HEALTHCARE

## Overview

Florida Hospital Celebration Health is a 174-bed, state-of the art hospital that serves as a showcase of innovation and excellence in healthcare. Celebration Health bases its care on a patient-centric philosophy. It has long recognized that nursing is a key factor in the efficient delivery of high quality patient care. Nursing also represents the hospital's highest cost of labor. Given these factors, administrators at Celebration Health sought business intelligence tools to better understand current nursing performance and pinpoint opportunities for workflow improvements leading to higher patient and staff satisfaction.

Celebration Health's Innovation Tower includes a 31-bed surgical/medical unit designed to be a "living laboratory" for innovation. In keeping with the hospital's patientcentric philosophy, Celebration Health made a strategic decision to invest in a real-time locating system (RTLS).

**Solutions Implemented**

- AeroScout Staff Workflow
- AeroScout Asset Tracking
- AeroScout Environmental Monitoring
- AeroScout Patient Flow

*With the advent of new reimbursement models and staff needing to work more efficiently, we saw a tremendous opportunity to use RTLS for ongoing research and process improvement.*

*- Patty Jo Toor, BA, RN, OCN
Chief Nursing Officer
Celebration Health*

With RTLS, the hospital aimed to address a range of operational and culture challenges, seeking not only to raise efficiency but also improve the patient experience and staff satisfaction. Building on the early successes in improving asset tracking and monitoring of temperature and humidity, the hospital turned its attention to using RTLS for business intelligence: understanding and improving complex processes related to clinical workflow.

## The Solution

Using STANLEY Healthcare's AeroScout® RTLS platform and MobileView® software, Celebration Health has pioneered the use of technology to track, analyze and enhance clinical workflow. This investment has been accompanied by proactive change management and communication to ensure that nurses understand and support process improvement initiatives. This initiative enables Celebration Health to more fully leverage the benefits of the STANLEY Healthcare Visibility and Analytics Platform, which it previously implemented for RTLS Asset Management and Environmental Monitoring.

*Celebration Health is leveraging the RTLS data provided by the STANLEY Healthcare solution to correlate staff actions with HCAHPS scores. The hospital can not only monitor care team processes and workflows, but understand the way the flow is viewed from a patient perspective.*

## The Results

By documenting travel patterns and time spent per location, administrators have been able to investigate specific aspects of nursing workflow, partnering with nursing staff to find new and better ways to optimize staffing levels, improve the efficiency of unit layout, and stablish and implement best practices for compassionate, compliant nursing care. The redesigned workflows have helped Celebration Health raise hourly rounding compliance to greater than 90%, while also driving the separation rate for registered nurses to 8.57%, well below the industry average.

## Solution Benefits

Since the unit's launch in 2011, Celebration Health has monitored staff workflow in the Innovation Tower; in 2013, it added oncology and elemetry patient units, and the OR, as well. Today, over 123 nurses and techs are part of the workflow improvement initiative across those four units.

"For years, hospitals have made certain assumptions about nursing staffing," says Director of Performance Improvement Ashley Simmons. "We realized we could use our STANLEY Healthcare solution to study nursing at a whole different level—to question many of those longstanding assumptions and to truly understand how and where our nurses spend their time."

In deploying the solution, Celebration Health gave particular attention to managing cultural change, working closely with the clinical staff to educate them on the intent of the technology and to address any "Big Brother" fears. By making it clear that the solution was intended to improve the work experience by making shifts run more smoothly and efficiently, and that the data would never be used in a punitive way, the hospital has been able to turn the clinical staff into engaged participants, eager to see and understand their own workflow patterns. This strategy has made Celebration Health highly successful in retaining its nursing staff, with a separation rate for registered nurses of just 8.57%, well below the industry average. Keeping staff turnover to a minimum reduces recruiting and training expenses, and helps foster a stable environment for care teams.

Having access to detailed data—and being able to run a wide range of analyses and reports—has revealed some important findings. With the ability to drill down by service line, by time of day and even by individual nurse or technician, the hospital has uncovered opportunities to make small but important changes.

Heat maps confirmed how much time and attention clinical staff members were devoting to Head and Neck Surgery patients. "The data showed that if you had multiple head and neck patients, you were just swamped," Ms. Toor notes, adding that the hospital has since made assignment changes to better balance workload.

Celebration Health has also started to understand and respond to the different dynamics of the day and night shifts. It has become clear to the hospital that, contrary to a widely held assumption, the night shift is just as busy as the day shift. The way it is busy, however, is very different. Activity on the day shift is more or less constant, whereas the night shift is characterized by periods of intense activity at the start and end of the shift, with a lull in between. By shifting some activities to the quieter hours, the hospital has helped reduce bottlenecks and addressed a point of dissatisfaction for the clinical staff.

Significantly, the nursing staff is now taking ownership of identifying ways to enhance processes. The spaghetti maps of movement across a shift enable each nurse to actually see how the day is spent, and identify areas for improvement; for example, by combining multiple trips to the supply room into a single visit to eliminate tiring "back and forth" movement. "When they see data, they're starting to think differently," Ms.Toor says. "It has been rewarding to watch them take control of their own environments—to ask the tough questions and then try to fix it."

Celebration Health follows a Purposeful Rounding practice, encouraging meaningful engagement between clinician and patient at every room visit. The data from the AeroScout solution provides objective validation that this is in fact occurring. Hourly rounding compliance stands at a healthy 90%, and the length of time nurses are spending in patient rooms provides evidence that they are doing so with intent. "Each time that they round they're spending at least 2 to 4 minutes in the room," says Ms. Simmons. "It's not just a quick poke your head in."

Looking to the future, Celebration Health is leveraging the RTLS data provided by the STANLEY Healthcare solution to correlate staff actions with HCAHPS scores. The hospital can not only monitor care team processes and workflows, but understand the way the flow is viewed from a patient perspective. "There is still a lot more we can learn from really understanding nurses and their workflow and how it impacts the bottom line for the hospital," Ms. Toor notes.

Read the full case study at www.stanleyhealthcare.com

# *Case Study*: Geisinger Tracks Patients with Disposable RTLS Wristband Tags

—STACEY ROBERTS, MARKETING MANAGER, CENTRAK

Approximately 80 percent of patients who visit the Geisinger-Community Medical Center (G-CMC) emergency department go home at the end of their visit. The other 20 percent are admitted to the hospital for overnight care, and might move from one area to another—such as to diagnostics, a patient room or a waiting area. In this dynamic, unstructured care environment it can be difficult and time-consuming for families or health-care providers to locate them. CenTrak's disposable wristband tag is intended to resolve that issue. G-CMC is using the disposable tags to provide patient location information to patients' families and care providers, as well as to its cleaning staff. What's more, the disposable wristband tag is more affordable than reusable versions—especially since the permanent wristband tags can get lost, and there is an additional cost of sanitizing them after use. "One of the barriers to patient tracking has been the cost of tags," says Ari Naim, CenTrak's president and CEO. Reusable tags can be expensive, while related activities—such as the cleaning and sterilization of tags, as well as the replacement of tags accidentally taken home by patients—can add an additional cost. To be economically and clinically efficient, the tag must be a commodity, not an expensive gadget.

## Accurate, Real Time Patient Location

At G-CMC, upon being admitted to the hospital, a patient is issued a disposable CenTrak tag attached to a standard plastic ID bracelet typically used by medical facilities. The unique identifier encoded on the tag is also printed on its front so that employees can input that number into the system to link it with the patient's other information in TeleTracking Technologies' software, which manages the tag data. The wristband tag also comes with a bar code utilizing that same serial number, enabling personnel to scan the bar code to enter the identifier as well.

CenTrak's second-generation infrared (Gen2IR™) beacons were installed throughout the hospital. The wristband tag receives the ID numbers transmitted by IR beacons within its range, and forwards that information, along with its own identifier, via an ultrahigh-frequency (UHF) signal using a proprietary air-interface protocol. The data is received by a CenTrak Gen2IR Monitor (RFID reader) and forwarded to a CenTrak location server. The location data is then passed on to the TeleTracking software, which displays the tag's location —and thus that of its wearer—on a video monitor.

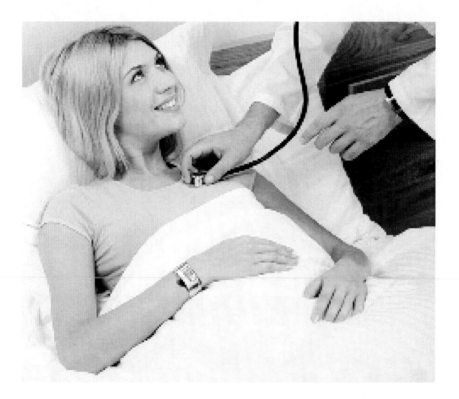

The hospital uses video monitors, known as tracker boards (three of which have been installed in the emergency department), as well as computers, to display the location of each patient by name in real time. The monitors are not intended for public viewing. A physician or family member looking for a patient can seek assistance from a staff member, who then refers to the monitor display and can tell that person the room in which the patient is currently located.

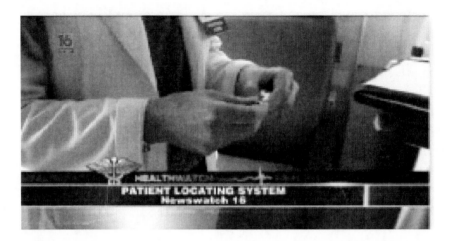

When G-CMC discharges the patient, the entire wristband is removed and placed in a CenTrak ITK 363 Tag Drop Box. A built-in Gen2IR Monitor captures each wristband tag's ID number and forwards that data to the software, which then updates the patient's status as having left the facility. The cleaning staff can then access the software to determine that that patient's bed has been vacated, as well as when this occurred, so that they can enter that room and begin preparing that bed for the next patient.

## An Extendable Technology Solution

Initially, the hospital intends to continue using the solution to provide location information to families and health-care providers. However, G-CMC notes , the solution could offer further functionality that the medical center might opt to take advantage of in the future. For instance, Kelly Worsnick, registered nurse and Operations Manager of the Emergency Department at G-CMC, says, the hospital could link the locations of medical equipment and patients, in order to better track which services a patient is receiving and when they are provided, not only for real-time information but for historical data as well. If a highly contagious infection were detected at the hospital, personnel could quickly access information about equipment used on an infected patient and address the sterilization issues accordingly. The system can also be used to monitor the time and duration of a visit between a healthcare provider and a patient, as long as that provider was also wearing an RTLS badge or tag. It's called "clinical grade" locating, and it's flexible enough to meet a variety of operational requirements; not only is location known, but key measures of performance can be tracked, processes can be streamlined, and predictive tools can be employed. These ondemand insights allows clinicians to more efficiently manage workflows, reduce patient wait times, and ensure that the correct clinical staff and equipment are in the correct place at the correct time. These expanded applications of CenTrak's "clinical grade" RTLS are being deployed in the emerging "smart" hospital.

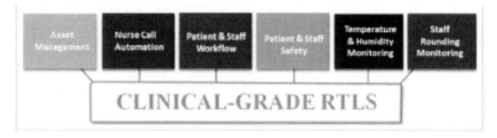

# "Smarter" RTLS in the "Smart" Hospital

In the smart hospital, smart RTLS is being employed to stagemanage patient movements and interactions throughout the facility, and to make predictions about likely bed use, admissions and discharges over the next several hours. With RTLS inspired contextual awareness, the smart hospital can glean insights into operations aimed at cost reduction, process optimization and clinical service quality.

Here are some examples:

### Extendable Workflow Solutions
Hospitals are building upon single purpose clinical solutions like hand washing monitoring, as the springboard towards a range of sophisticated mobile/RTLS patient care analytic and reporting tools, made available in real time.

Pre and Post-Op – Bed-level locating

Emergency Department – Bed-level locating with rapid location update speeds

Patient Transit/ Hallways deploy RTLS in all areas

Staff Locating – deploy RTLS in all areas

Room-level, sub-room level – Enable reliable nurse rounding compliance monitoring

Operating Rooms – Easy installation for non-disruptive full hospital deployment

### Remote Patient Monitoring

In the facility, staff can monitor (and act upon) patient throughput, wait times, and high value asset allocation. With multi-parameter monitoring devices for post-acute care, these tools are cheap, and prevent unnecessary health events and hospital re-admits.

### Wearables

Multi-purpose watch or badge captures location and process data in regard to patient services, enterprise workflows, and consumptive tasks. In nursing services for instance, wearable RTLS badges and wristbands are being mated with mobile and BI technologies, delivering a patient engagement and behavior change tool.

### Business Intelligence and Modeling

Mobile enabled RTLS data – including big data – can reveal a wealth of information at the staff level about the speed and effectiveness of clinical operations, identify weaknesses, allocate resources, and model solution sets. With these analytics, hospitals can make efficient use of staff time, allocate equipment, adjust appointments, boost quality and compliance, and increase capacity.

For the patient, smarter RTLS technology means better management of the patient experience, improved clinical quality, better coordination of the care team, and for the caregiver, family and friends – a sense of inclusion.

# *Case Study*: The Value of Enterprise-Grade Operation Intelligence

HOW WAKE FOREST BAPTIST HEALTH LEVERAGES REALTIME TECHNOLOGIES TO OPTIMIZE RESOURCES AND STREAMLINE WORKFLOWS

*"It is so rewarding to see our staff so engaged with technology. Every day they come up with new and innovative ideas on how to use sensory data to provide the ultimate patient experience."*
> — Conrad Emmerich, VP Clinical Operations, Wake Forest Baptist Health.

## The Situation

The goal of Wake Forest Baptist Health is to provide the best quality patient and family-centered care to improve the health of those who live in the communities they serve, and to do this more efficiently and effectively to lower medical costs. One of the key initiatives at Wake Forest Baptist is to use real-time technologies coupled with process improvements to optimize resources, streamline workflows, and assist in creating the "Ultimate Patient Experience."

## The Solution

In order to meet this strategic objective, Wake Forest Baptist established the Office of Enterprise Visibility. This office is responsible for the implementation of process, supporting technologies, driving Service Excellence, Patient Safety and Satisfaction, Operational Excellence and Efficiency, and the Transformation of Healthcare Delivery (SPOT). As the result of this focus, Wake Forest Baptist has been recognized as having the most comprehensive implementation of real-time technologies in the healthcare industry.

Wake Forest Baptist has successfully implemented more than50 use cases leveraging real-time location data, These use cases include asset management, temperature monitoring, wait=time management, infection control, patient/staff locating, milestone of care, and many more. Achieving breadth and depth of use cases enabled through the execution of a specific vision and multi-year plan along with an enterprise-grade operational intelligence platform. The platform's API's are being continually utilized to develop additional integrations and several additional high-value applications.

## The Benefits

The value of leveraging real-time technologies at Wake Forest Baptist is measurable and sustainable, accounting for more than $8 million in benefit - all in just the last 34 months. By automating temperature monitoring processes, Wake Forest Baptist is experiencing a savings of $970,000 per year. Additional benefits include asset management, which providing a savings of $2 million per year, and an increase in staff productivity that is valued at over $2 million per year. Wake Forest Baptist has also been able to save $3.5 million by eliminating the need to purchase redundant systems and avoiding unnecessary costs. The staff at Wake Forest Baptist fully embraces the value of technology and incorporates it in their daily operations.

Looking back upon the project, Wake Forest Baptist is able to justify the effort and cost based upon the return already received, and is looking forward to even more value as the ROI continues to grow with each new use case being deployed.

**Real-Time Location System Tracks Staff, Patients, and Equipment, Reducing Costs, Improving Infection Control and Room Turnaround, and Generating High Satisfaction**

## Description of the Innovative Activity

Two Texas Health Resources (THR) hospitals—a large 40-year-old facility and a new smaller facility—use a real-time location system enabled by radio frequency and infrared identification (RFID) technology to monitor the current location and recent movement of major pieces of equipment; one hospital (the new facility) also uses it to monitor the whereabouts of patients and staff, with the other hospital is currently adding this capability. Integrated into other THR information systems and overseen by a centralized mission control unit, the system is used to improve various clinical and nonclinical processes, including asset management, infection control, room turnover, and transportation. Hospital leaders prohibit its use in punitive manner with staff.

## Selecting Hardware and Software

THR already used a software system throughout the organization, and leaders decided to continue working with that vendor (Intelligent InSites) to integrate the real-time location system. With respect to hardware, the project manager first worked with the information technology team to investigate available options and then issued an extensive request for proposals. This process began about a year before the hospital opened and concluded roughly 4 months later with the decision to contract with CenTrak for the RFID tags, monitors, and other needed hardware and equipment.

## Results

The system has significantly reduced annual equipment costs, room turnaround time, and staffing costs, and contributed to high levels of patient, physician, and staff satisfaction.

*Significant reduction in annual equipment costs:* The system has reduced equipment-related costs at both hospitals. At the 650-bed flagship hospital, the system generated nearly $1 million in savings the first year, including roughly $285,000 on rental equipment, $100,000 on budgeting for "shrinkage" (the common practice of intentionally purchasing more equipment than needed because of missing items), and more than $600,000 in procurement related expenses because of better utilization of equipment. At the new hospital, the system allowed leaders to avoid budgeting any money at all for shrinkage—by contrast, many hospitals routinely add 35 percent or more to their equipment purchase budget to account for missing and lost items.

*Faster room turnaround:* At the 58-bed hospital, room turnover occurs more quickly than at any other THR hospital, averaging 40 minutes, well below the 47-minute average for the system as a whole.

*Lower staffing costs:* While hard data are not available, the centralization of communications, transport, and other operational functions requires fewer staff than the typical decentralized approach. For example, when working in separate departments, telephone operators and transporters often have significant periods of downtime. With the centralized approach, downtime tends to occur much less frequently.

*High patient, physician, and staff satisfaction:* The 58-bed hospital enjoys very high patient satisfaction rates, which leaders believe are due in part to the timely, high-quality services enabled by the real-time location system. For example, in 2013 the hospital ranked in the 95th percentile or higher on patent satisfaction ratings for the following categories directly related to the system: promptness of response to call bell, pain control, and wait time in the ED before being admitted to the hospital. Physician satisfaction with the hospital's information technology ranks in the 92nd percentile, with 10 percent of physicians specifically listing technology as one of the hospital's greatest strengths. In addition, overall employee satisfaction ranks in the 90th percentile at the hospital.

# References

1.   AHRQ Health Care Innovations Exchange. Real-Time Location System Tracks Staff, Patients, and Equipment, Reducing Costs, Improving Infection Control and Room Turnaround, and Generating High Satisfaction (Texas Health Resources). In: AHRQ Health Care Innovations Exchange[Web site]. Published: August 27, 2014. Available: https://innovations.ahrq.gov/pro-files/real-time-location-systemtracks-staff-patients-and-equipment-reduc-ing-costs-improving

# *Case Study*: Health System Overview

- HENRY FORD HEALTH SYSTEM

Henry Ford Health System (HFHS) is a Michigan not-for-profit corporation governed by a 25-member Board of Trustees. Advisory and affiliate boards comprising 153 Trustee volunteer leaders provide vital links to the communities served by the System. HFHS is managed by Chief Executive Officer, Nancy M. Schlichting.

HFHS is one of the nation's leading comprehensive, integrated health systems. It provides health insurance and healthcare delivery, including acute, specialty, primary and preventive care services backed by excellence in research and education. Founded in 1915 by mobile pioneer Henry Ford, the health system is committed to improving the health and well-being of a diverse community. HFHS is the fifthlargest employer in metro Detroit with over 2.1 million-squarefeet of medical facilities which treat 2.2 million patients per year.

The entire system centers around five main medical centers: Henry Ford Hospital, Henry Ford West Bloomfield Hospital, Henry Ford Kingswood Hospital, Henry Ford Macomb Hospital and Henry Ford Wyandotte Hospital. The System's flagship, Henry Ford Hospital in Detroit, is a Level 1 Trauma Center recognized for clinical excellence in cardiology, cardiovascular surgery, neurology and neurosurgery, orthopedics, sports medicine, multi-organ transplants and cancer treatment.

Highlighting the system's dedication to patient experience and improved patient care, Henry Ford West Bloomfield Hospital is leading the industry in providing excellence in the patient experience through the direction of a former CEO of The Ritz- Carlton chain of fine hotels. Towering atriums, comfortable patient rooms, pervasive wireless connectivity and an organic and healthy menu prepared by world-class chefs are just some of the features of this boutique facility.

# The Health IT Department

At HFHS, eight engineers are dedicated to supporting the wireless infrastructure for the entire organization. These engineers are regionally focused and are assigned to a geographical region to support each medical center network. Each location is designated either a Tier 1 (large main campuses, data centers) Tier 2 (bigger hospitals, clinics with emergency services/mission-critical locations) or Tier 3 facility with a total of 150 sites currently and growing. Each engineer is not dedicated to a particular site, but is assigned by subject matter and region. Wireless has its own architecture and operations responsibilities separate from the regular LAN operations and architecture.

Siemens Enterprise Communications provides all engineering services for HFHS, facilitating IT-level support and taking care of IT infrastructure, services, desktop engineering and help desk. OneIT is the HFHS solution for all outsourced solutions at HFHS, bringing all vendors under the umbrella of supporting the entire health system.

# The Challenges

## EHR Accessibility at the Point of Care

Henry Ford Health System required continuous availability of the Wi-Fi network to support their mobility initiatives, which included supporting a multitude of mobile biomedical devices, patient & visitor BYOD and the wireless infrastructure to support improved EHR access in conjunction with their massive, 20,000 user Epic deployment. A critical aspect of the mobility needs at the hospital, the Epic implementation supports the requirements to provide real-time patient data at the point-of-care. Phase 2 of the Epic implementation includes the MyChart mobile application which gives patients controlled access to the same Epic medical record their doctor's use, via browser or mobile app. It would be critical for the IT department to provide support for the MyChart application for patient devices as part of the EHR rollout and will begin the implementation of a BYOD policy rollout for patient access to the clinical Wi-Fi.

## Providing Wall-To-Wall Wi-Fi Coverage

Henry Ford Health System is comprised of diverse facilities. The main campus in Detroit is a 70-year old building that was constructed as a fallout shelter during the cold war. This facility contains 6-foot concrete walls and many features that make RF propagation challenging. On the other end of the spectrum, Henry Ford West Bloomfield Hospital contains an 80-foot tree-lined atrium with interior patient rooms that makes containing RF difficult. When presented with these issues, HFHS performed a predictive site survey and spectrum analysis to understand what RF is already present and to layout the installation to insure adequate coverage would be achieved. HFHS incorporated CADD drawings of the site or building to layout the Wi-Fi network based on the predictive analysis. In some cases they have had to adjust their RF to get rid of interference and at one location they had to turn off the 2.4Ghz spectrum altogether due to RF interference. They have also had to overcome RF interference issues such as the trees growing in the atrium blocking the RF signals to the access points.

Deployment came down to one of two scenarios, each representing their own set of challenges: a lot of small sites with Wi-Fi spread across many small buildings to provide connectivity or one very large deployment requiring a lot of access points to provide connectivity and address high density traffic.

## Supporting Biomedical Devices on the Wireless Network

When HFHS planned the wireless infrastructure, the needs of Technology Management Services (TMS) could not be ignored. TMS is responsible for assisting clinicians in planning the purchase of biomedical devices. For many years, TMS rarely consulted with HFHS IT when it came to

A Showcase in Providing a Superior Patient Experience through Wi-Fi Technology

implementing these biomedical devices on the wireless network. After many cycles of biomedical device failures when integrating with the wireless network, Ali Youssef, Wireless Solutions Architect within Henry Ford IT, determined there must be a better way. Clinicians became very disenchanted with the wireless network, prompting Youssef to spearhead a program to help clinicians understand what devices would work best on the wireless network.

"Prior to working with TMS, most biomedical devices were "bolt on" solutions that may or may not function properly within the dense Wi-Fi deployment at HFHS," said Youssef. "Using our ITIL v2 and v3 Foundations Certifications helped us work with the supply chain for early engagements when procuring biomedical devices. By producing a service catalog, HFHS IT was able to provide a menu of approved biomedical devices that have been tested to work with the Extreme Networks IdentiFi Wi-Fi infrastructure".

## *The Extreme Networks Solution*

Working with Siemens Enterprise Communications and Extreme Networks, Henry Ford Health System embarked on an effort to provide pervasive wireless coverage to all five of their campuses. The deployment is spread throughout Michigan and extends down to Toledo, Ohio with four main hospital campuses and additional 50-60 additional sites (clinics, medical buildings, etc.) which range in size between 2,000 and 80,000 square feet. During the upgrade of the HFHS wireless network, it was determined there would be two main initiatives:

- Using higher capacity controllers reduced the number of controllers from 16 to 12 in order to reduce support requirements as well as provide a more robust infrastructure
- Increase access point coverage to support the initiativesrevolving around telemedicine, VoIP, and the need for 100% Wi-Fi coverage to support biomedical device integration.

Overall up to 7 million square feet of facility has Wi-Fi access with another 1 million square feet to be opened in the near future.

At this point there are approximately 3,200 access points, 1,200 dedicated sensors (for security), and 12 wireless controllers deployed to support the entire Extreme Networks IdentiFi Wi-Fi architecture.

The IdentiFi Wi-Fi solution at HFHS was designed and built for continuous availability through the use of overlapping access points and fully redundant controllers. During the design process, wireless engineers overlapped access points as much as possible although they are not using dynamic radio management (DRM) due to restrictions on where access points can be physically deployed. Deployed access points are stationed along the corridors and in open areas so as to minimize patient interruptions.

As far as outdoor access is concerned, there is not a lot of adoption because most of the work in healthcare is done indoors. HFHS does have one outdoor access point deployed on the roof in an outdoor patio area in the Bloomfield facility; mainly for VoWLAN which is supported at this facility. There is a potential scenario being considered for outdoor Wi-Fi in the ER area, which would allow an outdoor care space for the triage and treatment of patients in the event of a large disaster, such as hazmat containment, or in the event of a fire. HFHS may be looking at mesh for this and they have a design template for possible future deployment.

As of December 1st, 2012, HFHS on-boarded 20,000 users onto the new Extreme Networks IdentiFi Wireless network using the Epic EHR system without incident. In the Spring of 2013, they will continue rolling out Mobile IAM and a complete patient and clinician BYOD program.

# Chapter 5

# Wearables for Chronic Disease

**Movie 7: Wearables for Chronic Disease by Donald Jones**
https://vimeo.com/156569598

# Introduction

— POUYA SHOOLIZADEH

Access to healthcare is now considered an important part of the basic human rights, and the excellence of healthcare is essential in the safety of the complex network of society. Not only does it affect our individual health but it also directly touches persistent problems such as financial inequality, international poverty, war and conflict, natural disaster emergency situations, and national security[1]. These problems are in turn further complicated through growing healthcare costs, an aging global population, and a growth in chronic illnesses[1]. In the intelligent hospital of the future, experts will try to address these problems by integrating technological advancements that have recently fueled the ongoing revolution in healthcare with the explosion in mobile computing power that consumers have experienced.

A doctor's expertise can be reached from a patient's pocket through a smartphone, as the doctor can remotely monitor the patient's vital signs, perform simple medical diagnostic tests, observe the progress of an ongoing illness, predict a near future health event, contact the patient, dispatch emergency services for help, or even provide simple immediate treatment if needed, before the patient has even noticed any symptoms. A decade or two ago, this level of excellence in healthcare monitoring and remote healthcare delivery was perhaps only thought to be reserved for astronauts on the space station, but is now available to the average person thanks to the concept of mobile health (mHealth); an industry based on health equality, patient involvement, emerging technologies, consumerism, and a convergent evolution of electronic equipment into smartphones.

The new establishment of a link between mHealth and the concept of Intelligent Hospital is a prerequisite in the upcoming success of this concept. The complex interconnectivity of technology, the need for efficient and cheaper workflow, and mHealth, now all cross paths at the Intelligent Hospital.

The first part of this review focuses on several particular examples of ideas, devices, and concepts that have used innovative and simple methods to try to improve healthcare outcomes. Gratefully, these methods are starting to become more scientifically rigorous and advanced. mHealth is no longer a thought-provoking oddity but is now an integral part of patient-centered medicine. The later part of this review focuses on the recent realization that smartphone apps are now being utilized to not only diagnose patients, but also deliver important basic treatment to them.

# Discussion

The concept of telehealth – particularly the application of smartphones in healthcare - is extremely broad and covers all specialties of medicine, from the family doctor taking care of chronic conditions such as diabetes and heart disease, to the cardiologist, ophthalmologist, dermatologist, and psychiatrist. Also pediatricians now have an option to "prescribe" smartphone apps to children that teach them how to manage their complex medical problems through simple video games. Other games and apps have also been used in adults to drive behavior changes and health interventions that support smoking cessation[2] or monitor asthma[3]. Dermatologists too, can "prescribe" apps that can take pictures of skin moles and use an image analyzing algorithm to determine symmetry, borders, and color, then calculate the probability of malignancy[4]. Geriatricians can hand out "smart slippers" with sensors that detect walking gait[4] and use a smartphone app to evaluate the existence of medical issues and calculate the risk of a fall, and communicate this information with the doctor.

Perhaps one of the most exciting developments in smartphone patient monitoring is in the field of cardiology, since the smartphone is such an accessible, cheap, and yet powerful device to measure the heart's electrical activity. Willem Einthoven has been credited as the creator of the electrocardiograph (ECG) more than one hundred years ago[5], and was awarded the Nobel Prize in medicine in 1924[6] "for his discovery of the mechanism of the electrocardiogram." By building upon the important work of many physiologists who predated him, Einthoven successfully constructed the "String Galvanometer" in early 1900s and contributed to the start of the science of electrophysiology. The galvanometer, along with the mathematical modeling for the correction of the tracings allowed such an accuracy and precision, that the resulting ECGs (Figure 1) were

**FIGURE 1 Top: Einthoven's mathematically corrected traving published in 1902. Bottom: One of the first electrocardiograms drawn using a string galvanometer published in 1902.**

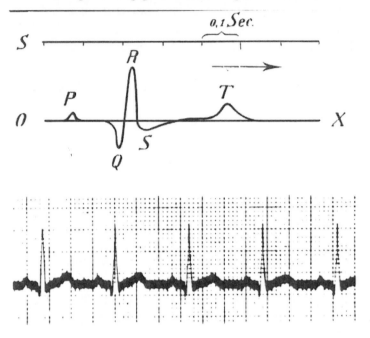

arguably as good as today's. An improved version of this large device that used water cooling for large powerful electromagnets, occupied a large room, and required five people to operate[7], can now be in your pocket: The iPhone. According to McManus et. al. at the University of Massachusetts Medical School, an application has been developed that uses the iPhone camera and lamp to obtain pulse recordings without the need for additional hardware[8]. This allows for an early detection of dangerous cardiac events such as atrial fibrillation (AF), a timely diagnosis of which is currently problematic with traditional tools[8]. Yet the novel algorithm "can accurately distinguish pulse recordings during AF from sinus rhythm."[8]

Patients in the 50+ age are generally seen as a group at high risk for cardiovascular issues and they can benefit immensely from mobile cardiovascular monitoring. A significant challenge in this field is that while currently about 79% of people aged 50+ own a cellular mobile phone, only 7% own a smartphone[9], although these numbers are certain to continue to increase. It is important to note that even though the 50+ age group is frequently shown in a few stereotypes, it is in fact a very heterogeneous group, and therefore the rate of adoption of new technology varies significantly among the group members[9]. One largely overlooked way to increase adoption of this new technology is to put it in the hands of the close caregivers who may also be age 50+. While 90% of 50+ persons who assist other 50+ persons are currently using cellphones, 83% of these caregivers do not use any mobile devices to help with the tracking of the health of the person they assist[9].

Another group at risk for cardiovascular issues is the seemingly healthy and superficially asymptomatic general population. It is thought that by 2015 more than two thirds of the population will own a smartphone, and a simple app such as the aforementioned iPhone application will be able to detect AF in the population that is hardest to monitor: the general population; while doing so, cheaply and efficiently[8]. The commercial market is also capitalizing on the new smartphone digital health revolution, such as AliveCor, a company that manufactures a small snap-on for smartphones that can take accurate ECGs[10]. This device can be used for the detection of atrial fibrillation in the general population[10], the same potentially dangerous condition that can be asymptomatic yet results in deadly strokes[10].

In a study, 109 patients had their ECGs recorded using the iPhone app as well as a gold standard 12- lead ECG10. Each of the patients were diagnosed by a cardiologist serving as a "gold standard", using only the 12-lead ECG, while two other cardiologists "A" and "B" – blinded to the 12-lead true diagnosis – had to diagnose each patient only using the iPhone obtained ECG. The results from cardiologist "A" showed 100% sensitivity, 90% specificity, and 94% accuracy, and the results from cardiologist "B" showed 95% sensitivity, 94% specificity, and 95%accuracy10. An automated optimized algorithm was then developed that could analyze the results directly. This algorithm was tested in a similar manner –blinded to the 12-lead ECG – this time tested on 204 patients (48 in AF), and the results showed 98% sensitivity, 97% specificity, and 97% accuracy[10]. A cheap and simple solution to detect atrial fibrillation in the general population will be a huge step forward since the current technologies are not costeffective enough to achieve this level of large scale screening[10]. In other innovations, smartphones have been used to complement already existing emergency services[11]. In the context of myocardial infarctions, the symptom-onset-toballoon time – the time it takes from a patient's onset of chest pain to their receiving of primary percutaneous coronary intervention (angioplasty) – has to be as minimal as possible. "Time is muscle" is an infamous saying in the hospital, as the earlier the reperfusion therapy is initiated the better the final clinical outcome is going to be, especially early in infarction[12].

Fujita et al have conducted a clinical trial for a newly designed system where an android smartphone is connected to a 12- lead ECG unit with Bluetooth[11]. Patients with myocardial infarction were placed into two groups: a control group receiving current standard of care, and an experimental group that utilized this smart phone system in addition to the standard care. This system successfully resulted in a significant reduction in the symptom-onset-to-balloon time, as the original control group without the ECG transmission resulted in 111±19.1 min, n=51, while the experimental group resulted in 91.5±11.1 min, n=22, p<0.000111.

Such time reduction of about 20 minutes which allows an accurate diagnosis of the patient's condition before arriving at the hospital can be a powerful solution with a substantially positive clinical outcome. Furthermore, if a patient can be diagnosed with an acute myocardial infarction early enough he/she can be taken directly to a hospital with an active catheterization lab, instead of having to be transferred there after arriving at an unspecialized facility, saving more time, and more heart muscle.

The above examples of smartphones complemented the diagnosis of patients, but interestingly smartphones can also be potentially used to deliver basic treatment for some conditions. Although the idea of smartphones helping physicians with diagnosis has been around for a while, the idea of smartphones performing treatment is relatively new.

One recently developed example is in patients who suffer from panic disorder. They are an important yet unnoticed group of patients visiting cardiologists with complaints of chest pain and palpitations[13].

Panic disorder is a condition in which a patient experiences panic or anxiety attacks, with symptoms such as shortness of breath, trembling of the extremities, chest pain, tachycardia, palpitations, sensation of extreme heat or cold resulting in excessive sweating or shivering, paresthesias, and psychological manifestations such as fear with an impending sense of doom, and depersonalization[14]. This disorder is usually successfully treated with a combination of Cognitive Behavioral Therapy (CBT), breathing exercises, and medication such as benzodiazepine for short term, and Selective Serotonin Reuptake Inhibitors (SSRIs) for long term therapy. Smartphones can be used to complement the breathing exercises, as well as deliver an internet based cognitive behavioral therapy, known as iCBT[15]. The efficacy of the smartphone and iCBT systems is under investigation, as a randomized controlled trial in Sweden is currently ongoing[15]. A smartphone game known as "Flowy" is proposed to be developed to teach the user "breathing retraining exercises" by translating their breathing pattern into a game. This game challenges the user to conform to a specific breathing pattern that can curtail the symptoms of a panic attack[16]. The anxiety, specifically the epinephrine excess associated with panic attacks is additionally linked to certain cardiac arrhythmias such as Premature Ventricular Contractions (PVCs)[17]. These contractions are found to be common among the general population[18], and are usually benign but they can be associated with other cardiovascular comorbidities.

PVCs can present in patients as a sensation of skipped beats followed by heart palpitations[17], which can in turn cause anxiety and trigger a panic attack and form a cycle of anxiety- PVC-panic, or rarely cause a fatal ventricular fibrillation[17]. It is then conceivable to construct a smartphone application that can accurately detect and record PVCs, assess the level of anxiety, and execute a treatment application if there are any ensuing complications such as a panic attack.

The "smartphone" is hard to define, as it is essentially a powerful computer with advanced sensors and digital communication capabilities, and many other smartphone-like devices have been made which have very similar abilities. Non-smartphone based smartphone-like wireless physiological monitoring has been entering the commercial market recently. BioHarness3 is a small device that can be fitted onto a person as a chest strap or be worn as a compression shirt, and monitor his/her vital signs as well as other physiological markers, and communicate this via a wireless network. With obvious uses such as for first responders or the military, similar devices by the same company Zephyr™ have been used in rescue operations such as monitoring of miners during the successful San Jose mine rescue operation after the Copiapó mining accident in hile in 2010 when 33 miners were trapped underground for 69 days19.

## Limitations

Perhaps an important yet mostly unnoticed barrier to implementation of these innovations is the stigma associated with bringing such medical procedures for diagnosis out of the hands of the physicians in the hospital and into the patient's own home. While some physicians may see this trend as potentially inappropriate, many other physicians, particularly the newer generation of doctors welcome and highly support this change. For example, at University of Central Florida College of Medicine, medical students have started a "Healthcare Innovations" society, specifically dedicated to bringing innovative and technologically advanced diagnostic and treatment apps and devices into a patient's own home20.

All new innovations and technology initially arrive with a bubble of excitement, publicity, and hype, and they must be put to the test by the rigors of the scientific method. But there must also be a balance reached, by "not letting perfect be the enemy of good"1. Developing nations are the ones that are in frantic need for innovation, and the 17 years it takes from bench to bedside "will doom an entire generation" according to the General Secretary for the International Telecommunications Union at the 2013 GetHealth Summit at the United Nations1. On the other hand, it is paramount to properly consider the safety, ethics, and scientific rigor of any idea, experiment, or design. It is therefore imperative for the more extensive and comprehensive projects to reduce translational latency as they expand internationally.

## Conclusions

Telehealth and in particular the application of smartphones in healthcare is a new and rapidly expanding field that can bridge the gap between the doctor and patient by using practical, ingenious, and resourceful techniques. Smartphones are now powerful computers that patients can carry around, empowering them with abilities that were not thought of before. They also give the physicians the power to diagnose or treat certain conditions from a distance, saving vital indispensable time, and limited money.

# References

1.  Abbott PA, Liu Y. A Scoping Review of Telehealth. IMIA Yearbook 2013: Evidence-based Health Informatics. 2013;8(1):51-58.
2.  Abroms LC, Lee Westmaas J, Bontemps-Jones J, Ramani R, Mellerson J. A Content Analysis of Popular Smartphone Apps for Smoking Cessation. American Journal of Preventive Medicine. 2013;45(6):732-736.
3.  Klasnja P, Pratt W. Healthcare in the pocket: mapping the space of mobile-phone health interventions. Journal of biomedical informatics. Feb 2012;45(1):184-198.
4.  Halim R. Unusual utilisation of mobile technology in medicine. Journal of Mobile Technology in Medicine. 2013;2(2).
5.  Moises Rivera-Ruiz, Christian Cajavilca, Joseph Varon. Einthoven's String Galvanometer. Texas Heart Institute Journal. 2008;35(2):5.

# *Case Study*: The Health Impact of Intelligent Home

CISCO • DAIS TECHNOLOGIES • FLORIDA BLUE • LAKE NONA INSTITUTE • US DEPARTMENT OF VETERANS AFFAIRS • UNIVERSITY OF CENTRAL FLORIDA • WELLNESS & PREVENTION INC. • A JOHNSON & JOHNSON COMPANY

## Intro

This white paper provides information on the research backdrop and the future potential for our Intelligent Home. We hope it will inspire individuals to think about ways to join or partner with Lake Nona Institute to further develop these technologies and explore potential use cases, using the home as a sort of "living laboratory" to pilot and assess new products and techniques.

## Organization

**Section I:** Rationale behind our approach to constructing and using the Intelligent Home.

**Section II:** The second section provides a review of some pertinent medical research that demonstrates the feasibility and effectiveness of many of the components of the home, and similar systems of health tracking and coaching.

**Section III:** A sampling of potential research questions the home may help answer in its function as a living test bed. Next, the report demonstrates examples of research and innovation opportunities made possible by the Intelligent Home. Finally, the report provides a brief overview of future health themes and events planned for the home.

Welcome to the Lake Nona Tour

**Intelligent Home Guided tour**

# Rationale for Approach

The design and intention here is to create a home that helps improve and sustain health; a nurturing environment. This can take form in the most technologically advanced device and the simplest pairing of an image and story in a frame. A nurturing environment is restorative and proactive. It cues the individual and spurs them towards where they find health and meaning —on a regular basis. The very act of creating this environment acknowledges that nurturing is a basic human need—not always something special or extravagant—but something essential. The attributes of a nurturing environment are attributes that connect people to their better intentions, to where they find purpose and inspiration for health (Shepherd, 1997). The Intelligent Home presents opportunities to find methods and measure the effects of creating a nurturing environment that address multiple dimensions of health.

With this home, we hope to illustrate ways that individuals and providers can work together to make their home a way to help improve and maintain the overall health and well-being of the family. A handful of conditions and health issues are currently being surveyed and addressed within the home, but we intend this model to be upgradable and flexible, such that we can accommodate and assess future conditions and points of concern.

Our aim is for the Intelligent Home to be useful not just as a single example or demonstration, but as a living laboratory and test bed to spur thinking and experimentation. In addition, we hope that the technologies and processes spurred by or vetted within the environment of the home will expand out from the individual family to the community level. Systems and models for families have the potential to interface and transfer out to the larger neighborhood and the population of patients served by particular practitioners or organizations.

### The Value of Wellness

The value of wellness is both personal and socio-economic. In addition to the impact that people can experience in their daily quality of life estimates show that of the nearly $3 trillion spent annually on U.S. healthcare costs, 69% are heavily influenced by consumer behaviors, over 30% can be directly attributed to behaviorally-influenced chronic conditions, and medication compliance alone costs $100 billion (Dixon-Fyle, Gandhi, Pellathy, & Spatharou, 2012).

Observably, lifestyle has a significant impact on healthcare expenditures – so much so that employers, major players in healthcare, and now retailers are seeking ways to help individuals improve their daily well-being and ultimately reduce healthcare spending.

Most recently, health promotion – in the form of wellness programs – has been gaining traction for its diverse array of potential impact on population health management. Wellness programs engage participants in a broad range of health education initiatives, create environments conducive to healthy lifestyles, and provide convenient access to healthoriented resources. While they have only recently started to receive large amounts of mainstream publicity, these programs have a history of success that is well documented in the scientific literature, ranging from improvements in biometric values, to improvements in health-related behaviors such as exercise and diet, to even more complex health issues, such as substance abuse and mental health (Loeppke 2013; Osilla 2012; Byrne 2011; Merrill 2011).

### The Intelligent Home

To maximize the potential for wellness initiatives to succeed, efforts must go further than merely implementing programs. An individual's ambient environment (or living space) must also be optimized to create a setting in which success is made easier and more achievable.

Intelligent homes are state-of-the-art residences designed with multiple cooperative and connected interfaces that encourage individuals to make healthful choices.

These smart homes transform the way individuals "make themselves at home" into ways they can help make themselves healthier. The interfaces connect residents more closely with the community, providers, insurers, and employees to minimize behavior-influenced healthcare costs. Inspired by innovations from Cisco, Florida Blue, GE, UCF, the VA, and Wellness & Prevention, Inc., a Johnson & Johnson company, among other partners, the Ashton Woods model is an Intelligent Home that helps individuals re-imagine everyday living.

### *The Art of Presentation*

One way to optimize an individual's environment is to support positive behaviors by influencing daily decisionmaking. Understanding what impacts our everyday choices will enable us to shape the environment to support and promote positive behaviors. Choice architecture teaches us that we can structure our environment in ways that maximize the probability of making healthier choices by making them both easy and desirable while simultaneously creating subtle barriers to prevent making less healthy decisions. For example, convenience and accessibility of calorically dense fast foods encourages their consumption - it is much faster and easier to go to the local drive-thru for a greasy cheeseburger and an enormous, sugary drink than it is to cook a balanced, healthy meal at home. But what if this wasn't the case? What if your kitchen was specifically designed to make cooking a healthy meal for your family quick and convenient, and was even stocked with healthy foods that were organized in such a way that made them seem more accessible and appealing? Or with smaller plates that provided visual cues that made consuming appropriate portions easier? Having a plan for how your kitchen is organized will help you keep the healthy foods in reach, and the not-so-healthy ones stashed away for when you want a treat! (Ferriday & Brunstrom, 2008) Such an environment would make the choices required to live a healthy lifestyle much easier and would support healthy decisions.

In the same way that choice architecture can impact decisions, reframing the way that people think about concepts like nutrition can also support healthy changes. For example, it's important to eat a balanced diet and do so with moderation. (Schwartz & Byrd-Bredbenner, 2006.) Yet in America, many people believe that more is better; portion inflation is a major contributor to obesity and its comorbidities. Therefore, helping people appreciate the benefits of appropriate portion sizes, as well as understand the consequences of overconsumption, supports positive behavior change. (Schwartz & Byrd-Bredbenner, 2006).

Similarly, Americans could be encouraged to embrace frequently eating small meals and snacks as a way to enhance performance rather than skipping meals, or consuming fewer or only one large meal, as a way to lose weight or manage time. It has been estimated that 95% of people who lose weight regain it. Healthy lifestyles could be made more palatable and sustainable by replacing the belief that a healthy diet means being deprived of your favorite foods with recommendations that encourage consuming a balance of desired or "want" foods with nutrient dense "need" foods.

# Background Evidence

## *mHealth*

Mobile technology is increasingly being used for assisted living for chronic conditions by offering ongoing monitoring, self-tracking, coaching/support, and reporting. In a literature review on mobile health-enabling technologies, Von Bargen, Schwartze, and Haux (2013) found that the most common disease addressed in these studies was diabetes, followed by AIDS, cardiac insufficiency, cancer, asthma, COPD, and schizophrenia, in addition to vitals monitoring. The cell phone features used for communication are primarily SMS and MMS messaging, along with some usage of telephone and videophone calls.

SMS messaging to help patients manage ongoing chronic conditions such as diabetes have shown promising results for patient self-monitoring/tracking as well as for providers to send supportive and coaching messages. In their pilot of a telemedicine system to support glycemic control for adolescents, Rami et al. (2006) saw improved control when using the telemedicine solution for tracking versus using a paper diary method, as well as general high perception scores rating the program very good and wanting to continue. These programs are primarily helpful when combined properly with regular treatment plans to offer additional convenience and bridge gaps between consults. Sweet Talk, an SMS system for young persons with diabetes, improved selfefficiency (rating increased from $56.0 \pm 13.7$ to $62.1 \pm 6.6$) and self-reported adherence (rating increased from $70.4 \pm 20.0$ to $77.2 \pm 16.1$) when combined with conventional therapy; 82% of surveyed patients felt Sweet Talk improved their self-management, and 90% wanted to continue receiving messages (Franklin et al., 2006). With their Mobile Prescription Therapy (MPT) system for diabetes condition tracking, records access, and coaching, WellDoc has seen positive results in all components of care, including declines in HbA1c levels of 1.2% more among participants using the MPT solution versus patients receiving usual care, estimated cost savings per user per month of $390 - $630, as well as a 58% reduction in ER visits and 100% reduction in hospitalizations from the prior year among patients using the MPT (Quinn et al., 2011; Peeples & Iyer, in press; Katz, Mesfin, & Barr, 2012).

## *Telehealth*

Mobile and telemedicine technologies within the home can also help patients stay in touch with their doctors and other healthcare providers in more convenient ways, allowing for increased doctor-patient communication while still lowering costs. In his two-year assessment of a system for mobile evisits with doctors, Dr. William Thornbury (2013) saw approximately 15% increase in practice capacity alongside an almost equivalent percentage drop in per-capita costs, with a 97% rate of patient satisfaction and an average turnaround time of less than three minutes per consult.

### *Fitness and Wellness*

The concept of the intelligent home is intended to help make a healthy lifestyle easier, and one of the ways this is accomplished is by making certain health-promotion resources available and easily accessible. One such resource, available to those who choose to participate in the Lake Nona Life Project, is Digital Health Coaching (DHC). DHC is an internet-based tool that uses participant feedback (guided by intelligent algorithms and established therapeutic techniques) to help individuals achieve a healthier lifestyle. Put simply, DHC provides immediate, private access to some of the same evidence-based behavioral recommendations and interventions you might receive from a face-to-face session with a clinician – all tailored to your specific needs and situation. The specific evidence for Digital Health Coaching spans across wellness and disease management, and has been associated with meaningful economic value in each of these areas. Participants in the Highmark BCBS employee wellness program (which included health risk assessments, online programs, coaching, biometric screenings, and fitness campaigns) showed health care costs lowered by $176 per participant per year, an ROI of 1.65:1 (Naydeck et al., 2008). Assessment of the HMSA BCBS plan in Hawaii's use of HealthPass demonstrated ROI ranging from 1.16:1 to 1.16:1 to 2.83:1, with an average cost savings per participant of $350 (Schwartz, et al., 2010). 2.83:1, with an average cost savings per participant of $350 (Schwartz, et al., 2010).

Among specific health related topics, some studies have shown improvements as well. Kaiser Permanente (2010) has shown consistent positive results with their HealthMedia® digital coaching programs, demonstrating weight loss, smoking cessation, and stress reduction among more than 50% of participants that provided feedback following their completion of a related digital coaching program. Another study, published just this year, showed that participants experienced significant reductions in pain intensity and unpleasantness scores following completion of tailored DHC for chronic pain management (Nevedal, et al., 2013).

The advancement of wellness research now includes longitudinal community health studies. The community based approach to research was made famous by studies such as the Framingham Heart Study (http://www.framinghamheartstudy.org/), which focused on cardiovascular disease using a cohort of nearly 5,000 residents of Framingham, Mass. Now in its third generation, the Framingham Heart Study has contributed much of what we know today about heart disease and the associated risk factors. The Nurses' Health Study, another widely-cited study, has made similar invaluable contributions to our understanding of breast cancer and other women's health issues by studying data from more than 200,000 nurses over more than 35 years (http://www.nhs3.org). The Lake Nona Life Project is a modern-day version of these landmark efforts, conducted within a master-planned community, developed with sophisticated technology, and in a community focused on sustainability, education and health and wellness. By combining these cutting edge technological components with a deliberate and informed design, the intelligent home will be a valuable addition to the living laboratory utilized by the Lake Nona Life Project.

# Future Research & Collaboration

The beauty of the Lake Nona Life Project is collaboration. Already, leaders from industry, science, government, and academia have come together with a common goal in mind: to explore our greatest health challenges. We believe technology can play a large part in developing solutions and through collaborations like the Lake Nona Life Project and the Intelligent Home, we will be looking into:

- How are mobile devices being integrated into daily health and wellness regimens?
- Whether exergames are effective for motivating people to exercise?
- What is the combined effect of multiple nutrition and fitness interventions in a home setting?
- How do we extend individual health activities to an entire community?
- What are some of the social and collaborative tools that are most effective in promoting wellness and prevention plans and activities?
- Does the layout of a kitchen affect food choices?

- What are some of the planning and motivational techniques that can help achieve health outcomes at low cost?
- What is the optimal tool kit of health oriented apps, methods, and education that produces the maximum effect with vthe minimum financial and time impact?
- Does ambient health monitoring in CHF provide a capability that is similar to that of current remote monitoring capabilities through standalone equipment OR done through manual reporting of self-collected monitoring data?
- Does ambient health monitoring provide a Quality of Life benefit that is statistically better than the same achieved through other traditional means (remote monitoring or selfmonitoring) in CHF patients?
- Does ambient health monitoring lead to long-term health care outcomes related to lowered disease burden, improved quality of life, and lowered cost of care at the individual and system levels in CHF management within a community setting?
- What criteria can be used to identify an engaged patient and delivery system/care team that define the greatest likelihood of success for ambient health monitoring in CHF?

## Example Opportunities

In CHF, the success of the care plan in a community setting can be defined by the following:

1. Quality of life – the ability of a member to engage in activities they enjoy without limiting factors caused by CHF
2. Compliance to care plan
3. Physical abilities in Activities of Daily Living
4. Affordability of care
5. Delaying transition to assisted living
6. Reduction in interruptions caused by ER visits/hospital admissions

The experience in the living laboratory allows us to test different hypotheses as well create different case control experiments that test out the interdependence of various controllable variables, such as:

- Impact of physical activity
- Impact on health habit formation
- Impact of nutritional interventions related to changes in calories, sodium, eating times as well diet types
- Impact of monitoring vitals as well as morbidity indicators that can provide just-in-time patient controlled actionable interventions, as well its long term impact on health outcome
- Understanding the outcomes in engaged patients (or Activated patients) in comparison to those who are not
- Systems-based interactions for family members and technologies
- Social effects of health behaviors among family
- members

# Future Themes/Events

As you can see from the prior sections on background evidence and future opportunities for collaboration, the Lake Nona Institute team would welcome other partners who wish to conduct studies, pilots, or community testing to answer some of the many research questions presented herein.

Preparation has already begun for the HIMSS '14 Annual Conference and Exposition and the Intelligent Health Association Symposium, both scheduled for the week of February 23 in Orlando. We also welcome attendance and contact at future events like J&J Ignite and next year's Lake Nona Impact Forum.

# Contact Our Members

- For inquiries related to HIMSS, please contact Dr. David Metcalf (dmetcalf@ist.ucf.edu)
- For inquiries related to the Lake Nona Life Project, please contact Dr. Shawn T. Mason (SMason5@ITS.JNJ.com)
- For all other inquiries and Medical City partners please contact Gloria Caulfield (gcaulfield@lakenonainstitute.org)

# References

1.  Armstrong, A. W., Watson, A. J., Makredes, M., Frangos, J. E., Kimball, A. B., & Kvedar, J. C. (2009). Text-Message reminders to improve sunscreen use: A randomized, controlled trial using electronic monitoring. Archives of Dermatology, 145(11), 1230-1236. doi:10.1001/archdermatol. 2009.269

2.  Benardot D. (2007). Timing of energy and fluid intake: New concepts for weight control and hydration. ACSM's Health & Fitness Journal, 11(4), 13-19.

3.  Bachman, et al. (2011). Eating frequency is higher in weight loss maintainers and normal-weight individuals than in overweight individuals. Journal of the American Dietetic Association, 111(11), 1730-1734.

4.  Bourke, A. K., Prescher, S., Koehler, F., Cionca, V., Tavares, C., Gomis, S., ... & Nelson, J. (2012, August). Embedded fall and activity monitoring for a wearable ambient assisted living solution for older adults. In Engineering in Medicine and Biology Society (EMBC), 2012 Annual International Conference of the IEEE (pp. 248-251). IEEE.

5.  Byrne, et al. (2011). Seven-year trends in employee health habits from a comprehensive workplace health promotion program at Vanderbilt University. Journal of Occupational and Environmental Medicine; 53(12), 1372-1381.

6.  Dixon-Fyle, S., Gandhi, S., Pellathy, T., & Spatharou, A.(2012). "Changing patient behavior: The next frontier in healthcare value." Health International, 12, 64-73. Retrieved from http://www.mckinsey.com/~/media/McKinsey/ dotcom/client_service/Healthcare%20Systems%20and%20Services/ Health%20International/Issue%2012%20PDFs/HI12_64-73%20 PatientBehavior_R8.ashx

7.  Ferriday & Brunstrom (2008). How does food-cue exposure lead to larger meal sizes? British Journal of Nutrition, 100(6), 1325-1332.

8.  Fjeldsoe, B. S., Miller, Y. D., & Marshall, A. L. (2010). MobileMums: A randomized controlled trial of an SMS-based physical activity intervention. Annals of Behavioral Medicine, 39(2), 101–111. doi:10.1007/s12160-010-9170-z

9.  Franklin, V. L., Waller, A., Pagliari, C. and Greene, S. A. (2006). A randomized controlled trial of Sweet Talk, a textmessaging system to support young people with diabetes. Diabetic Medicine, 23, 1332–1338. doi: 10.1111/j.1464-5491.2006.01989.

10. García-Herranz, M., Olivera, F., Haya, P., & Alamán, X. (2012). Harnessing the interaction continuum for subtle assisted living. Sensors, 12(7), 9829-9846.

11. Gold, J., Aitken, C. K., Dixon, H. G., Lim, M. S. C., Gouillou, M., Spelman, T., ... Hellard, M. E. (2011). A randomised controlled trial using mobile advertising to promote safer sex and sun safety to young people. Health Education Research, 26(5), 782–794. doi:10.1093/her/cyr020

12. Hedman E, Ljotsson B, Lindefors N (2012). Cognitive behavior therapy via the internet: A systematic review of applications, clinical efficacy and cost-effectiveness. Expert Review of Pharmacoeconomics & Outcomes Research, 12(6), 745-764.

13. Hervás, R., Fontecha, J., Ausín, D., Castanedo, F., Bravo, J., & López-de-Ipiña, D. (2013). Mobile Monitoring and Reasoning Methods to Prevent Cardiovascular Diseases. Sensors, 13(5), 6524-6541.

14. Hurling, R., Catt, M., De Boni, M., Fairley, B. W., Hurst, T., Murray, P., ... Sodhi, J. S. (2007). Using internet and mobile phone technology to deliver an automated physical activity program: Randomized controlled trial. Journal of Medical Internet Research, 9(2), e7. doi:10.2196/jmir.9.2.e7

15. Kaiser Permanente. (2010). Health information technology: How can technology enhance care and reduce costs? Retrieved from http://consultants.kaiserpermanente.org/ info_assets/mercer/pdf/TIHP_IT_012610.pdf

16. Katz, R., Mesfin, T., & Barr, K. (2012). Lessons from a community-based mhealth diabetes self-management program: "It's not just about the cell phone". Journal of health communication, 17(sup1), 67-72.

17. Loeppke, et al. (2012). The association of technology in a workplace wellness program with health risk factor reduction. Journal of Occupational and Environmental Medicine, 55(3), 259-264.

18. Merrill, et al. (2011). Effectiveness of a workplace wellness program for maintaining health and promoting healthy behaviors. Journal of Occupational and Environmental Medicine, 53(7), 782-787.

19. Metcalf, D., & Krohn, R. (Eds.). (2012). mHealth: From smartphones to smart systems. Chicago, IL: HIMSS Publications.

20. Middleton, L., Buss, A. A., Bazin, A., & Nixon, M. S. (2005, October). A floor sensor system for gait recognition. In Automatic Identification Advanced Technologies, 2005. Fourth IEEE Workshop on (pp. 171-176). IEEE.

21. Naydeck, B. L., Pearson, J. A., Ozminkowski, R. J., Day, B. T., & Goetzel, R. Z. (2008). The impact of the Highmark employee wellness programs on 4-year healthcare costs. Journal of Occupational and Environmental Medicine, 50(2), 146-156.

22. Nevedal D, Wang C, Oberleitner L, Schwartz S, Williams A (2013). Effects of an individually tailored web-based chronic pain management program on pain severity, psychological health, and functioning. Journal of Medical Internet Research, 15(9), e201.

23. Osilla, et al. (2012). Systematic review of the impact of worksite wellness programs. The American Journal of Managed Care, 18(2), e68-e81.

24. Peeples, M., & Iyer, A. K. (in press). Mobile Prescription Therapy (MPT): Extracting healthcare and economic outcomes at the nexus of clinical and technology innovation. In R. Krohn & D. Metcalf (Eds.), mHealth Innovations. Chicago, IL: HIMSS Media.

25.  Prescher, S., Bourke, A. K., Koehler, F., Martins, A., Sereno Ferreira, H., Boldt Sousa, T., ... & Nelson, J. (2012, August). Ubiquitous ambient assisted living solution to promote safer independent living in older adults suffering from co-morbidity. In Engineering in Medicine and Biology Society (EMBC), 2012 Annual International Conference of the IEEE (pp. 5118-5121). IEEE.

26.   Quinn, C. C., Shardell, M. D., Terrin, M. L., Barr, E. A., Ballew, S. H., & Gruber-Baldini, A. L. (2011). Cluster-randomized trial of a mobile phone personalized behavioral intervention for blood glucose control. Diabetes Care, 34(9), 1934-1942.

27.  Rami, B., Popow, C., Horn, W., Waldhoer, T., & Schober, E. (2006). Telemedical support to improve glycemic control in adolescents with type 1 diabetes mellitus. European Journal of Pediatrics, 165(10), 701–705. doi:10.1007/s00431-006-0156-6

28.  Rothert K, Strecher V, Doyle L, Caplan W, Joyce J, Jimison H, Karm L, Roth M (2006). Web-based weight management programs in an integrated health care setting: A randomized, controlled trial. Obesity, 14(2), 266-272.

29.  Schwartz & Byrd-Bredbenner (2006). Portion distortion: Typical portion sizes selected by young adults. Journal of the American Dietetic Association, 106(9), 1412-1418.

30.  Schwartz, S. M., Ireland, C., Strecher, V., Nakao, D., Wang, C., & Juarez, D. (2010). The economic value of a wellness and disease prevention program. Population Health Management, 13(6), 309-317.

31.  Shapiro, J. R., Koro, T., Doran, N., Thompson, S., Sallis, J. F., Calfas, K., & Patrick, K. (2012). Text4Diet: A randomized controlled study using text messaging for weight loss behaviors. Preventive Medicine, 55(5), 412–417. doi:10.1016/j.ypmed.2012.08.011

32.  Shepherd, Donald. (1997) Ambient Design—Towards the Nurturing Environment.

33..  Thornbury, W. C. (2013). Mobile e-visits within the medical home [PDF document]. Session presented at HIMSS 13 Interoperability Showcase, New Orleans, LA. Retrieved from http://www.pcpcc.org/sites/default/files/mevisit_pcpcc_webinar_4-4-2013.pdf

34.  Van Ittersum, Koert, and Brian Wansink (2012). "Plate size and color suggestibility: The Delboeuf Illusion's bias on serving and eating behavior." Journal of Consumer Research, 39(2), 215-228.

35.  Villacorta, J. J., Jiménez, M. I., Val, L. D., & Izquierdo, A. (2011). A configurable sensor network applied to ambient assisted living. Sensors, 11(11), 10724-10737.

36.  Von Bargen, T., Schwartze, J., & Haux, R. (2012). Disease patterns addressed by mobile health-enabling technologies-a literature review. Studies in health technology and informatics, 190, 141-143.

37.  Zhou, Y. Y., Garrido, T., Chin, H. L., Wiesenthal, A. M., & Liang, L. L. (2007). Patient access to an electronic health record with secure messaging: impact on primary care utilization. American Journal of Managed Care, 13(7), 418-424.

# Additional References

1.  Frankl, V. (2006). Man's search for meaning. Boston: Beacon Press.
2.  Groppel, J. L., & Andelman, B. (2000). The corporate athlete: How to achieve maximal performance in business and life. New York: John Wiley & Sons, Inc.
3.  Johnson, R. W. (2004). Trends in job demands among older workers, 1992-2002. Monthly Labor Review, 127, 48.
4.  Loehr, J., & Schwartz, T. (2003). The power of full engagement: Managing energy, not time, is the key to high
5.  performance and renewal. New York: Free Press.
6.  Loehr, Jim. (2007). The power of story: Rewrite your destiny in business and in life. New York: Free Press.
7.  Newberg, A., & Waldman, M. R. (2006). Why we believe what we believe: Uncovering our biological need for meaning, spirituality, and truth. New York: Simon and Schuster.
8.  NIOSH Working Group. (1999). Stress at work. NIOSH Publication No. 99-101. Retrieved from http://www.cdc.gov/niosh/docs/99-101/
9.  Nygård, C. H., Huuhtanen, P., Tuomi, K., & Martikainen, R. (1997). Perceived work changes between 1981 and 1992 among aging workers in Finland. Scandinavian Journal of Work, Environment & Health, 23(Sup 1), 12-19.

# Acknowledgements

We would like to acknowledge the following contributors to this white paper:

*Cisco*
Surendra Saxena

*Dais Technologies*
Michael Voll, Vice President

*Florida Blue*
Jim Abdullah, IT Business Analyst
Jessica DaMassa, Innovation Consultant
Uday Deshmukh, MD, Sr. Medical Director, Care Management
Kathy Freyman, Sr. Director Business Innovation
Terry Murphy, Sr. Manager, Care Programs

*Lake Nona Institute*
Gloria Caulfield, Program Director
Ron Domingue, Program Director
Thad Seymour, PhD, President

*US Department of Veterans Affairs*
Ken Goldberg, MD, Chief of Staff

*University of Central Florida*
Michael Eakins, 3D Team Lead
Clarissa Graffeo, Faculty Researcher
Angela Hamilton, Program Coordinator
Brian Mayrsohn
David Metcalf, PhD, Director METIL

*Wellness & Prevention Inc., A Johnson & Johnson Company*
Eli Carter, Research Associate
Jennifer Farina, Creative Consultant
Rebecca Genin, Communications Manager
Cindy Heroux, RD Performance Coach (Human Performance Institute)
John Hetrick, Creative Director
Caren Kenney, Communications Director
Shawn Mason, PhD, Associate Director of Research
Outcomes and Analytics
Christopher Mosunic, PhD, MBA, RD, Director of Science
Raphaela O'Day, PhD, Manager Behavioral Science

# Chapter 6

# Global Best Practices and Evidence of Healthcare Outcomes Using Wearable Devices

Movie 8: Healthcare and using wearable devices by Alisa Niksch
https://vimeo.com/156575176

# Introduction

— LYNNE DUNBRACK - RESEARCH VICE PRESIDENT
  IDC HEALTH INSIGHTS

Three lifestyle behaviors — smoking, diet, and lack of exercise — contribute to poor health and exacerbate chronic conditions, which account for nearly 75% of healthcare costs. It is very difficult to address all three behaviors at once, especially since smoking and diet require individuals to make significant behavioral changes. But, addressing just exercise or activity can make a difference. Increasing activity can have a major impact on many chronic conditions including hypertension, coronary heart disease, diabetes, obesity, and mental health according to the CDC. The challenge is getting consumers to be less sedentary and more active. The CDC reports that 60% of U.S. adults are not regularly physically active and 25% of all adults are not active at all.

Consumers are showing an interest in tracking their health. A 2013 survey by the Pew Research Center's Internet & American Life Project reveals that 60% of U.S. adults say they track their weight, diet, or exercise routine and 33% of U.S. adults track health indicators or symptoms, like blood pressure, blood sugar, headaches, or sleep patterns. However, much of this health tracking is done informally and without the aid of technology, specifically trackers. Education about the availability and benefits of wearables will be important to the long-term success of health and wellness initiatives. Particularly if the recommendation to track health status comes from the consumer's trusted medical advisor.

Enter wearables that passively collect activity and biometric data such as number of steps taken, duration and distance, calories consumed and burned, and sleep patterns, via embedded sensors in the device. More advanced wearables not only track activity but also biometric data such as heart rate, skin temperature, skin galvanic response (i.e., sweat).

The devices are then synced with the mobile or Web-based companion application that features dashboards and activity logs for tracking this

# FITNESS & ACTIVITY
# WEARABLE TRACKERS

Slightly Less than
**1 in 3 CONSUMERS**
**Use** or **Have Used**
a Fitness & Activity
**TRACKER**

## Are you currently using a Fitness and Activity Tracker?

**10.8%**
Have stopped Using it

**19.2%**
Are still Using it

**70%**
Have never used a Tracker

## WHO IS THE TYPICAL
## FITNESS WEARABLE USER ?

**34 YRS**  $

61% are women

44.1% are 34 years old or younger

58.1% earn more than $50,000

87.3% have a smartphone

**DOWNLOAD**

**66%**
Have downloaded
a fitness Mobile
App that connects to
their Fitness Device

# Wearable Users
# & FITNESS MOBILE
# APPS USE

**56%**  Are still using the
Mobile app

IDC
Health Insights

IDC Health Insights study " Perspective: The Consumer Experience — Why Consumers Stop Using Fitness Trackers", Document #HI249611. For more information on IDC's research for IT executives contact us at 508.872.8200 or visit www.idc.com/itexecutive

information over time and against consumer-defined goals and provide feedback and opportunities for encouragement by online coaches and connections to social communities. The typical form factors for wearable activity trackers are wristbands including smartwatches, armbands, and devices that can be clipped on to clothing or footwear. Other form factors include sensors embedded into clothing, patches that can be worn discretely under clothing, temporary sensor tattoos "printed" directly on the skin, contact lenses that measure glucose levels, and even ingestible. Medical grade wearable devices used in the delivery of direct patient care must go through a rigorous approval process (e.g., FDA clearance, CE Mark).

Most common wearables for activity tracking are sold directly to consumers through traditional and online retail outlets. However, healthcare organizations (HCOs) are evaluating activity trackers and considering how they can be incorporated into their health and wellness initiatives as a means of better engaging their members and patients in their quest toward reaching their health goals. Lower-priced devices and data integration with HCOs' clinical systems will facilitate rolling out wearables as part of a larger population health strategy. Similarly, medical grade wearables for tracking biometrics for consumers with multiple chronic conditions or vital signs while in the hospital are also gaining traction.

## Results from Early Pilots are Encouraging

A number of pilot programs testing the efficacy of wearables have been conducted over the last few years by health plans and provider organizations.

- *Cigna and BodyMedia.* In a pilot program with BodyMedia, Cigna tested the efficacy of using digital health and fitness trackers along with health coaches to help members better manage their diabetes and reduce the associated risks of the disease. The program showed positive improvement in risk profiles with some participants moving from "chronic" to "at risk," and from "at risk" to averting diabetes.

- ***Cleveland Clinic and FitLinxx.*** Social networking plays an important role when it comes to consumer engagement. FitLinxx provides social networking for consumers through partner oganizations. For example, the Cleveland Clinic is working with Shape Up, a social wellness program that offers the Pebble to Cleveland Clinic employees. The Cleveland Clinic has distributed 24,000 Pebbles to their employees (85% of the eligible population) and set a goal of 600 minutes or 100,000 steps per month; 96% of participants have met their monthly goal. Employees (and their families) who use the Pebble enjoy lower health insurance premiums.

- ***Ochsner Health System and Apple Watch.*** As a beta tester of Apple's data-sharing platform, HealthKit, Ochsner was one of the first health systems in the United States to use the Apple Watch and iPhone to manage patients with chronic conditions. The first program remote health monitoring program was for hypertensive patients with blood pressure greater 140/90. While patients were given an Apple watch for the program, they had to provide their own iPhone and it and wireless blood pressure cuff, both of which were capable of connecting to HealthKit. Initial results look promising; seven weeks into the program 40% of the enrolled patients achieved controlled blood pressure status. Based on initial results, Ochsner is looking to grow the hypertension program using the Apple watch from 40 to 125 patients by the end of 2015.

- ***National Health System and SensiumVitals.*** In 2014, Montefiore Hospital in Brighton, England was the first hospital in the U.K. to use wireless patches from SensiumVitals to provide continuous vital sign monitoring of patients on the ward. Every two minutes, the patch's sensors collect vital signs such as heart rate, respiration and temperature and sends it wirelessly to the nurses station and handheld devices. If the readings are out of pre-set bounds, alerts are sent and nurses can intervene immediately. Continuous monitoring replaces the current method of taking vitals every four to five hours. Nurses on the ward where SensiumVitals patches are being use report that they can manage their workload more effectively and spend more time with patients who need immediate attention. The ability to continuously monitor vital signs means that clinicians can respond more quickly to patients whose conditions are deteriorating. In fact, early detection of a significant number of patients (12%) in the pilot meant that received care before their condition worsened, thus leading to better outcomes. A 2013 study conducted by SensiumVitals in the U.S. demonstrated that patients who received early intervention had their hospital stays reduced on average by four days.

- *China-Japan Friendship Hospital, Ministry of Science and Technology of the People's Republic of China and Wearables for Diabetes Management.* Based in Beijing, China, the China-Japan Friendship hospital is a tertiary Alevel hospital. In 2012, the institution embarked on a threeyear demonstration involving 1,000 patients with type 2 diabetes to test the efficacy of using a Xikang watch from Neusoft to encourage adherence to exercise recommendations. While the study is expected to conclude at the end of 2015 so no formal findings have been presented, early findings indicate that if the consumer made even a modest investment in the watch that they would be more active participants in the program. Providing additional services beyond the services provided by physicians in the local community centers (where patients must go to pick up medications) would also enhance the consumer experience and promote engagement between consumers and their clinicians.

# Success Requires Careful Planning to Overcome Challenges

A well-documented challenge of wearables, particularly those designed for activity tracking, is that after the initial infatuation with their device consumers lose interesting in tracking their health status and stop using their activity tracker. Various industry studies suggest that most consumers stop using the device regularly after 60–90 days or use it sporadically. The IDC Health Insights' Cross-Industry Consumer Experience Survey reveals that 1 out 3 consumers using a fitness tracker stopped using it in the past 12 months. If health and wellness programs that use fitness and activity trackers are to be successful, they must create sustained interest among consumers to continue using these devices and their accompanying health applications. Careful attention must be paid to program design to ensure ongoing consumer engagement and success outcomes.

Key questions to consider include:

- ***Who will pay for the fitness trackers?*** Sponsorship of the devices is an important consideration because many consumers will not pay $125 to $150 out of pocket for an activity tracker or hundreds of dollars for a smartwatch. Volume discounts from wearable vendors will be help to address this issue since most employers and HCOs will find these price points cost prohibitive for large-scale programs. Thus, few healthcare organizations or employers will give an expensive wearable to consumers for free with "no strings attached." Instead, financial incentives will be provided to encourage consumers to continue to use the device. One option is to have consumers buy their device, and upon meeting certain health goals, they are then reimbursed for the device. Though this may limit participation to those consumers with more discretionary spending. Another option is to provide a free device in return for doing something. Optima Health provides a free $100 Fitbit to OptimaFit members – if they have completed a personal health risk assessment – as part of new rewards program it launched in December 2014. Members are then eligible for an additional $175 in cash rewards for managing their health.

- ***How will behavioral health be incorporated into the program?*** While technology plays an important role by helping the consumer to be more aware of health status indicators (e.g., weight, exercise levels, sleep quality), coaching, motivation, and accountability will go a long way to bring about the changes needed to address unhealthy behavior. Social networking opportunities will provide opportunities for consumers to share their experience with others with similar health goals and to provide and receive encouragement to stay on track.

- ***How actionable is the information presented to the consumer?*** Readings from the device should be readily available to the consumer, ideally from the device itself or at least a mobile application. Dashboards presenting information to the consumer should be well organized and easy to understand by people with average health and data literacy. Color coding (e.g., red, yellow, green) is a useful way to depict progress toward goals. Some metrics, such as number of steps walked, are easier to understand

and are more actionable. Sleep duration and quality, on the other hand, is at best a proxy based on accelerometer algorithms and more difficult for the consumer to address on his or her own.

- **How accessible is the data generated by the device for the health and wellness program administrator?** HCOs and employers should carefully evaluate how easy it is to aggregate data from across the population using the fitness trackers. This is beyond consumers downloading their data to the mobile or Web-based application to review their activity. The ability to track activity data easily and accurately will enable organizations to develop incentive programs, report group progress, and identify consumers who may be abandoning the program.

## Best Practices from Early Pilots Emerge

Before beginning the selection process, including identifying potential vendor solutions to evaluate, HCOs should define what they wants to accomplish and the goals and objectives for health and wellness or chronic conditions management program. This will help to inform many of the decisions that must be made along the way. It is important to get this right or HCOs will risk selecting the wrong solution to meet illdefined objectives.

- **Consider ease of use and the ergonomic design of the device.** Wearability, ease of use, and valuable insights are two important factors when it comes to sustained used of wearables. It is important to recognize that wearables are mechanical devices that have their limitations such as battery life, charging time, and ability to get wet or not. Ease of syncing the device with the mobile app to export data to be presented in dashboards that are easy to understand will be important to keeping consumers engaged in the health and wellness program.

- **Don't underestimate the logistical requirements of device Management.** Key questions to consider are how will devices be distributed? In the case of devices for monitoring chronic conditions, physician offices handle this step or will the vendor? Consumers will have questions about how to use the device and what to do if it malfunctions. HCOs will need to determine if they, the vendor, or a third party will provide logistical support for the HCO and customer support for consumers.

- ***Involve clinicians, especially for remote health monitoring programs.*** As with any clinical project, there has to be a strong advocate for the program who will tout the benefits of the RHM program to his or her colleagues. Collaboration and communication among physicians will  be instrumental to ensuring clinical buy-in. Success lies with the clinical team. If they perceive that the RHM program will upend their clinical workflow, require a complete reengineering of their processes, and create additional steps that make them less efficient, they will resist participating in the program. Nor will they encourage their patients to participate.

- ***Understand how clinicians will use patient reported information.*** In order to create complementary clinical workflows for accessing patient information collected through wearable devices, HCOs should evaluate how physician practices will use the information as well as how they would like to receive clinical alerts. Look for solutions that provide the most flexibility when it comes to communicating patient data and alerts to clinicians because practice patterns will vary by specialty, technical expertise and care management resources within the practice.

- ***Control the flow and volume of data.*** Integration of biometric data into the physician's EHR system must be done carefully. Some physicians will want this data included in the patient's medical records, but will want to control which data values and how much to include. Physicians do not want thousands of biometric readings inserted into the patient's records. Other physicians will prefer to view data in a physician dashboard that presents data graphically for either individual patients or patient populations. Or will want it available to their nurse care managers who provide a summary report for the patient's next office visit. Surveying physicians to determine what works for them is a useful step before rolling out wearables for monitoring chronic conditions on a wide scale basis. HCOs would be well advised to ensure the vendor can support multiple approaches to data integration and presentation.

- ***Be prepared to invest in inoperability, analytics, and security technology.*** While getting the "gadget" right is important for user acceptance, getting the infrastructure correct is critical to long term success at scale. Integrating data collected from wearables with electronic health records is challenging because most wearable devices rely on proprietary technology. The Apple HealthKit, Google Fit, and Microsoft Health platforms provides APIs that enable data from multiple devices to be aggregated for analytics and uploaded to EHRs. Aggregating more consumer data, including consumer generated data, will require additional investments in analytics and privacy and security to assuage consumer concerns regarding breaches of their personal health information. Consumer concerns regarding privacy and security may inhibit adoption of wearable, so must be addressed head on by HCOs and the vendor community.

- ***Educate consumers and their caregivers about the benefits of wearables.*** Education of the benefits of using wearable devices to track fitness and activity, or monitor chronic conditions will play an important role in ensuring program success. This is true not only for consumers but for their care providers. Creating the proper incentives to use the device and providing actionable information that consumers can use to change their behavior will ensure consistent use by the consumers and ultimately help them achieve their health goals.

- ***Promote the success of wearables programs.*** Let the healthcare community know about the success of the telemonitoring program on an ongoing basis to encourage further adoption by clinicians and consumers. Clinicians will respect evidenced-based data that demonstrates positive outcomes of telemonitoring using wearable devices. They will also appreciate talking with other clinicians when it comes to learning more about the telemonitoring services being offered and how those services will impact them and their practices.

## Parting Thoughts

The use of wearables – whether they are consumer or medical grade – will create a highly personalized consumer experience and enable clinicians to customize care plans for their patients' individual needs. A key to success is understanding what will motivate consumers to begin to use the device and continuing using it on a long term basis. For some consumers the motivation will come from the desire to meet certain health goals such as controlling their diabetes or hypertension. For others the goal might be to lose weight before a special event such as a wedding or college reunion. Consumers with multiple chronic conditions, are disproportionately older, less affluent than the early adopters of activity trackers. They will not have the same level of enthusiasm for tracking their health status and view it as work. These consumers will need more encouragement and coaching to participate in health and wellness or chronic condition management programs. Even younger, healthier consumers will respond better if their trusted medical provider recommends they use a wearable device to improve their health. Deploying wearables is not just a matter of getting consumers and clinicians to use technology, but leveraging what they perceive to be the value proposition of using that technology and providing services that they compliments the wearable technology such as actionable insights, coaching, social outreach, and active interventions to encourage use of the wearable device on an ongoing basis.

# *Case Study*: Extreme Networks Purview Solution Improves Customer Satisfaction & Delivers Better Patient Outcomes

- INDIANA UNIVERSITY HEALTH LA PORTE HOSPITAL

## Introduction

Indiana University Health is Indiana's most comprehensive healthcare system. A unique partnership with Indiana University School of Medicine, one of the nation's leading medical schools, gives patients access to innovative treatments and therapies. IU Health is comprised of hospitals, physicians and allied services dedicated to providing preeminent care throughout Indiana and beyond. To meet the mobile needs of a modern mission-critical hospital environment, IU Health chose Extreme Networks to replace their existing network infrastructure. The network visibility that the Extreme Networks Purview solution provides has enabled the hospital to deliver a consistent experience to all users, increase customer satisfaction and improve patient outcomes.

*"We have seen a direct correlation with how our network and applications run with patient experience. Everyone's job is made easier with a fine-tuned network and we are able to do that with Extreme Networks and Purview."*

**JOSH MANDEVILLE, NETWORK SECURITY ADMINISTRATOR AT IU HEALTH**

## Hospital's Challenge

With more and more network devices (EHR, Diagnostic Imaging, Wireless/ Network Capable Medical Equipment, BYOD) being on-boarded to their mission-critical hospital network, IU Health needed a stable infrastructure with 365X24X7 availability that would allow them to be proactive and more agile.

One of their greatest challenges was network management and visibility. "We didn't know what was going on until there were problems," said Josh Mandeville, Network Security Administrator at IU Health. "With no insight into the network and no redundancy, if something failed it could be a matter of life or death." With only 1.5 people managing the network, IU Health needed a system that would bring the entire network into one view and allow them to see the network and everything running on it at a much more granular level to better serve their end-users.

Providing a robust, reliable wireless experience for guests has become a must-have for hospitals — directly correlating with patient experience and satisfaction and ultimately affecting the bottom line. With 2,500 unique guest devices per day, bandwidth was becoming an issue for IU Health's GuestNet. IU Health required a wireless solution that would allow them to provide a consistent experience to staff, patients and guests.

## Extreme Networks Solution

IU Health decided to replace their Cisco and Juniper infrastructure with an Extreme Networks solution that offered redundancy, unified management, granular visibility and topnotch support at a better price point than the competition. Mandeville says that the transition has been "amazingly smooth" and in one building, the conversion from Cisco to Extreme Networks was performed with less than two hours of downtime.

The Extreme Networks solution, designed to meet the high demand and high-availability requirements of a hospital environment, includes S-Series switches at the core, C- and B-Series switches at the edge and IdentiFi Wireless. The entire infrastructure is easily managed by the Extreme Networks NetSight network management solution and Extreme Networks Purview provides visibility into applications for improved decision making to create a better user experience.

## Results

The Extreme Networks solution has given IU Health a stable, reliable infrastructure that can handle the mobile needs of a demanding and mission-critical hospital environment. The NetSight and Purview tools have given their small IT staff the ability to view, manage and control the entire network and all the applications running on it, allowing them to make informed decisions to provide a consistent user experience, improve customer satisfaction and improve patient outcomes.

1. **Central management, visibility and control of the entire network** – The unified NetSight network management console enables IU Health to manage their entire network from one system. According to Mandeville, "We couldn't find anything that could do that until we found NetSight." Extreme Networks Purview gives IU Health complete visibility and insight into all the applications running on the network, enabling them to proactively shape and direct traffic to better serve end-users. "Purview allows us to give the same consistent experience to all of our users. It truly is an MRI for the network," remarks Mandeville.

2. **Improved patient satisfaction** – IU Health has seen definite customer survey improvements. Their customer satisfaction rate went from 85% to 94% as a result of the improved time and productivity savings that Purview has enabled. "Because we are able to tweak and shape traffic to better serve our customers, doctors and nurses are able to spend more time with patients rather than being frustrated at their computer," says Mandeville.

3. **Consistent user experience** – Within two weeks of having Purview up and running, IU Health was able to actually yield numbers to prove that if they had a better firewall to stop torrenting, they could provide an improved and consistent experience for all users by provisioning equal amounts of bandwidth to all patients and visitors.

4. **Improved decision making and cost savings** – By using Purview to measure application usage and adoption by physicians and staff, IU Health has been able to confidently support the decision to reduce the amount of licenses for software that are not being used, thereby increasing their cost savings. "We were debating on housing internal or moving to Office 365 and Purview allowed us to make that decision based on usage numbers by staff. We're also seeing more traffic in the new EHR that has been rolled out, which means an uptick in adoption of it," says Mandeville.

In Mandeville's opinion, the Extreme Networks technology has made diagnosing issues much easier: "Our systems are much more complicated than they were two years ago, however I believe we have a better handle on the network now which helps all of our user experiences – doctors are spending more time with patients and patients and their guests can relieve the stress of being in a hospital by streaming Netflix or FaceTiming with friends and family – all of this has had a positive effect on patient outcomes."

With the support of GTAC, IU Health will continue to upgrade all 25 locations with Extreme Networks to provide a consistent user experience to benefit patients, guests and the bottom line. "Extreme Networks has helped us achieve what we couldn't even dream of before. We wanted to deliver the best experiences possible to improve patient outcomes, and now we can." concludes Mandeville.

# Chapter 7

# Compliance

**Movie 9: Compliance in Healthcare by Lisa Suennen**
https://vimeo.com/156570677

# Editor's Note

Compliance and regulation represent huge challenges for a complex communication environment like the IoT – an environment in which layers of information are being exchanged, stored and distilled. Fortunately, standards organizations are working now to create guidelines for wireless communications between monitoring devices and with care providers. The Continua Health Alliance is a coalition of healthcare and technology companies that was founded in 2006 to establish guidelines for interoperable personal health solutions. The organization has already published a set of specifications to help ensure interoperability. In the future, organizations that buy a Continua-certified device will have the assurance that it will connect with other certified devices in IoT-driven applications.

Continua's device standards are part of a larger standards environment that includes information technology standards established by the International Organization for Standardization (ISO) and engineering standards set by the Institute of Electrical and Electronics Engineers (IEEE®). In wireless technology, IEEE standards for LANs define Wi-Fi (IEEE 802.11) and ZigBee (IEEE 802.15.4) networks. Standards for PANs include Bluetooth and BLE, as well as IEEE 802.15.4j and IEEE 802.15.6, which are the IEEE standards associated with the body area network (BAN). Standards for cellular networks include GSM/UMTS and CDMA. Proprietary wireless networks still play something of a role in healthcare environments in general and IoT applications in particular, but that role seems to be shrinking as the industry continues to move toward standards-based architectures. For more on standards see: http://www.atlanticcouncil.org/images/publications/ACUS_Intel_MedicalDevices.pdf

— Rick Krohn

# Policy

— THOMAS MARTIN

**Movie 10: Introduction to Policy and Standards by Rick Krohn**
https://vimeo.com/156571005

## Chronic Care Management and Reimbursement – Policy meets practice

A number of opportunities present themselves with regards to the intersection of wearable devices and timely management of care. The burden of chronic disease is significant in the U.S. healthcare system. The opportunity to shift a clinical encounter from episodic to preventative in nature only occurs when providers have a vested interest in the behaviors and tendency of a patient when they are not present; be it before, during, or after a clinical encounter.

A number of policy shifts need to occur to incentivize the evaluation of information from wearable devices. First, Accountable Care Organizations (ACOs) need to have greater flexibility within the application process to proactively manage populations by utilizing technology to the fullest extent

An overt focus on the Certified Electronic Health Record has prevented many technologies from being fully leveraged by the ACOs focus on managing patient populations. Many population health tools vary widely in their complexity and ability to meet all, some, or none of the criteria established by the CEHRT process. However, many tools are being created which have an impact on the monitoring of patients and the ability to create meaningful data.

The second area or opportunity is to continue to evaluate the Current Procedural Terminology (CPT®) base overseen by the American Medical Association (AMA) and the mechanism by which the Centers for Medicare and Medicaid Services (CMS). The major policy tool, which is updated yearly, is the Physician Fee Schedule (PFS) that establishes effort and monetary rates for professional healthcare services billed to Medicare. With the publication of the 2015 Medicare Physician Fee Schedule Final Rule, it is now certain that Medicare will pay for chronic care management, or CCM, beginning January 1, 2015.

The exploration and research focused upon the identification of the types of professional services that "involves medication reconciliation, the assessment and integration of numerous data points, effective coordination of care among multiple other clinicians, collaboration with team members, continuous development and modification of care plans, patient or caregiver education, and the communication of test results." These services, which require significant professional time but are not delivered face to face - are not currently reimbursed - are among those that comprise the heart and soul of quality care management, patient-centered care, and patient engagement and self-management. The following represent a set of services, highlighted in recent comments by the Personal Connected Health Alliance regarding the physician fee schedule:

- Review of patient generated biometric data and revision of a care plan based on patient generated biometric data (CPT Codes 99090 and 99091). CMS should unbundle these CPT codes to permit reimbursement for services for patients with a disease or condition which requires care plan modifications based on fluctuations in biometric data. For example, diabetes, heart failure, asthma, chronic obstructive pulmonary disease are all conditions for which monitoring of PGHD provided biometric data leads to improved care.

- Review of patient generated biometric data and revision of a care plan based on patient generated biometric data (CPT Codes 99090 and 99091). CMS should unbundle these CPT codes to permit reimbursement for services for patients with a disease or condition which requires care plan modifications based on fluctuations in biometric data. For example, diabetes, heart failure, asthma, chronic obstructive pulmonary disease are all conditions for which monitoring of PGHD provided biometric data leads to improved care.

- Online or electronic evaluation and management for established patients (CPT 99444). CMS should add this CPT code 99444 as a reimbursable code to the PFS for the purposes of care plan modification, patient and caregiver education, and communication with patients in a time sensitive and efficient manner.

- Data analysis, care protocol development, and creationof patient registries for care management, medication reconciliation, and patient engagement outreach. This work, which requires extensive clinician cognitive work to develop clinical evidence based models and algorithms, is an essential base to the data analysis, care protocol development, and creation of robust patient registries which is fundamental to provision of patient centered care management. The opportunities associated with digital registries or digital cohorts are discussed later in this chapter.

Finally, while a bit beyond the scope of this chapter, a shift needs to occur whereby consumer oriented technologies play a more important role in telehealth or telemedicine. The use of remote and wireless technologies has had a profound impact on addressing cost and improving outcomes. The challenge faced currently is updating definitions and requirements of technology in 42 USC 1395m which do not sufficiently incorporate new and contemporary technologies which – are often wearable in nature and consumer oriented – should play an increasingly important role as healthcare delivery structures move towards outcomes and quality.

# HIPAA and Wearables in a Consumer Driven World

Increasingly, technology focused for consumers is encroaching on technology once only available for clinicians or healthcare professionals. The ability for patients to monitor their own vital signs represents a major opportunity to more fully engage patients in their health and plan of care. Information collected by consumer oriented health and wellness devices is not subject to the onerous privacy protection requirements set forth in Health Insurance Portability and Accountability Act (HIPAA) of 1996. By and large, information collected by patients using consumer oriented wearable devices for their own use fails to meet the requirements of Protected Health Information under HIPAA. The tipping point within the industry currently is to develop best practices on how, when, and where to further integrate this information into a healthcare providers workflow, at which point the information becomes PHI classified material.

One of the primary issues with importing patient-reported data into an EMR is how to identify the collector of the data (see the discussion below regarding the need for UDID). EMRs are designed to store provider's clinical entered data, not patientreported data. The Health Level 7 (HL7) organization is working on initiatives to label patient data, to be able to differentiate the data between consumer generated and provider generated . Given the movement by the healthcare sector towards value based outcomes purchasing, there continues to be unique challenges presented to the wearable community. A comprehensive transition from consumer oriented generation and aggregation towards a provider analysis of such data is needed. The options include vendors continuing to remain siloed with regards to open access of information by other systems. A mitigated risk approach, where by intermediaries simply facilitate the hand off, is becoming increasingly likely to successfully move information back to a centralized healthcare repository.

Broadly, industry should be cognizant of the following emerging best practices. For instance, the University of Washington has provided guidelines for healthcare providers who want to further integrate glasses type technologies into their practice. At this point in time industry stakeholders should continue to focus on the following issues as it relates to the use of wearable technology to advance clinical health delivery and consumer health.

1. **Disclosure** – Vendors and end users should both understand the limitations and capabilities of the technology to monitor information.

2. **Permission** – 3rd party applications should be clearly outlined in the disclosures. Further, any additional use of information by 3rd party applications should trigger a reauthorization by the data generator.

3. **Transport and Protection** – The point in time at which data from a wearable device becomes protected health information is important to understand. Industry stakeholders operating in this space should consider reviewing applicable state and federal laws to more fully understand the impact of their device on the policy landscape. The means to comply with HIPAA are widely covered here http://www.hhs.gov/ocr/privacy/hipaa/administrative/breachnotificationrule/brguidance.html

# Unique Device Identifiers: Is there a need?

Broadly, Unique Device Identifiers (UDIs) are employed to more efficiently manage data streams and sources. Many traditional medical devices -depending on Food and Drug Administration Classification- require a UDI. UDIs serve a unique roll in other aspects aside from managing data sources or streams. UDIs help facilitate product recalls, can improve registries and clinical trials, and strengthen abilities to respond to sentinel or never events. The unique device identification system, which will be phased in over several years, offers a number of benefits that will be more fully realized with the adoption and integration of UDIs into the health care delivery system.

The challenge associated with the deployment of UDI to assist in tracking of devices is an all or nothing proposition, especially among unregulated consumer oriented devices. To gain the benefits of adoption of UDI standards, all firms within an industry sector must adopt the approach. If industry consensus is that understanding data streams from distinct devices within a consumer health monitoring environment is important, UDI should be adopted widely. Conversely, the need to register and track UDIs is an expense often borne by the manufacturer. Another challenge is the appropriate location for the storage of such information. Many electronic health records are becoming the location by which UDIs are stored and tracked. While wearable technology has operated largely outside the confines of the traditional device regulatory regime, there is a growing convergence between consumer oriented technology and the traditional practice of medicine. So too will the need appropriately identify information as the acceptance of patient generated data into electronic health records becomes more widely accepted among practitioners. Also, a UDI only identifies a device, and not an individual. However, for conducting large scale deployments of consumer oriented devices, UDI represents and interesting and pragmatic policy issue. The true value of a UDI system, however, lies in its broad adoption and subsequent use by manufacturers, distributors, payers, providers, patients, and other stakeholders with important roles throughout the medical device lifecycle.

## Policy Impact: Research and Clinical Applications

The rise of mobile devices as data aggregation platforms has created new opportunities for researchers to collect and analyze patient generated health data. Increasingly academia and industry are collaborating to enable applications of technology which ease the burden of recruitment for clinical trials, minimize recall bias of participants, or increase the number of participants in a study. This large scale tracking and analysis of data gathered in a longitudinal manner enables new lines of investigation for researchers and the opportunity to speed the rate at which rigorous research is conducted. The ability to market digital health studies broadly to patients via consumer oriented medium is profound. The largest Parkinson's clinical trial conducted to date yielded 1,700 participants, yet a recent ResearchKit app gained more than 640 downloads after three hours in the Apple App Store. Another large initiative is HealthKit which allows for the aggregation and transmission of 60 discrete elements of physical health and wellbeing. The fact that so much can be accomplished with so little presents a number of challenges for the researcher and affiliated organizations.

This research oriented section seeks to provide emerging best practices and limitations surrounding the role of digital platforms for the formation of cohorts. As data from digital health cohorts becomes more prevalent, researchers will need to understand the limitations associated with the application of technology. The section will address the following topics.

First, discussion will cover the capabilities of digital platforms to aggregate both social and physical determinants of health. Second, the issues associated with data integrity issues and data management when employing digital health data sets for either prospective or retrospective research methods are discussed. Third, highlights regarding the role of digital health platforms to obtain digital consent. Finally, the research section concludes with examples of challenges confronting both academic and industry analysts which may present themselves during Institutional Review Board assessments.

# Aggregating Physiological and Social Determinants of Health

There are two separate and distinct open source frameworks provided by Apple. HealthKit is the open source platform for the aggregation of data originating from biosensors and wearable devices and other end user generated information from applications employing the framework. HealthKit aggregates numerous "type identifiers" within the framework. These identifiers include both physiological values and self-reported end user values. For example, blood oxygen saturation (sensor generated) or workout type identifier (end user input). The articulation between Health-Kit and ResearchKit requires that specific type identifiers be added to the HealthKit platform by Apple. For example, a researcher could not track unique patient reported metrics such as results from complex blood panels unless this information was already included in the HealthKit platform.

# Data Integrity and Data Management

There are three key components of ResearchKit as a research oriented data collection platform. These include surveys, consent, and "active tasks". Current limitations of the platform include the capability for ResearchKit to prompt surveys on a scheduled time frame or active tasks. This limitation significantly impacts the ability to conduct structured surveys on a recurring temporal basis. One of the biggest opportunities for Re-searchKit to have an impact on data collection and validity is the capability to minimize recall bias. For example, a participant within a digital cohort would not be prompted to complete a dietary schedule on a reoccurring interval.

# Digital Consent and Marketing

Digital consent represents another major feature of Apple ResearchKit. Individuals seeking to leverage this feature should understand the requirements set forth by Office for Human Research Protections (OHRP). There is no specific format for digital signatures. However, OHRP provides general guidance regarding the use of digital signatures. IRBs reviewing protocols which leverage digital signatures should consider the following:

1. How the signature is created
2. Legitimacy of the signature
3. Hard Copy Production for the Signature (use of a secure system which provides encryption)

In addition, there are advanced features and functionality regarding the use of low energy Bluetooth Beacons to market or solicit participation within a cohort. Applications which an end user has downloaded could be modified to communicate with low energy beacons. For example, a hospital with an endocrinology clinic -which has an app for the hospital-could be programed to alert patients in the waiting room that a clinical trial is being conducted. IRBs should be mindful of new and novel approaches to recruit and retain participants via digital health platforms.

# Industry and Academic Uncertainty and IRB Requirements

Despite many of the enablers offered by technology when creating digital health cohorts, there are barriers and considerations for the academy, private industry, and IRBs reviewing protocols leveraging digital health platform. First, a number of challenges exist for establishing processes for ensuring data integrity of data and authenticity of participants. In addition, researchers leveraging digital health platforms for the purpose of data collection should be aware of the requirements set forth by Apple. This includes use of HIPAA compliant servers for the storage of protected health information. In addition, prior to review and publishing of any app leveraging ResearchKit to the iTunes store, developers and researchers must submit an IRB approval letter for the study protocol.

# Precision Medicine

Finally, there are initiatives such as the Precision Medicine effort currently underway which could further leverage the benefits associated with widely deployed digital health platforms. However, there is a tendency for many large databases of patients to remain siloed without appropriate standards to effectively exchange information. While many of the digital health platforms can technically overcome these hurdles, there is a need for policy to appropriately identify key metrics that should be accomplished from both and academic perspective and spending of federal funds on research. Items needed to successfully deploy precision medicine using mobile and connected health devices include:

1. A focus on "leave behind" data sets with open access for future researchers

2. Shared decision making between researchers and healthcare providers regarding data access, privacy and security, and necessary compliance with existing laws

3. A greater movement towards collaboration between federal agencies such as the Patient Centered Outcomes Research Institute (PCORI) and the Patient-Centered Clinical Research Network (PCORnet)

4. Data sets which leverage industry standards for data aggregation eg – MySQL or other nonproprietary formats like HL7 and FHIR based on PCORnet principles

# Chapter 8

# Standards and Security

**Movie 11: Standards and Security by Matthew Dolt**
https://vimeo.com/156571563

# Editor's Note

In its report The Healthcare Internet of Things: Rewards and Risks issued by the Atlantic Council and INTEL, the authors estimate the number of devices connected to the internet of things will increase to more than 5.4 billion connections by 2020. As the use of networked medical devices becomes prevalent in the healthcare world, security breaches are growing and, if not addressed and mitigated, they threaten to undermine technology development in the field and result in significant financial losses. Security issues loom large in healthcare, with 44 percent of all registered data breaches in 2013 targeted at medical companies. In addition, information security breaches reported by healthcare providers skyrocketed 60 percent from 2013 to 2014 – representing more than double the increase seen in other industries, with financial losses up 282 percent.

Networked devices are vulnerable to accidental failures in technology that can undermine consumer trust and inhibit the development of new tools; privacy violations, in which stored data on devices is targeted; and widespread disruption, where connected devices are infected by malware of all kinds. Other vulnerabilities to networked wearable devices include accidental failures, intentional device tampering to cause harm, theft of personal data, and widespread disruption of the devices.

Networked healthcare devices come with four main overlapping areas of concern, including accidental failures that erode trust. Should any high-profile failures take place, societies could easily turn their backs on networked medical devices, delaying their deployment for years or decades. Protecting patient privacy and sensitive health data is a second immediate concern, as malicious online hackers consider healthcare information especially valuable.

Intentional disruption is also a concern because networked medical devices face the same technological vulnerabilities as any other networked technology. Viewed through the lens of wearables and implantables, the potential for harm is ominous. When a networked device is literally plugged into a person, the consequences of cybercrime committed via that device might be particularly personal and threatening. For further depth, see (http://www.atlanticcouncil.org/images/publications/ACUS_Intel_ MedicalDevices.pdf

Even more dangerous than the potential for targeted killings, though also far less likely, is the threat of widespread disruption. Theoretically, a piece of targeted malware could spread across the Internet, affecting everyone with a vulnerable device. Such a scenario has materialized in governmental and business IT and industrial control systems. Recent examples include Anthem, the IRS and SONY pictures.

Despite the growing security threat to healthcare, and the liability issues that result from the violation of patient privacy, the current focus in wearable device development is dominated by manufacturers' preferences and patients' needs. In addition to developing features, industry and government should also focus on implementing an overarching set of security standards or best practices for networked devices to address this growing threat. And the solution set is going to demand an unprecedented degree of cooperation among developers, vendors, regulators, and users – no small hurdle.


— Rick Krohn

# Standards

— JEFF BRANDT

**Movie 12: Introduction to Policy and Standards by Rick Krohn**
https://vimeo.com/156568010

Standards, while not the most exciting topic in the book, provide us a path to developing or purchasing products and tools that protect investments and protect you the user. Of note, IoT standards to-date are still somewhat limited. The following organizations are some of the leaders working on new standards and provide some of the existing standards and guidance applicable for IoT.

## HL7

Health Level Seven International, an ANSI-accredited standards organization is the leader in healthcare communication standards. Its primary focus is on communication between terrestrial based healthcare facilities, i.e., hospitals. As mentioned previously, HL7 is beginning to change it's focus with the acquisition of FHIR. First developed by Graham

Grieves, FHIR is based on Thomas Fielding Phd thesis, Architectural Styles and the Design of Network-based Software Architectures. (https://www.ics.uci.edu/~fielding/pubs/dissertation/top.htm)

FHIR is a technology that supports a "RESTful" interface, better known as "REST" via an Application Programmers Interface (API), which provides a simple access facility for vendors to expose internal functionality and data requests for a patient's medical record. REST provides a framework to access and expose legacy systems data, e. g., EHRs.

# IEEE

Institute of Electrical and Electronics Engineers organization provides standards for wireless devices such as IEEE 11073 for smart sensor and wireless device to gateway and smartphone communication. The IEEE-SA group for IoT includes IEEE P2413, Draft Standard for an Architectural Framework for the Internet of Things Working Group.

# International Health Enterprise (IHE), Patient Care Devices (PCD)

The International Health Enterprise, organization acts as a framework to fill the gaps between the health standard groups, such a DICOM and HL7.

Of particular interest, the IHE PCD does not currently cover security. They state, "The assumption is made that the Infusion Pump Event Communication, (IPEC) Profile is implemented in a single enterprise on a secure network."

Are they concerned about security behind the enterprise firewall, i.e. within the walls of the hospital?

On May 1, 2015 the FDA issued as Safety communication concerning the vulnerability to hacking of the Hospira Lifecare Infusion pumps.

Wireless devices have opened vulnerabilities everywhere, even behind the organizations firewall. All Connected devices are vulnerable and we must think, "Security first".

# Industrial Internet Consortium (IIC)

Though IIC is not a standards committee, the consortium plays an important role in providing guidance to it's members and the IoT healthcare community. One of their primary areas of focus is security, where IIC provides guidance through use cases, frameworks, and testing facilities for new technology.

# Continua

The Personal Connected Health Alliance a LLC formed in 2014 with HIMSS as it sole stockholder, manages the mHealth Summit and Continua4. Continua was the primary sponsor of the IEEE 11073, a device communication standard. Continua also offers a certification program to it's members to insure interoperability.

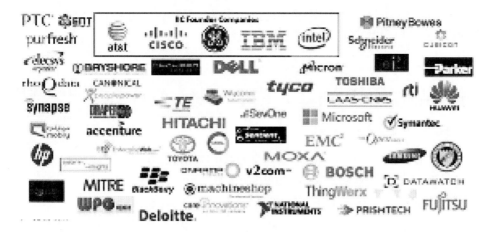

# ONC S&I Framework

The Office of the National Coordinator of Health (ONC), though not a recognized standards organization was established as part of the HITECH Act. The S&I framework is part of the ONC charter to provide Health IT solutions.

The Provenance Workgroup, part of the S&I framework focuses on trusting the data. Provenance, from the French word provenir, "to come from", the chronology of the ownership, origin, custody or location of an artifact, one of the most important components of healthcare.

Currently the S&I Framework Work Group concentrates its work on EHR (Electronic Health Records) interoperability using HL7 communication; it doesn't currently include wireless devices or the wireless domain. I mention this to make you aware of a Standards Gaps between mobile and embedded devices and EHRs. However, IEEE 11073 a health device communication standard and Continua both support Data Provenance within their standards.

# Open mHealth (non recognized Standard)

Open mHealth (OmH) by their own classification is a Framework, however it has the properties of being the welldesigned "non-standard" standard in mobile health. Dr. Ida Sim, Professor of Medicine and Co-Director of Biomedical Informatics of the Clinical and Translational Science Institute at UCSF, a co-founder along with advisors such as Dr. John Mattson, CMIO Kaiser Permanente formed OmH to fill the Gaps in the official standards. Most of the current standards focus on traditional behind the walls EHR tethered care. This leaves a huge underserved community of new healthcare companies and developers that are diligently working to solve our worldwide health crisis. Dr. Sim explains, "As mobile extends the boundaries of IoT, Open mHealth is working to ensure that IoT health data is usable and meaningful for personal disease prevention and chronic care."

Mobile is different from traditional technology; the available wireless bandwidth and memory is smaller, meaning that the overhead must be reduced in order to transmit or store usable data. OmH has taken these issues into consideration when designing their framework. First, the data isn't tethered to any EHR. The immediate issue to be addressed is that there are many providers around the world that do not have access to an EHR and bandwidth is always an expensive commodity and data is exponentially growing. Healthcare Standards which serve a worldwide community tend to overlook that LMIC (Low to Middle Income Countries) and rural areas do not have access to 4G or any Internet. HL7 is currently working on a solution to send health-data over SMS/Text. OmH has provided a framework that reduces the need for high-speed networks.

OmH has taken on one of the most difficult technical issues in mHealth, interoperability. One of OmH's partners offers a OmH to HL7 v2.0 duplex converter which allow the developer to convert OmH data into a standard protocol (V2.0), which EHRs understand and transmit from V2.0 back to OmH. This is a non-standards organization to put on your watch list.

# Food and Drug Administration (FDA)

One of the many roles of the FDA, is regulating medical devices, and that includes standards via the Center for Devices and Radiological Health (CDRH) Standards program. Their role, as stated by the CDRH, "the world's leader in standards implementation and utilization for medical device innovation and manufacturing, and radiation-emitting product safety". The CDRH provides a searchable standards database, FDA Recognized Consensus Standards Database, e.g., search of "implantable" devices returned eighteen results shown below:

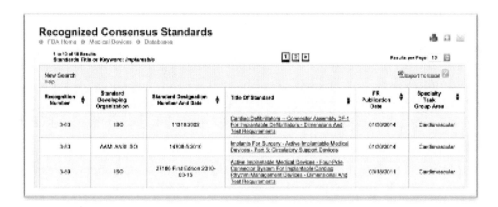

The FDA also provides guidance on Cyber security and has taken steps to strengthen Cyber security of medical devices with their "final" guidelines and recommendations of device manufactures .

# Federal Communication Commission (FCC)

The FCC controls allocation of radio airwaves or spectrum used by devices. The majority of wireless IoT devices today use unlicensed radio frequencies, also known as "trash band", 900 MHz for Electronic Product Code (EPC), which host Zig-bee, Bluetooth, some WIFI and garage door openers. "There are no spectrum bottlenecks for dedicated IoT systems yet, as Wi-Fi services get maxed out, there are only so many channels which will fit into the available spectrum," Kevin Ashton, co-founder and former executive director of Massachusetts Institute of Technology's Auto-ID Center5. We will be hearing more from the FCC on IoT as the eco-systems grows and bandwidth becomes an overburdened commodity.

# Federal Trade Commission

The FTC provides consumer protection on the Web, they also provide guidance and enforcement for privacy and identity issues.

Recently a Federal appeals court granted the FTC more authority in the landmark case FTC v. Wyndham Hotels. After several breaches the judges ruled that Wyndham didn't provide adequate protection of it's customer data, states HealthcareDive online magazine. This new ruling continues to empower the FTC in their watchdog and enforcer role of the consumer's security and privacy.

# Security

— JEFF BRANDT

Nearly everyday the media is full of stories of security, data breaches and attacks on our privacy. Attacks originating from all over the world and on every piece of connected electronics in our homes, cars, businesses and healthcare networks. Soon, everything from your coffee pot to Infusion pumps will be connected to the Internet, opening more opportunities for attacks.

Security of the IoT may seem daunting, a huge opportunity for cyber criminals, however in many ways the same rules such as processes and procedures apply to securing any device on the network. Not to say it is going to be easy, the endpoints on the network will experience exponential growth.

The shear volume of sensors and devices placed into service in the next few years will be the challenge for organizations. How will they keep these devices in service? To provide some perspective, think about all of the battery-operated devices in your home today and the challenge it is to keep them all charged or having the batteries available when one fails. Now multiply that by 100's or 1000's. There will be sensors in everything from your toaster, your bed, car and shoes. Providers and organizations depending on sensors to monitor patient's health will also depend on services to provide the maintenance and administration of these devices.

Many monitoring devices will be inexpensive and disposable; others such as gateways may be rented. Keeping up with the devices, the ssociated devices and all the entitlements (warrantee, support, contracts) will be a formidable task.

Currently there are two primary areas of concerns in data security. "At Rest" data within a machine such as a database or cache and "In-"Flight", data that is being transmitted. I believe there is a new dimension, "In-Space" or floating, an unattended device, e.g., Infusion Pump, heart-valve, A-FIB, a brace sensor. Security for the "In-Space" scenario is similar to "At Rest", however, different in the sense that it's unattended, unmanaged, simple mobile "write only" devices.

Privacy is what we achieve through security. The IoT world will places stress on all aspects of security, which reduces privacy. Apple was granted a patent for a "Seamlessly embedded heart rate monitor" to help to identify a user, i.e., Bio-Identifier, which includes a feature to monitor mood. The patent states, "Using the detected signals, the electronic device can identify or authenticate the user and perform an operation based on the identity of the user. In some embodiments, the electronic device can determine the user's mood from the cardiac signals and provide data related to the user's mood." Opportunities abound for using the information generated. Who will be allowed to access this information and for what purpose? Even if we regulate the access to this data, how can we protect it from being exploited? How do we empower the source of the data to control how it's to be used, even for their own care.

The following is part of the NCCoE Cyber Security Challenge; illustrating applicable standards and best practices for the Use Case, Wireless Medical Infusion Pumps6; part of Federal Risk and Authorization Management Program (FedRAMP) e.g., Security Control MA-3.

**Federal Risk and Authorization Management Program**
**Control Enhancements:**

(3) The organization prevents the unauthorized removal of maintenance equipment by one of the following: (i) verifying that there is no organizational information contained on the equipment; (ii) sanitizing or destroying the equipment; (iii) retaining the equipment within the facility; or (iv) obtaining an exemption from a designated organization official explicitly authorizing removal of the equipment from the facility.

**Enhancement Supplemental Guidance:** None.

**LOW** Not Selected    **MOD** MA-3 (1) (2) (3)
**Control Parameter Requirements:**

None.

**Additional Requirements and Guidance:**

None.

FedRAMP MA-3

The following "Security Map" produced by NIST and NOCCCe provides applicable standard and best practice for Critical Infrastructure Cyber Security Framework (CSF). Note: for more information on the content of the table, refer to NIST publications Special Publication 800-53 e.g., SC-8 Security Control 8 or CM-6 Configuration Management -6

| Technology | Description and functionality | Security Control (SP 800-53) | NIST Cybersecurity Framework (Section 2.1) |
|---|---|---|---|
| access controls | selective restriction of access of system capabilities, physical access, and ability to perform certain functions | AC-1, AC-2, AC-3, AC-19, AC-24, PE-3, PE-4, PE-5 | Protect Identify |
| asset management system | system which monitors and maintains organizational assets | PE-20 | Protect |
| authorization system | identification system authentication of user local authentication to device remote authentication authentication of device remote authentication | CA-6, IA-1, IA-2, IA-3 | Identify |
| anti-virus | software intended to prevent, detect, and remove malicious computer viruses | MA-3 | Respond Recover |
| anti-malware | software intended to prevent, detect, and remove malware | MA-3 | Respond Recover |
| computer security response system | system implemented for immediate response to information security jeopardizing events | IR-1, IR-7, IR-8 | Respond |
| credentialing system | holds the authentication information | IA-5 | Identify |

| | | | |
|---|---|---|---|
| data encryption | encoding data to make it unreadable to unauthorized parties<br><br>data at rest<br><br>data in transit<br><br>baseband isolation | SC-8 | Protect |
| infusion pump provisioning | remote wipe | CM-6, CM-7, MP-6 | Protect |
| infusion pump integrity checks | showing accuracy and consistency of data on device | CM-7, SA-19 | Protect |
| infusion pump resource management | ability to enable/disable device peripherals<br><br>device integrity checks<br><br>application verification [CM-6]<br><br>verified application and OS updates<br><br>trusted integrity reports<br><br>policy integrity verification<br><br>application white listing/black listing | IR-4 | Protect<br>Respond |
| geolocation system | GPS tracking of organization owned devices | CM-8 | Identify |
| firewall | hardware and software-based network security which controls incoming and outgoing network traffic | SC-7 | Protect |
| honeypots | trap to detect and or counter unauthorized access | SC-26 | Protect<br>Detect |
| intrusion detection system | device or software application that monitors the network for malicious activity such as policy violations | SI-4 | Protect<br>Detect |

| | | | |
|---|---|---|---|
| physical monitoring system | device that keeps constant watch on organizational assets to prevent tampering | PE-6, CA-7 | Identify |
| physical security | implementation of security measures to best protect organizational assets | PE-2, PE-3, PE-4, PE-5, MA-5 | Identify<br>Protect |
| port monitoring system | monitors network packets entering and leaving the organizational network | CA-7 | Identify<br>Protect |
| scanning system | constant sweep of systems owned by organization for malicious activities | AU-6 | |
| session verification | reauthorization of the authorized user during their login session | AC-10, AC-11, AC-12, AU-14, IA-1, IA-2, SC-23 | Identify<br>Detect |
| system monitoring | review of actions taken place on organization owned devices<br><br>anomalous behavior detection<br><br>canned reports and ad-hoc queries<br><br>compliance checks | AU-6, AU-13, CA-7 | Identify<br>Detect |
| trusted key storage | trusted location for the safe storage of keys | SC-12 | Protect |
| vulnerability scanner | software that scans mobile devices, workstations and networks for vulnerabilities | RA-5 | Identify |

# Trust

Trust can be an overlooked component in today's high tech world, however in security, trust is an essential part of protecting data. The abundance of data breaches has given us pause to consider who do we trust to secure our data?

Credit Card companies reassure us that customers are protected from financial loss when their instruments are used for purchases. Healthcare is different, for that same guarantee is not available. Once health data is compromised there is no ability to retrieve privacy. CIO's of healthcare organizations must trust every component and vendor within their organization's network when assessing risk.

# Identity

Who are You? Whether it is a waiter, an ATM machine, even a new acquaintance, it is normally the first question that should comes to mind, before placing trust, e.g., do you trust those no-name ATM machines in a little convenience store or bar?

Identities are public, they have to be; drivers license, ATM cards and digital certificates, e.g public keys or public objects/ tokens that we use for claims of our identity7.

Identity Management (IdM) and Identity Access Management (IAM) are the beachhead of security in IoT , Identifying and granting access to a machine or human at a point of access.

Organizational networks depend on these tools to grant access and to share data such as email and portals. These tools will also be used as the gatekeeper in the cyber world of IoT.

Identity plays a very important role in healthcare because devices, medications and lab testing results and other clinical data are linked to a specific human and unlike a social media account, if someone spoofs an account it may be life threatening.

Identity fraud plagues the healthcare industry. In January 2014 the "Identity Theft Resource Center produced a survey showing that medical-related identity theft accounted for 43 percent of all identity thefts reported in the United States in 2013.", as stated in the Kaiser Newsletter8. IoT, with the right guidance, may be able to reduce this issue with stronger identity capability, resulting in lowering cost of operation.

Not only do we need to identify the patient for care, we must also identify the devices used for care. There are always challenges of fraud with mobile devices because of their inherent ability to move. Other than implantable devices, it is challenging to know where the device is really located and who is wearing it.

Example:

> Husband was diagnosed with diabetes and was prescribed intravenous insulin pump to delivers insulin to the patient based on the blood sample from his wirelessly paired glucose monitor. His wife, also a diabetes patient, doesn't have an insulin pump. The wife runs out of glucose monitor test strips and decides to use her husband glucose monitor, which in turn delivers to the husband her required insulin. Though this is a fictitious story, it is feasible and the outcome of such an event could result in death.

## Authentication

When asked the question, who are you? Authentication is the step you take to answer the question, proving it , a pin code, a fingerprint or a trusted person to vouch for you. Authentication insures that only the right people or machines gain access. With IoT, most of the authentication will be between machines, many of which are currently not secure, such as simple home devices. These unprotected devices provide opportunities for breach of privacy. An example is the LIFX Light bulb hack [9], where passwords were compromised from a connected light bulb, as was demonstrated by security experts in the UK.

## Biometrics

Biometrics are used for 2-factor authentication, such as fingerprint swiping a screen lock on a iPhone or Samsung smartphone. This is not considered to be Strong Authentication, as stated by cyber security expert, Professor Alan Woodward of Surrey University, "Biometrics that rely on static information like face recognition or fingerprints - it's not trivial to forge them but most people have accepted that they are not a great form of security because they can be faked". However, using a combination of factors, such as fingerprints to authenticate, the likelihood of being spoofed is reduced. Biometrics will most likely become a major part of IoT identity and authentication in the very near future.[10]

## Unique Device Identifier (UDI)

The FDA established a Unique Device Identifier to be adopted by all medical device manufactures upon their final release of the specification. The UID will provide patient safety through surveillance, reporting and identifying devices. The FDA hopes that the program will lead to a worldwide adopted UDI system. Manufactures will also provide information for the FDA's Global Unique Device Identification Database (GUDID). The Access GUDID, a public portal is being built to empower the public with device information.

## Data Retention

IoT devices have the potential of generating petabytes (1,000,000 gigabytes) of data for transit and storage. Many devices will "store and forward" data when connectivity is limited. To reduce the chance of data being compromised, it is a best practice not to store information on a device. However, as we push analytics to the edge, more data will need to be temporarily stored on the device. Care must also be taken when retiring a device that the memory is cleared of any vestige of data.

## Administration

One challenge of IoT in Healthcare is the administration of the devices for both in-patient and remote settings. Administration includes procuring, enabling, monitoring, tracking, supporting, repairing, replacing and disposing devices.

The FDA Released Guidance on Securing Wireless Medical Devices in August 2015 titled Radio Frequency Wireless Technology in Medical Devices

## FDA Guidelines include[11]:

- Identification of the device's assets, threats, and vulnerabilities
- Impact assessment of the threats and vulnerabilities on device functionality
- Assessment of the likelihood of a threat or vulnerability being exploited
- Determination of risk levels and suitable mitigation strategies
- Residual risk assessment and risk acceptance criteria

## Governance

Gartner defines governance as "the specification of decision rights and an accountability framework to ensure appropriate behavior in the valuation, creation, storage, use, archiving and deletion of information. It includes the processes, roles and policies, standards and metrics that ensure the effective and efficient use of information in enabling an organization to achieve its goals."12 Taking this into account, now we must decide how to apply IoT governance and what it means to your organization and our society.

Governance provides the framework for protecting the privacy of all of our data. IoT data stewardship and security will become exponential in volume as more data points are added to the network. Currently, there is little formal guidance in this area, however organizations may want to start to consider the impacts as part of their IT agenda.

# International Consideration

In the United States of America there are many federal and state organizations that govern healthcare. Outside of the USA there are also agencies, which provide guidelines on security and Personal Health Information regulations. It is essential to understand regulations in each country you do business with or transmit patient or consumer data.

In 2012 the European Commission proposed a comprehensive reform of data protection rules in the EU to strengthen privacy laws and provide for a EU wide single law to balance enforcement. One of the main points of law is specific governance of personal data when exporting across EU boarders. Vendors and health organization must be aware of the restrictions when selling products or providing services.


# Blockchain – the future?

Blockchain is relativity new security and audit mechanism which supports BitCoin's cyber-currency. Blockchain has the potential to be the next solution for securing medical records. Blockchain uses an open ledger system to track transaction or Blocks, in a linear chronological order. Data such as a medical record, when closed by a user or system, such as an EHR, is encrypted and signed by the producer and the evidence of that transaction is stored in a Block. The Block is appended to a chain, which is written to multiple public open ledgers on the network/Internet, providing a trust relationship between unrelated entities on an untrusted network such as the Internet[13]. Blockchain also provides a secure framework to share records within an Health Information Exchange (HIE) or with anyone or organization that is part of the network. Companies such as Phillips are reported to be exploring the use of Blockchain technology for healthcare[14].

# Devices

— JEFF BRANDT

## Medical Devices

Medical Devices according to the FDA (US Food and Drug administration) can range from a simple tongue depressor to intelligent equipment such as a Rapid Infuser; devices that are intended to provide medical information for diagnosis, care, and treatment. See FDA.gov for more information.

On July 31, 2015 the FDA issued a Class 1 recall of the Simbiq infusion pump system for wireless vulnerabilities. The FDA strongly advised the discontinued use of the system until Simbiq provides a fix. The vulnerably allowed unauthorized access to the system that controls the dosage, which could lead to a life-threatening event.

In December 18, 2014, the previous year, the National Institute of Standards and Technology (NIST) and the National Cyber security Center of Excellence (NCCoE) released a "Use Case" document on cyber security of a Wireless Medical Infusion Device. The document states, "Describes potential security risks affecting wireless medical infusion pumps". Did Simbig fail to acknowledge this risk or did the hospital(s) administration and staff overlook the vulnerability? In a "Security First" environment all parties need to take responsibility.

## Smart IoT Devices

Smart IoT Devices are small computers with the ability to connect to a network and run software, they are also called Microcontrollers. These devices must implement the same security measures and take the same precautions as Smartphones when securing data.

These devices are often classified as "Edge" devices, i.e., devices that are located at the furthest edge of the network or the endpoint, such as an Internet connected ECG. Security of Edge devices have special needs because of their location and access. They are also vulnerable to attacks such as man-in-the-middle where a hacker intercepts the transmission of data to a device.

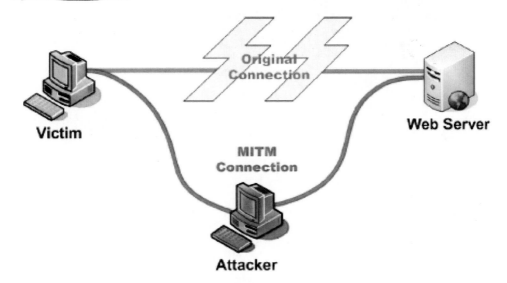

Most Smart Devices are inexpensive to manufacture, which will allow them to become ubiquitous in our lives. At the time that this chapter was written you could buy a consumer grade PC-104, a Raspberry Pi mini computers-on-a-chip for under $10 USD.

It is difficult for the untrained eye to know which devices contain microcontrollers, e.g., activity trackers and smart watches. These will lead to more vulnerability to privacy. If a device is not secure, hackers can access and reprogram the device, essentially taking control of it.

Some of the features of Microcontrollers

- Enable sensors that collect patient data
- Process, analyze and wirelessly communicate the data
- Enable rich graphical user interfaces
- Provide robotic control
- Analyze and send sensor data to the cloud through Healthcare-specific gateways

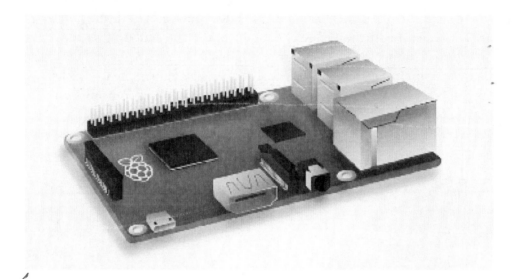

# Write Only Sensors

Connected sensors will provide the majority of the information collected in the world of IoT. Excluding FDA approved devices; the cost will be inexpensive and can be placed into everything from our shoes to our cars.

The service issue with these devices is that their communication is one way from the edge to the server; if an update is needed, the device will have to be physically serviced. System Architects must take this into consideration, needed updates can be very expensive.our cars.

Hacking of "Write only" devices is lower than Smart devices because there is little that can be collected for the effort; there is no storage and little control that a hacker can exploit. However, that doesn't preclude malicious hackers from compromising the data being collected.

Disruption of service or eavesdropping is a concern with sensors and steps should be taken to secure and monitor. Disrupting service of a sensor can be achieved as easy as removing or destroying the sensor; since it is impossible to electronically "ping" or contact a "Write only" sensor, (i.e. contact the sensor to determine if the device is still operating properly).

# Wearable

A PwC 2014 report stated that 1 out of 10 adults surveyed used wearable devices everyday15. These numbers are expected to grow as new form factors are released with more services and capabilities. The manufacturer of the wearable's, the apps, and the providers of the connectivity are responsible for the security, privacy and trust relationship of managing your data securely. Do you trust the vendor of the wearable to protect your privacy? Security and privacy of your data and how it is used is presented to all users in a form of "Terms and Conditions" and "Privacy policies", it's the verbiage that you are asked to agree on to use the app, device or service. Most people including professionals do not take the time to read these binding documents, but simply accept the conditions presented. I once asked a group of classmates; mostly doctors in a Bio-medical Informatics Grad program, if they ever read the Terms and Conditions of the medical equipment that they used everyday in their practice. The bottom line on most T&Cs, is the doctor is responsible if the device fails. One doctor told me at the end of the class that he would never look at a rapid infuser the same.

Wearable devices provide access, or said another way, a window into someone's life that may not initially be realized by the user. Consider the devices worn to be bed that monitor sleep , the data being collected, and who has access to it. Fitbit when they first got started was unwittingly sharing users sex lives data on the Internet i.e., sexual activity states GIZMODO16.

The following is a list of wearable types:

- Consumer -Fitbit, Pebble
- OTC (over the counter) – AliveCor ECG
- Non-Consumer, prescribed – Google non-released device
- Implantable Medical Device (IMD)- pacemakers
- DME (Durable Medical Equipment - Prosthetics, Orthotics

# Conclusion

— JEFF BRANDT

"A society without privacy protection would be suffocation, and it might not be a place in which most would want to live." Prof. Daniel J. Solove

We must all take a "Security First" attitude, if we are to have privacy. This will take people, organizations and companies that care about security and have an unbending desire to ensure it. Yes, everything is a compromise and there will be breaches in security, however when companies have a "Security First" attitude, our privacy will be more assured.

When thinking about any aspect of IoT in healthcare, security is "the elephant" in the room; we must bring the topic front and center. Vendors should lead the discussion with their customers and team, "Don't wait for them to ask, (the Customer) they won't", Russ Dietz GE.

We must train these same people, organizations and companies on how to engender a "Security First" culture. This will take leadership that have the fiduciary responsibility to instill a Security First mantra within their organization.

> "Lack of talent can be the biggest vulnerability."
> Tim Holman, CEO of 2-Sec and director of ISSA

It is, as it has always has been, our responsibility to guard and protect our privacy and security. Many that I speak to about privacy and security believe that it no longer exists. In some ways it appears to be true, however we do not have to accept this notion. We must all strive to support privacy or we will certainly lose it.

We possess the power to voice our security and privacy concerns and demands. As a customer we may simply tell our merchants such as Amazon or Facebook and others what we will and will not accept, they will listen. As constituents we can call or write our representative and voice our opinions to initiate laws and guidelines around privacy and security. As employees we have the power to help protect our company and customer privacy, as well their customers privacy. It is, as it has always has been, our responsibility to guard and protect our privacy and security.

The more we consider the magnitude and complexity of the Internet of Things, the more security and privacy issues arise, as well, opportunities. In no other space in history will the "Butterfly effect" be more realized, the ubiquitous endpoints will provide multitudes of non-linear information[17] leading to multitudes of new theories and findings.

We must all do our best to provide the security needed to insure privacy for the patient. Without it, we will not be able to collect quality data. For data quality is higher when there is trust between the collector and the collectee18.

# References

1. After car hack, Internet of Things looks riskier [Internet]. [cited 2015 Aug 4]. Available from: http://www.betaboston.com/news/2015/08/03/after-car-hackinternet-of-things-looks-riskier/
2. What is a White Hat Hacker? - Definition from Techopedia [Internet]. Techopedia.com. [cited 2015 Dec 12]. Available from: https://www.techopedia.com/definition/10349/white-hathacker
3. Gartner Says the Internet of Things Installed Base Will Grow to 26 Billion Units By 2020 [Internet]. [cited 2015 Aug 27]. Available from: http://www.gartner.com/newsroom/id/2636073
4. New HIMSS unit to focus on mobile, home-health market [Internet]. Modern Healthcare. [cited 2015 Jul 22]. Available from: http://www.modernhealthcare.com/article/20140224/NEWS/302249979
5. Barbagallo P, 2014. As "Internet of Things" Evolves, FCC's Spectrum Strategy Will Be Put to the Test [Internet]. [cited 2015 Aug 19]. Available from: http://www.bna.com/internetthings-evolves-n17179912070/
6. Wireless Medical Infusion Pump Use-Case, G. O'Brien, G. Khanna 2014 Dec. 18 https://nccoe.nist.gov/sites/default/files/nccoe/NCCOE_HIT-Medical-Device-Use-Case.pdf
7. Riley S. It's Me, and Here's My Proof: Why Identity and Authentication Must Remain Distinct [Internet]. TechNet. [cited 2015 Aug 28]. Available from: https://technet.microsoft.com/en-us/library/Cc512578.aspx
8. Ollove M, Stateline. The Rise Of Medical Identity Theft In Healthcare [Internet]. Kaiser Health News. [cited 2015 Aug 15]. Available from: http://khn.org/news/rise-of-indentity-theft/
9. Wakefield J. Smart LED light bulbs leak wi-fi passwords - BBC News [Internet]. [cited 2015 Aug 29]. Available from: http://www.bbc.com/news/technology-28208905

10    Biometric security: Authentication for a more secure IoT | ITProPortal.
      com [Internet]. [cited 2015 Aug 15]. Available from: http://www.itproportal.
      com/2015/08/08/biometricsecurity-authentication-for-a-more-secure-iot/

11.   The Internet of Things: FDA Releases Guidance on Securing Wireless
      Medical Devices -- What Medical Device Manufacturers Should Know |
      InfoLawGroup [Internet]. [cited 2015 Aug 28]. Available from: http://www.
      infolawgroup.com/2013/10/articles/information-security/the-internet-of-
      thingsfda-releases-guidance-on-securing-wireless-medical-deviceswhat-
      medical-device-manufacturers-should-know/

12.   Information Governance - Gartner IT Glossary [Internet]. [cited 2015
      Aug 9]. Available from: http://www.gartner.com/itglossary/information-
      governance13. Why Bitcoin Matters - The New York Times [Internet]. [cited
      2015 Dec 12]. Available from: http://dealbook.nytimes.com/
      2014/01/21/why-bitcoin-matters/?_r=0

13.   Why Bitcoin Matters - The New York Times [Internet]. [cited 2015 Dec
      12]. Available from: http://dealbook.nytimes.com/2014/01/21/why-bitcoin-
      matters/?_r=0

14.   Philips Looks to Bring Blockchain Technology to Healthcare [Internet].
      CCN: Financial Bitcoin & Cryptocurrency News. [cited 2015 Dec 12].
      Available from: https:// www.cryptocoinsnews.com/philips-looks-to-bring-
      blockchaintechnology-to-healthcare-2/

15.   Wearable Devices: Privacy, Security Worries Loom Large -InformationWeek
      [Internet]. [cited 2015 Jul 22]. Available from: http://www.informationweek.
      com/healthcare/mobile-andwireless/wearable-devices-privacy-security-
      worries-loomlarge/d/d-id/1316833

16.   Loftus J. Dear Fitbit Users, Kudos On the 30 Minutes of "Vigorous Sexual
      Activity" Last Night [Internet]. [cited 2015 Aug 29]. Available from: http://
      gizmodo.com/5817784/dearfitbit-users-kudos-on-the-30-minutes-of-
      vigorous-sexualactivity-last-night

17.   Internet of Things May Disrupt Predictive Analytics in Big Data Clouds
      [Internet]. DATAVERSITY. [cited 2015 Aug 23]. Available from: http://www.
      dataversity.net/internet-of-thingsmay- disrupt-predictive-analytics-in-big-
      data-clouds/

18.   Blackburn S. The link between data relevance and
      accuracy, and consumer trust: a Q&A with Rick Erwin [Internet]. Marketing
      Forward. [cited 2015 Aug 30]. Available from: http://www.experian.com/
      blogs/marketing-forward/2013/10/11/the-link-between-data-relevance-and-
      accuracyand-consumer-trust-a-qa-with-rick-erwin/

# Part Two: Wearables and the IOT

**Movie 1: Robert Wachter and the Internet of Things**
https://vimeo.com/156572060

# Part Two Introduction

-RICK KROHN

## The IoT

In these pages we argue that across the spectrum of healthcare, a spike in innovation that leverages technology is transforming the industry from a disaggregated, bricks-andmortar system to a higher-quality, more efficient, and accountable delivery architecture. Integral to this system transformation is the employment of digital solutions that connect the elements of care – people, places and things. The aim – to streamline healthcare delivery both within the facility and at the point of care – in the facility, at home, anywhere. These digital solutions include diagnostic and treatment tools, remote monitoring, education, alerts and reminders, monitoring and early intervention based solutions. The tools of this "care anywhere" include wearable devices, apps, outreach, and clinical collaboration based on information liquidity. And the enabler of this catalog of solutions is the Internet of Things (" IoT"). The IoT is the next stage in the evolution of smart technologies, where devices "talk" to each other and to humans. It has the potential to change the dynamic of health care itself. It's about how different devices are all connected with one another, and how we are able to better share information and make wellinformed, data-driven decisions. But the IoT in healthcare is not simply about making digital connections, it's about recasting the complex interplay of the industry's stakeholders – with an increasingly central role assigned to the patient. Making the leap to the IoT isn't a seamless process - making the transition to a unified data architecture will require careful planning and execution.

## Managing IoT Transformation within the mHealth Ecosphere

In addition to the challenges associated with digital and cultural transformation that the IoT will create, Health IT innovators must also tailor digital solutions that address the unique requirements of a highly mobile "customer" base. Booz Allen Hamilton has identified four key competencies to manage this transformation.

## 1. Activation

This term refers to patients taking a more dynamic role in their own care, through self-management, monitoring, staying informed, and more. It covers a wide range of high- and low- technology activities, including conversations with doctors about care options, or use of mobile apps that track eating and exercise habits.

## 2. Connection

The mobility of patients and providers makes it difficult to ensure that patients and providers have seamless access to the people, information, and resources they need. The vision of the IoT in healthcare includes full connectivity of the care team and information. Via the IoT, physicians from different departments, physical locations and disciplines will be able to work together to deliver team-based care, and information will flow freely and securely among networks and with patients.

## 3. Optomization

A health system is optimized when it "makes the most of what it's got" in terms of facilities, equipment, and teams working toward achieving the best possible outcomes, the lowest possible cost, and the greatest efficiencies. A few ways to achieve an optimized system include reexamining processes, decreasing use of unnecessary care options, and leveraging data to help people make the right care decisions. Another way is to apply best practices from other industries.

## 4. Learning

The good news about IoT transformation is that much of the raw material on health needed to guide efforts is already there, manifested in the work providers do every day. The trick is figuring out how to gather relevant information, mine it for insights, put these insights into practice, and refine efforts through a data feedback loop. To these ends, health entities must become continuous learning organizations—collecting data, identifying best practices, and feeding both back into the system for ongoing, on-the-fly improvement. A 2013 report by the Institute of Medicine enumerates the capabilities needed: creating continuously learning organizations that generate and transfer knowledge from every patient interaction will require systemic problem solving; the application of systems engineering techniques; operational models that encourage and reward sustained quality and improved patient outcomes; transparency on cost and outcomes; and strong leadership and governance that define, disseminate, and support a vision of continuous improvement.

# Anticipating and Mitigating Risk: Things to Watch Out For

Major transformations are rarely smooth or simple. However, planning and anticipation can help mitigate risks in vulnerable areas. Often mistakenly viewed as a mainly IT initiative, digital transformation entails risks that are predominantly process related. Some of these include:

## Information Technology

Even the best technology will not help a health system achieve its goals if aligned leadership and processes do not support it. As Michael E. Porter and Thomas H. Lee wrote in "The Strategy That Will Fix Health Care": Information technology is a powerful tool for enabling value-based care. But introducing EMR [electronic medical records] without restructuring care delivery, measurement, and payment yields limited benefits. And siloed IT systems make cost and outcomes measurement virtually impossible, greatly impeding value improvement efforts. If the IoT simply adds complexity to workflows without addressing problems like information disaggregation and process inefficiency, it is part of the problem, not the solution.

## Capacity

Health systems need to thoroughly think through how transformation activities will affect their ability to deliver care. For instance, a patient recapture effort that gets a booming response in the short term may ultimately fare poorly if a facility is not ready to keep up with the increased demand and deliver high-quality care and service. Patients dissatisfied with their experience may prefer to receive care elsewhere.

## Productivity

The change to a team-based, data-driven model of care presents challenges and opportunities not unlike a merger or acquisition. One lesson from these experiences is to set realistic, mission-based productivity targets and then plan the workforce accordingly. Productivity monitoring and evaluation processes should be closely linked to the established targets.

In this final section we take a look at the intersection of the IoT with two of mHealth's rising stars – Big Data and analytics. We close with a panel of industry experts who give us their take on the future of wearables and the IoT.

# Chapter 9

# IoT Overview

**Movie 2: Eric Topol and the Internet of Things**
https://vimeo.com/156567446

# Editor's Note

The Internet of Things (IoT) is swiftly emerging as the third wave of the Internet – and the fastest growing one yet. While the first "fixed" Internet wave (1990's) connected 1 billion users and the second "mobile" wave (2000's) connected 2 billion, and in the third wave, the IoT has the potential to connect 10X as many (28 billion) "things" to the Internet by 2020, ranging from bracelets to cities.

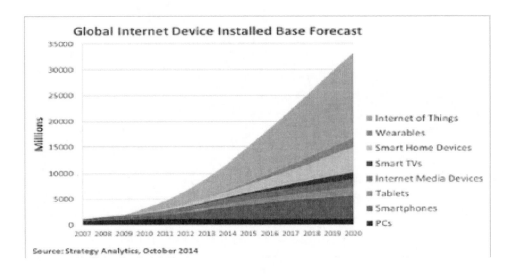

And just as the previous waves altered the way we work and live, the IoT is changing social behavior, workplace productivity and personal consumption. IoT solutions enable organizations to use smart interconnected devices to get more visibility into the identification, location, and condition of products, assets, transactions, and people. The range of IoT applications span the personal (healthcare, homes, cars) to the foundational (environments, industries) and likely in ways still unseen. Once realized, the Internet of Things will deliver an infinite array of smart connected solutions designed to improve our health, environment, services, and productivity through the intelligent use of data.

"The Internet of Things (IoT)… is expected to be the next great technological innovation and business opportunity. It will exceed in size and importance both the personal computer and mobile communications markets, and even the development of the Internet itself." ABI Research

What is the IoT? The Internet of Things connects devices such as everyday consumer objects and industrial equipment onto a data network, enabling information gathering and management of these devices and creating new services. The term was first proposed by Kevin Ashton, a British technologist, in 1999. The IoT sometimes is described in global terms with reference to industrial deployments like connected electrical grids and oil exploration, but the IoT can be intensely personal as well. As shown below, the IoT radiates from the individual (health, fitness), to broader consumer services, to entire populations and industries. It's changing the technology landscape, again.

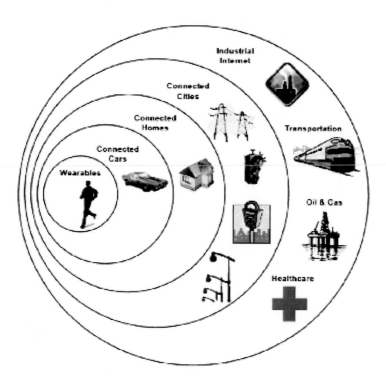

"In our view, it (IoT) can be broken up into five key verticals of adoption: Connected Wearable Devices, Connected Cars, Connected Homes, Connected Cities, and the Industrial Internet." Goldman Sachs

It's an interconnected world. As long ago as 2009, the number of internet-connected devices exceeded the number of people who own them. In healthcare, those devices are becoming increasingly sophisticated, from body area networks to implantable monitors. Taken together with apps that capture and interpret data, and integrated enterprise and cloud data repositories, the networks of these devices form the underlayment of Healthcare's IoT. Looking ahead, patientgenerated health data from IoT devices will be the key to population health management, to gleaning reimbursement in a value based world, and to producing measurable gains in outcomes and patient satisfaction.

-Rick Krohn

# Capitalizing on the IoT with Visibility and Intelligence

-COURTESY OF ZEBRA TECHNOLOGY

On any given day, each moment matters to someone, somewhere. From a retail manager responsible for asset tracking and inventory control to a clinician charged with ensuring accurate patient identification and medical records, enterprises have the opportunity to positively impact their customer and employee experiences - and bottom line. We live in a connected world and technology is embedded in everything we do, and the Internet of Things (IoT) momentum is reaching critical mass. With cloud technology, organizations have access to their devices from any location for remote monitoring, management and data capture. While accessibility to devices and data enables productivity and quality improvements, the real potential of the IoT may not be realized without a broader set of enabling technologies and insight.

It is these enabling technologies that allow enterprises to go beyond the incremental productivity and quality improvements to gain actionable intelligence on assets, people and transactions across their organization. This enhanced business insight is what enables more informed decision making and improved performance. Put simply, Enterprise Asset Intelligence helps businesses yield maximum value from IoT solutions.

According to Peter Middleton, research director at Gartner Research, "The growth in the IoT will far exceed that of other connected devices. By 2020, the number of smartphones, tablets and PCs in use will reach about 7.3 billion units. In contrast, the IoT will have expanded at a much faster rate, resulting in a population of about 26 billion units at that time."i

# IoT: Opportunities and Challenges

## Opportunities

Cloud and mobile technologies are increasingly available and affordable, and the IoT specifically, presents businesses with a multitude of opportunities. By leveraging the IoT, organizations can transform their business models to drive innovation and strategic advantages, utilize advanced analytics to become more predictive and automated and deliver more personalized customer experiences. Additionally, organizations can gain enhanced insight into their business operations to increase efficiency, reduce costs and improve security and safety, among other things.

Given the vast potential that the IoT brings, industry leaders are not hesitating to implement IoT solutions. In fact, many have already started to gain a competitive advantage with its use. However, without the proper set of enabling technologies, businesses may not be able to extract this value from the IoT. In order for businesses to gain real-time visibility into their assets, people and transactions and turn data into actionable intelligence, they need a portfolio of technologies, including:

- Devices that are equipped for data sensing, tracking and capturing in order to manage assets, people and transactions.
- Cloud technology that provides the interconnection of smart devices and the hosting of enterprise applications.
- Mobile technology that is extending business processes and information accessibility throughout the workforce.
- Big Data solutions that provide the advanced analytics necessary to gain actionable business insight from the raw data that is generated by these devices

## Challenges

Though the IoT stands to deliver various benefits, it also presents challenges. And while the momentum doesn't seem to be slowing down anytime soon, there are factors that should be taken into account when making a business decision to adopt an IoT solution. Among the main challenges faced when deploying IoT solutions are:

- Complexity
- Connecting legacy devices
- Security standards
- Device management
- Data analytics

Regarding complexity, an IoT deployment has various moving parts. Between planning, integrating and testing the ecosystem, organizations have their work cut out for them.

Specifying and connecting devices to the cloud can often be challenging, because device manufacturers typically use protocols and firmware for particular devices. This challenge is often a barrier to success adding risk and cost.

As it pertains to the connectivity of legacy devices, Forrester Research suggests that there is no standard to integration across IoT devices, applications and services.ii And while many devices are capable of connecting to Wi-Fi® and similar networks, a significant amount of devices are still Internet unaware, relying on basic LAN connectivity. In order to connect legacy devices to an IoT system and cloud technology, businesses will need to upgrade and/ or replace their networking capabilities. As the number of devices grow, various types of formats, information sources, etc., can make it hard to manage all of them while in sync with one another, thus generally requiring a set of proprietary tools. Not to mention, many applications can only consume specific data from the field and support only specific process needs. The results fall short of end-to-end visibility into the data. Moreover, as the number of connected devices continues to dramatically increase, so does the amount of available data. Two issues that are often presented by this phenomena include: data sets increasing in volume, velocity and variety, which make it difficult to process with standard database management systems, and the disjointed data silos in which much of this data sits - making it inaccessible across the enterprise.

Security also becomes an issue when physical assets are converted to digital and thus, susceptible to cyber attacks. The security of the device's data is also an issue when dealing with devices that are Internet aware. Though the aforementioned are just a few of the major challenges, successful IoT deployment requires solid connectivity, simple scalability and  collaboration at every point. Connected devices don't yield intelligence by simply producing more raw data. Insight must be gained through the interpretation of the data. But to obtain real value, end-to-end solutions need to be delivered that address the challenges of implementingIoT technologies.

## ..erprise Asset Intelligence

### Enables Businesses to Capitalize on the IoT

Once IoT deployment challenges are evaluated and met, organizations need to execute their strategy to reach Enterprise Asset Intelligence. Obtaining intelligence is about transforming an organization into a predictive and automated enterprise - which is a new way of doing business that drives innovation and revenue.

However, when it comes to allowing trusted, automated decision making, the intricacy lies in compiling intelligence, enabling the technologies to work together, defining processes and implementing workflow and security. Enterprise AssetIntelligence then enables machine-tomachine interactions that don't require human intervention, rather devices that act on signals in an automated manner. This automation is enabled by processed data with advanced analytics, which is transformed into predictive algorithms and programmed automated systems.

Enterprise Asset Intelligence provides the visibility organizations need to leverage the IoT, but beyond that, it provides enterprises the business insight they need to be innovative and earn their competitive advantage. Without this enhanced knowledge, enterprises have endless amounts of data and no sound interpretation and insight into how to use it to transform their business.

# Five Essentials for Deploying IoT

### Solutions

When building an IoT organization, it's critical that the system supports both legacy and new smart devices. Further, it should provide support for multiple connectivity options (i.e., wired, wireless, etc.). IoT solutions should also have centralized and remote device management to allow for dayto-day provisioning, device setup and maintenance.

- Devices
- Connectivity
- Account/device management and security
- Application programming
- Analytics and reporting

To support application connectivity, the system should offer consistent application programming interfaces across a wide range of devices, while affording easy scalability and connectivity to the data center. Once an IoT solution is in place, it needs to be capable of comprehending advanced analytics in order to process Big Data. Business intelligence, enterprise resource planning and other applications enrich data collected, which ultimately yields insights, as well as predict outcomes and actions.

## Conclusion

At the end of the day, the IoT enables a transformative business opportunity. However, businesses that don't navigate the complexities and take advantage of the technology won't be able to compete.

Businesses that leverage IoT technologies and data in such a way that supports strategic and innovative business models, advanced analytics and better customer service, are truly raising the bar for performance. Businesses need to partner with a company that has the technology, knowledge and experience to address the challenges in solution deployment and management. Zebra and its technologies enable Enterprise Asset Intelligence, which addresses the critical challenges enabling businesses to realize the competitive advantages afforded by the IoT.

As the IoT continues to advance, so does the adoption of machine-to-machine (M2M) communications. Vodafone suggests that around 50 percent of companies will have adopted M2M technologies by 2020. The solution is accelerating companies' ability to remotely monitor equipment to improve external factors such as customer service. And like the IoT, M2M is becoming a critical component to company strategy and competitive advantage.iii

# References

1.  Gartner Research, "Gartner Says the Internet of Things Installed Base Will Grow to 26 Billion Units By 2020," December 2013.
2.  Forrester Research, Inc., "Preparing IT for the Internet of Things," April 2013.
3.  Vodafone Ltd., "The M2M Adoption Barometer," July 2014.

# *Case Study*: How the Collective Can Keep Us Healthy by using IOT-Enabled Mobile Healthcare Solutions

ATHELLINA ATHSANI, DIRECTOR OF STRATEGIC

According to CDC, chronic illness in the US is a serious problem causing 7 out of 10 deaths, affecting 133 million Americans who live with at least one chronic illness, and taking up more than 75% of total health care costs. While chronic diseases are among the most common and costly of health problems, they are also preventable1. In fact, the leading cause of death in the US and in the world - cardiovascular diseases - can be prevented by simply engaging in healthier activities such as exercises, better food choices and tobacco/alcohol avoidance. Clearly, a health care system that focuses more on preventing diseases as opposed to the existing model of treating illness is a better option. With technology advances, ubiquitous connectivity, lowering costs of sensors and wellness-related devices, as well as individuals' propensity towards smartphone usage, mobile healthcare for chronic disease management is ripe for adoption. Add the role of the collective as the catalyst for lifestyle change and adherence, preventing chronic diseases is made all the more viable. Today's mobile healthcare for disease management is in its early stages. Individuals have to navigate through 97,000 iOS and Android health and fitness mobile applications. Individuals have to determine for themselves the effectiveness and usefulness of the apps. Even if they find something, the onus is on them to follow through and validate the program/ information.

There is also the issue of privacy and security of the data captured/ exchanged and the cost burden for the individual to overcome. Having a champion to advocate and mobilize efforts - as well as putting resources toward achieving health targets - is more powerful than putting self-care solely in the hands of the individual. The ideal champion is a collective body that can motivate individuals, encourage compliancy, and mobilize resources and efforts towards health targets[2]. The collective can be institutional bodies such as government agencies, schools, community groups, hospitals/senior homes as well as corporations such as business and towns/municipality/cities.

US corporations serve as a great example of a collective change agent for preventive mobile healthcare. In the US, nearly 80% of its people have health insurance through an employer or a federal program like Medicare. One of the top challenges for US corporations has been to manage health benefit costs since health insurance is used to attract and retain employees. General Motors, as an example, historically spent more on employee health care than they do on raw material for making cars ($5.2 billion in 2004)[3] . Corporate health insurance is obtained through group plans priced according to several factors including company size, worker age, claim history and most importantly, availability of health and wellness programs.

American corporations are highly motivated to implement innovative and engaging health management programs. Two key trends affirming this argument are the increased adoption of health management programs and the increased offering of incentives for employees who meet health goals (e.g. target BMI, cholesterol and/ or blood pressure levels, etc.).

Few companies are beginning to implement interactive webbased technology and mobile applications to improve participation levels. Corporations recognize the need to manage health issues caused by highly stressful work environments and are turning to technology to better manage their employee's wellbeing. One use case is EMC's Health-Link4 by which employees can access and track their healthcare information via their PC or mobile devices using the HealthLink portal. This medical content management platform allows the employee to track wellness programs, gain access to medical information on care providers and medical diagnoses. In turn, the portal also allows the employer to track statistical medical cost reports such as claims and wellness performance statistics. Since implementation in 2004, EMC has seen savings of more than $223 million in health care costs and has kept its healthcare cost 2.4% below the national average.

The second trend driving the adoption of innovative and engaging mobile healthcare programs is the wellness program ROI. Currently, corporate employers spend an average of $594 per employee on their health care programs[5] yet the impact of chronic diseases in lost productivity is roughly valued at $1.3 trillion dollars loss while another $338 billion is spent annually on treatment[6]. With today's spending rate on healthcare programs, corporations realize an estimated $1.5 trillion in recovered productivity and nonmedical claims. With more effective, well-measured wellness programs, the savings can potentially be bigger. Hence, corporations are offering incentives to employees who actively participate in wellness programs.

IOT solutions for mobile healthcare can up the ante for corporations and individuals. The consumerization of healthcare technology for these programs is inevitable, especially factoring the pervasiveness of mobile devices in people's daily lives. In addition, lower costs and improved technology in mobile devices and mobile peripherals has made health data collection and exchange easier and more accessible. Ubiquitous connectivity of wireless technology via Wi-Fi and Bluetooth has made medical content collection, consumption and dissemination more prevalent and increasingly more secure through the latest encryption and authentication technologies, thus increasing the employee's confidence in the application and providing the potential to monitor their wellbeing anytime and anyplace.

Corporations, in turn, can leverage these advantages to create interactive and engaging wellness programs that ensure compliancy to the programs, add a fun element via gamification, provide better measurements of effort and effectiveness of the program, adjustable privacy levels and much more. Importantly, the IOT ecosystem can leverage already existing infrastructure, such as corporate-issued mobile devices and PCs, as well as secured connectivity and corporate buildings/structure thus keeping the solution cost relatively low. Another reason such a solution is ideal for corporations is the inherent security and inclusiveness of the enterprise's walled garden nature.

Mobile devices, sensors and connectivity used in the corporate environment are a part of the corporate network presumably protected by the corporate security policies in place. Leveraging corporate resources also ensures a degree of expected adoption/opted-in participants. Furthermore, the added bonus of a highly quantifiable wellness program is the likelihood of the insurance provider to partner in providing such a solution, thus distributing the burden of cost to more vested parties. In fact, having insurance provider partners will also help ensure that employers are using the system purely for health insurance purposes.

## Continued growth in use of outcomes-based incentives

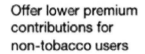

**More large employers linking incentives to what employees do about their health**

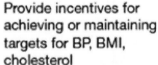

Offer lower premium contributions for non-tobacco users

Provide incentives for achieving or maintaining targets for BP, BMI, cholesterol

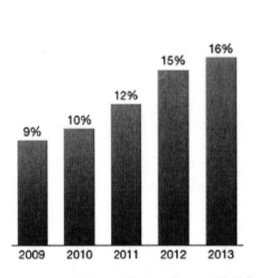

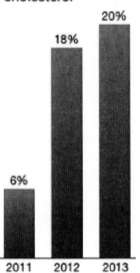

*Mercer's National Survey of Employer-Sponsored Health Plans*

**Figure 1:** Employer trends in outcomes-based incentive, Mercer's National Survey of Employer Sponsored Health Plans

From the employee's perspective, mobile healthcare is a natural predisposition of individuals who are already using their mobile devices for various aspects of their lives, whether in financial management, travel, shopping, navigation, media consumption, information gathering, etc. Not to mention, corporate sponsored wellness programs will put fitness/ wellness devices and apps into the hands of more individuals who otherwise would not or do not use them.

Furthermore, innovative and engaging wellness programs leveraging mobile applications can increase productivity, offer a sense of community, satisfaction, happiness and the benefits the wellbeing of employees.

Today, 91% of organizations already have some type of wellness program in place[7]. Many of the popular wellness programs - including weight management, smoking cessation programs, fitness programs, alcohol/drug abuse, stress management, health education and so on - can benefit from an IOT ecosystem. An example IOT enabled wellness solution can include a mesh of Bluetooth Smart beacons interacting with the employees' mobile devices. Strategically placed beacons in the work environment serve as a tracking and check-in mechanism and a profile based broadcast system. Additionally, hardware and software peripherals make the effectiveness of the activities more easily measured.

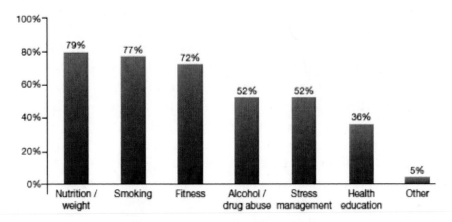

Source:   RAND Employer Survey, 2012.
Notes:    The graph represents information from employers with at least 50 employees that offer any lifestyle management
          intervention as a component of a wellness program.  51% of employers offer a wellness program, and 77% of those
          have a lifestyle management intervention.

**Figure 2:** Types of Lifestyle Management Programs offered by Employers RAND Employer Survey 2012

The tracking and check-in mechanism can be programed to automatically or manually track an individual in proximity of a beacon. These check-ins help the company measure collective activity levels (For the month of April, 10% of the engineers walked a total of 1000 meters daily) and ensure some level of compliancy with wellness programs (Jean checked into the gym 4 times in January). The system can even track distance/ places traveled by individuals or anonymous groups of time.

Where individuals can fool fitness devices or smartphones by simply mimicking movement on their devices, i.e. shake the device, a Bluetooth-lined track can measure actual distance travelled more accurately as the individual needs to pass all the beacons to trigger check-ins by the beacons. Leveraging Bluetooth Smart beacons also has other technological advantages such as low power consumption making the solution last longer and require less maintenance. Bluetooth Smart beacons also offer ease of pairing with mobile devices and peripherals if at all required. Furthermore,the mesh of beacons also ensures continuity in tracking even in problem Wi-Fi or cellular connectivity areas.

The Bluetooth solution also allows the company to tailor activity or content based on profiles such as individual employees (Jane, John, Joe), types of employees (engineers, assembly line workers) or location profiles, e.g. cafeteria, 400m track from the reception desk through the stairwell and back, etc., making the program more interactive and flexible. For example, location-based content from the solution can announce today's menu with caloric count as employees approach the cafeteria or announce that the granola bar is healthier than the chocolate one when an employee approaches the vending machine. The solution can also send out a group-based reminder to the factory workers to take a mandated 15-minute break every 2 hours while alerting the engineers on the second floor to stand up from their work stations every 30 minutes. An individual based prompt can alert to Larry to step away from the ice cream dispenser machine. Furthermore, the ability for flexible profiling can potentially allow corporations and insurance companies to track all employees anonymously by allowing employees who opt-in to be tracked as individuals while those opted-out can be tracked as anonymous group types.

Hardware and software peripherals can be equally useful in a mobile wellness program. Purpose built devices such as Garmin GPS watches, Fitbits, Bluetooth heart rate monitors, and custom-built devices with advanced MEMs targeting specific measurements can be used to measure effectiveness of the activity/ workout. This in turn provides better caloric burn rates or effectiveness of effort in relation to the activity. For example, the system is able to distinguish Jane's effort, who ran the 400m track twice, from Larry's, who used his chair to propel himself through the track. Adding a heart rate monitor into the mix will also measure the intensity of the individual's workout and allow health-related triggers. For example, if Larry's heart rate goes up over 200 beats per minute when he tries to run the track, the system can send him an alert by making his smartphone sound or vibrate, notifying him to slow down and prevent injury.

Having a wellness solution with these features helps corporations gamify their wellness programs. Workout intensity goals, abstinence from vending

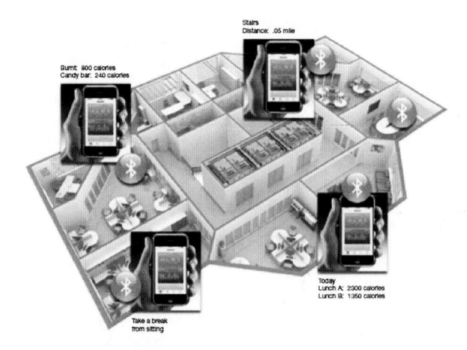

Burnt: 800 calories
Candy bar: 240 calories

Stairs
Distance: .05 mile

Today
Lunch A: 2300 calories
Lunch B: 1350 calories

Take a break
from sitting

**Figure 3:** Sample Bluetooth-enabled Wellness Program

machine candy bars, frequency or duration away from the chair, group vs. group activity, treasure-hunt or Easter egg surprise in personalized content are just some examples to make wellness programs more fun. Check-in activities and quantifiable measurements allow the program to be point-based, which in turn can help the company determine tiered-level incentives more effectively by rewarding those who work harder.

Why should IOT hardware and services providers care? Healthcare industry represents 18% of the US GDP, while most of Europe's healthcare spend is at 10% and Canada is roughly at 11%. In 2013, 149 million non-elderly people were covered by employer-sponsored insurance. With today's rudimentary wellness programs, corporations are already spending $594 per employee. This is a current approximate value of $88.5 billion for total available market in the US alone. Would such solutions cause privacy or Big Brother-type concerns? Potentially. Employees will naturally have a distrust of a system that can potentially be abused by the employers or insurance providers. The implementation of such a system will have several vested parties: corporations, insurance providers as well as institutions governing the corporations, groups of workers and insurance providers.

One way of managing the concern is to have administration of such a program run by the insurance provider or a neutral third party so that employers and insurance providers cannot abuse the system. Another concern is the security of data collected. As mentioned previously, corporations are the ideal collective to deploy IOT enabled mobile healthcare systems as corporations are naturally walled garden environments where there should already be heavy investments in secured, encrypted connectivity and data repositories.

Engaging and highly quantifiable wellness programs are the tip of the iceberg for what IOT and mobile technology can offer for the healthcare industry. In a not too distant future, doctors can prescribe mobile applications to their patients. As an example, a gynecologist can request an expecting mother to download an app that can track her health parameters throughout her pregnancy. Care for the elderly and the  incapacitated can be made all the more precise with ingestible sensors8 capable of giving care givers real time wellness updates. Children in schools where obesity is a problem can be pitted against each other in wellness leagues to compete for the healthiest or the most physically active school where their activity and food intake is tracked via an IOT-enabled mobile system.

# References

1.  Chronic Diseases, The Power to Prevent, The Call to Control: At A Glance 2009 http://www.cdc.gov/chronicdisease/resources/publications/aag/chronic.htm
2.  Michigan Ross School of Business paper on the role of collective change agents in closing the gap of healthcare disparities. 2006.
3.  Wellness programs get boost from new technologies - Matt Dunning April 29 2012 http://www.businessinsurance.com/article/20120429/NEWS03/304299980#
4.  Fidelity® and National Business Group on Health Find Average Wellness Incentives to Increase to Almost $600 per Employee, More than Double the Average Incentive in 2009 2/20/2014 http://www.fidelity.com/inside-fidelity/employer-services/health-care-survey-finds-spending
5.  An Unhealthy America: The Economic Burden of Chronic Disease -- Charting a New Course to Save Lives and Increase Productivity and Economic Growth - Ross DeVol and Armen Bedroussian, with Anita Charuworn, Anusuya Chatterjee, In Kyu Kim, Soojung Kim and Kevin Klowden Oct 01, 2007 http://www.milkeninstitute.org/publications/view/321

6. American Institute for Preventive Medicine study - Characteristics of Successful Wellness Programs - Don R. Powell http://www.healthylife.com/template.asp?pageID=41

7. American Institute for Preventive Medicine study - Characteristics of Successful Wellness Programs - Don R. Powell http://www.healthylife.com/template. asp?pageID=41

8. Proteus Digital Health Announces FDA Clearance of Ingestible Sensor http://www.proteus.com/proteus-digitalhealth- announcesfda-clearance-of-ingestible-sensor/30Jul2012

# *Case Study*: Forget Smart Phones - What You Need Are Smart Pumps

CATHY SULLIVAN, RN. NP. DIRECTOR OF PATIENT CARE SERVICES •
BETH ISRAEL MEDICAL CENTER, NEW YORK, NY

## Objective

Medication Safety is a primary goal for our system of 4 major medical centers in the New York City area. To reduce errors associated with IV infusion, we evaluate several infusion pumps with smart pump technology and selected the B. Braun Outlook 400ES based on the following key safety features.

- real time data monitoring
- wireless retrospective reporting software
- ease of use
- light-weight, single channel device

After implementation, we used the real time view and retrospective infusion data to identify opportunities to further enhance patent safety.

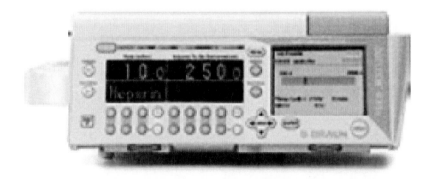

# Methods

A multidisciplinary team from all hospital sites met weekly to standardize our hospital formulary, including drug concentrations, diluents, and weight-based dosing. The new formulary was updated in our electronic medical record and computerized physician order entry. A smart pump drug library was created with input from various departments, establishing parameters such as soft and hard dosing limits, clinical advisories, and bolus dosing. We created a single uniform drug library for all smart pumps across our system.

# DoseTrac Real Time and Retrospective Data

Real time monitoring allowed us to see all of our infusions, confirm whether they were programmed in the drug library, and immediately identify if any infusions were outside the dosing limits. We were pleased to find drug library utilization in critical care at 100%. Retrospective reports allow us to identify trends with drug library utilization, dose overrides, corrections, and to drug associated with alerts. Six month data analysis (Jan - June 2012) showed the following.

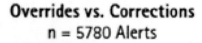

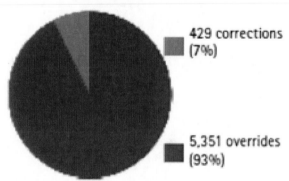

- Few dose corrections indicate low incidence of programming error
- Only 3 insulin corrections over 6 months!
- High number of overrides led us to look at our soft limits and practices
- 493 herapin ACS overrides - exceeding soft limit of 1000 units/hr

- 46 fentanyl "good catches" - all corrected to within the soft limits
- 396 RBC's overrides - 52% due to infusing 80 - 100 ml/hr (soft max 75 ml/hr)
- 198 dexmedetomidine overrides - exceeding soft limits and bolus dosing
- 250 propofol overrides - 23% due to bolus dosing
- 2988 bolus doses - using bolus feature

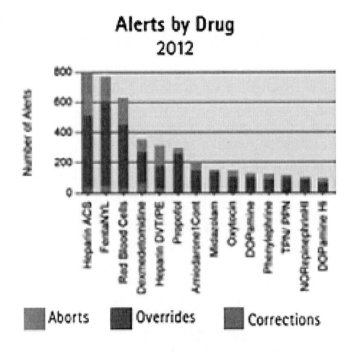

# Results

Significant reduction in alerts was achieved through dosing limit modifications, education on use of bolus feature, cheat sheet for staff, and distribution of weekly DoseTrac reports to pharmacy, and administration.

- Continue to evaluate RBC's due to incidence of overrides

Reduction in alerts for target drugs:
- 88% reduction in heparin ACS alerts
- 88% reduction in fentanyl alerts
- 48% reduction in RBC alerts
- 45% reduction in dexmedetomidine alerts
- 63% reduction in propofol alerts

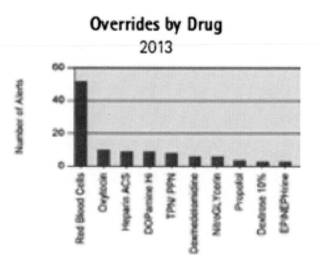

# *Case Study*: Smart Pumps: Achieving 100% Drug Library Compliance & Averting Medication Errors

CHRISTINE RUHL, BSN. CCRN, NURSE MANAGER CVU, ICU, CARDIOLOGY SERVICES. • CHERYL GROGG, BSN, NURSE

## Introduction

### Goals of the Project

- Uphold the health system culture of patient safety by improving medication administration processes and monitoring
- Standardization of practices, supplies, and implementation of new technology to decrease potential for pump related errors and associated patient harm

### Problems identified

- Old technology with limited safeguards
- Clinician manual programming for IV drip infusions
- Customized medication concentrations and infusions leading to large variability
- Multiple types and models of IV pumps and accessories throughout the organization
- Reporting of medication errors relied solely on direct observation and self reporting.

### Implementation

#### Phase I

- Development of the multidisciplinary team with members from Pharmacy, Nursing, Education, Biomed, Materials Management, and Management

• Research and investigation regarding different enders and technology available including site visits and testing of IV pumps in-house with our wireless system.

Over 400 Outlook ES IV pumps were installed throughout the health system, almost a full year from the start of the project!

**Phase II**

**Drug Library Development**

> • Development of the multidisciplinary team with members from Pharmacy, Nursing, Education, Biomed, Materials Management, and Management

Examples:

- Fenoldopam in both 10 mg/250ml and 20 mg/250ml standardized to 20 mg/250ml
- Norepinephrine prescribed both mcg/kg/min and mcg/min dosing-standardized to mcg/min
    - Epinephrine and phynlyephrine dosed both mcg/min and mcg/kg/min-standardized to mcg/kg/min
- Collaboration between Pharmacy, Physicians, and Nurse Clinicians to evaluate practices and preferences
- Safety "double-checks" including clinician advisories on high risk medications Heparin and Insulin
- Soft minimum and soft maximum dosing limits set for all drugs to alert clinicians of programming that is above or below the customized limit set
- Soft limit designed to warn but not restrict
- Hard maximum limits set for high alert drugs preventing clinicians exceeding specified dosing limit

**Phase II**

- Drug Library Validation Workshop
    - Multidisciplinary review of the drug library by all areas
    - Nurses, physicians, and pharmacists included
- Training Workshops
    - Clinical mentors (Resource staff for each area)
    - All Nurses received hands on training immediately before pump implementation
- Patient ID scanning procedure with handheld and built in pump scanners for patient specific real time monitoring

## Innovation

DoseTrac Real Time Data

- Monitoring by clinicians and pharmacy to view pump settings, alerts and active alarms
- Pharmacists use real time monitoring to improve workflow and decrease turnaround times

DoseTrac Reports
  • Retrospective reports of pump infusions and alerts to understand
  trends, identify education opportunities and drug library improvements

Technology Integration
  • Smart pump IV solution is embedded with BMV process
  • Smart pumps are integrated with nurse call and portable
  phone technology
  • Alarms from IV pumps are directed through nurse call
  system directly to the phone of the primary caregiver.

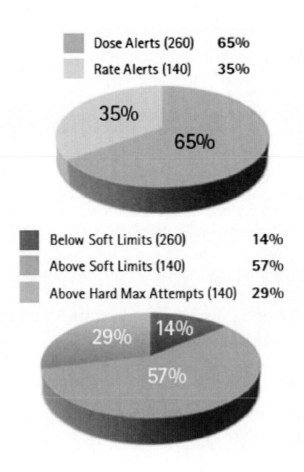

Post Implementation:
Total 400 Alerts in 11,784 Infusions

Dose Alerts (260)          65%
Rate Alerts (140)          35%

Below Soft Limits (260)          14%
Above Soft Limits (140)          57%
Above Hard Max Attempts (140)    29%

# Data Analysis Results

- Initial data analysis was completed 6 weeks post implementation
  - Total of 11,784 infusions - 35.34% used drug library

# Intervention

- Weekly unit-based audits to assess and document drug library utilization and compliance due to:
  - Overall low drug library utilization (35%)
  - High number of aborts
  - Wrong care area/location selections
  - Targets of 95% established across key infusion pump metrics:
  - Dose delivered infusions, rate delivered infusions, correct location, and correct care area.

## Compliance Rates

| | Target | 12/2011 | 07/2012 |
|---|---|---|---|
| Dose Delivered | 95% | 93% | **100%** |
| Rate Delivered | 95% | 49% | **100%** |
| Correct Location | 95% | 92% | **100%** |
| Correct Care Area | 95% | 62% | **100%** |

- **Compliance increased to 100% through awareness, education, and process improvements**
- **Within the first three months of implementation, seven (7) adverse drug events were averted**

## Outcomes
Lessons Learned

- Alert fatigue from soft maximum limits set too low vs. actual infusion practices was a concern
  - limit adjusted to prevent potential alert fatigue and maintain safe dosing

- Ongoing education: Bolusing, oncology drug infusions
- Communication with staff
  - Outcomes, good "catches" and averted errors
- Custom concentrations could possibly increase errors:

  - Propofol entered as 10mg/100ml instead of 1000mg/ml could result in 100 times higher rate
  - Norepinephrine 8mg/250ml programmed as 4mg/250ml could result in an infusion rate double the intended rate

  - These examples demonstrate opportunities for error when custom concentrations are enabled
  - Support decision to limit entering custom concentration on as many drugs as possible
- Smart pump technology resulted in improving medication safety, preventing patient harm, faster recognition and response to alarming pumps, and further promoting a culture of safety

# Chapter 10

# The IoT and Big Data

**Movie 3: Robert Wachter on IoT and Big Data**

https://vimeo.com/156573661

# Editor's Note

Today healthcare data resides in multiple, independent locations, including the physician office, the electronic health record (EHR) systems, insurance claims databases, siloed personal health apps, research and clinical trial databases, imaging files and of course paper. To bring order to these "islands" of information. there is an enormous opportunity to establish a unified data repository, an architecture that delivers a complete picture of the patient. Here the IoT, Big Data and wearables are a natural fit. Arguably the biggest winner in the wearables sweepstakes, Big Data derived from wearables can be used to extract value, identify long term patterns and risk factors for clinicians and researchers. Evidence distilled from this treasure trove of clinical information, and particularly genomic data, can improve diagnoses, trigger earlier interventions, and discover more effective treatments. There are of course, hurdles. Who owns the data and who has access? How much is too much? What security provisions are being employed to "bulletproof" protected information? Managing huge volumes of data – we are now in the realm of "exabytes" of data produced daily- is going to require deft handling.

-Rick Krohn

# The Internet of Things and Big Data in Healthcare

-STEVE KASTIN, MD

**Movie 4: Introduction to The Internet of Things and Big Data in Healthcare by Rick Krohn**
https://vimeo.com/156573897

To understand the relationship between so-called "big data" and the Internet of Things (IoT), one must first have a good understanding of each. Unfortunately, each term suffers from being used in a variety of ways by different people. For example, IoT is sometimes used to refer to any set of devices which can communicate with one another. Other definitions include additional requirements. One such definition, contained in a recent whitepaper from Verizon1, states that in order to be considered part of the IoT, three attributes must be present:

1. the connected asset must be able to sense something about its surroundings
2. the data from that asset must be transferred seamlessly and automatically, and
3. the analysis of the data must be integrated into the business process

Other definitions require that each item must have a unique identifier or that the communication must involve the Internet.

Similarly, "big data" is a term that creates lots of confusion, in part because it's used to mean different things by different people. At its most general, "big data" simply means "LOTS of data." But just as the definition of IoT above contains an element of how it's used, so too do some definitions of big data. These definitions emphasize the analysis of large (or huge) datasets in order to discover patterns or associations that might not be evident when looking at smaller datasets. A good example of this is when new pharmaceuticals come onto the market and begin to be used by very large numbers of people. Side-effects or other problems often crop up that were not seen during pre-market testing. Why? Because the testing was on hundreds or perhaps thousands of people, yielding a comparatively small dataset. Once millions of people start using the drug, the dataset is much larger, and new insight become evident.

With the advent of the IoT, we have a situation where large numbers of connected devices are each generating potentially HUGE quantities of data. This is what generates the huge datasets that are the hallmark of "big data." In a medical context, these devices could be a variety of wearable and non-wearable sensors on your body or in your home. Over time, people will likely use more and more devices, and each device will likely become capable of monitoring more and more things. Devices might be reporting your heart rate, blood pressure, oxygen saturation, chemical composition of your tears, and many more things. And they might be reporting these things every minute or more. As you can imagine, that very quickly leads to extremely large amounts of data.

OK, so now we have this huge pile of data that we've collected from the IoT devices.

That leads to a number of questions, such as where and how we'll store it, and how we can analyze all this data to make it useful. Remember, the whole point of having all this data is to be able to use it to make helpful, intelligent decisions – and no quantity of data will help us to make good decisions unless:

- it's good quality (valid, reliable) data to begin with, and
- we use the right tools to analyze the data in the proper way.

Just as with the example of a new drug entering the market and then being used by very large numbers of people, the huge datasets that become available due to the IoT do two things for us:

1. they provide additional data (new data or simply more data) that we never had before
2. they provide new insights into how one type of data might be related to another type of data

It's the second item that causes the most excitement when people talk about the limitless possibilities of the IoT. But unlocking that potential will require powerful (and easy to use) tools to allow us to properly analyze the data that the IoT devices provide.

Part of the challenge of analyzing any data is to make sure you're asking the question you think you're asking! That may sound odd, but there's an old saying that "computers do what you tell them to do, not what you want them to do." What this means is that computers are very literal. Humans understand our imprecise communication and (hopefully) understand what we really meant to ask (or say), based on context and "common sense." Computers, on the other hand, don't typically do that. If our query to the computer is merely imprecise, that's arguably not so bad, because the computer can usually detect that we didn't provide enough information, and inform us of that fact. The real problem is when we are sufficiently precise for the computer to be able to give us an answer, but we accidentally ask for the wrong thing. When humans create a query in a database, accidentally asking a question different from what you intended to ask turns out to be surprisingly easy! What you need, therefore, is a query language that's straightforward enough to make it easy for you to understand what you're asking, in order to help you identify any errors you might have made. The more "natural" (i.e. human-like) the query language is, the better. The ultimate goal, of course, is to be able to ask the question in standard human language and have the computer ask you for any clarification it feels it needs. (Think of the computer on board the USS Enterprise in Star Trek. No special query language needed there!) There are programs referred to as "NLP" (natural language processing) that do just this – they take a query in "natural language" (the way we would ask the question to another person) and convert it into the appropriate query that the database program can understand.

Assuming that you form your database query correctly, (i.e. asking for "blood pressure" when you really do want to know about blood pressure) the next obstacle is assuring that all data that pertains to blood pressure is labelled as such in the database, so that the computer "knows" which pieces of data are blood pressure data and which aren't. It's very important that all relevant data gets included, while all irrelevant data is excluded. This speaks to the need for data naming standards, which will be discussed in more detail in an upcoming chapter. Similarly, if the data on blood pressures, for example, is coming from more than one device, we need another type of data standardization, to assure that the same actual blood pressure in the patient yields exactly the same results (data) on all devices. Essentially, all devices need to be calibrated to a common standard. If that doesn't happen, the data coming from the multiple devices, when aggregated, will be confusing, at best. You might think that the person's blood pressure is bouncing up and down, when in reality, all that's happening is that the readings are alternately coming from Device A and then Device B. Meaningful analysis of Big Data, (well, all data, actually) relies on high quality and high reliability of the data.

# Challenges with Big Data

As hinted at above, there are a number of challenges faced when dealing with "big data." The first, and perhaps most obvious, is where to store it, especially in the context of a home user storing his or her own data. Relatively inexpensive hard drives are currently available with a capacity of up to 6 TB (Terabytes). (1 TB equals 1,000 Gigabytes or 1 million Megabytes.) And while a Terabyte may sound like a lot of storage, the sheer volume of data generated by multiple devices, each potentially putting out multiple data points every few minutes (or perhaps as frequently as every few seconds!) quickly adds up, even when each individual message is fairly small.

It's probably worth a quick sidebar to talk a bit about the messages themselves. When data is staying internal to a single device, the context of the data is known – at least in terms of the source of that data. It's from the device in question. Even then, the device will likely need to add the date and time to each bit of data, and if the device supports multiple users, it needs to include an identifier for which user the data pertains to. Other contextual data will also likely be needed, such as the units the value is measured in, the operating mode of the device, and other selectable device parameters. When data from multiple devices is pulled together into a single database, we also need to include the name or type/model number of the device, and perhaps a unique serial number of the device. The important thing is for all necessary context to be included with the actual data "payload" (such as a blood glucose value).

In addition to the need for lots of physical data storage space, the software (such as the database program that will be used to store and access the data) also needs to be able to support huge database sizes of perhaps millions (if not tens or hundreds of millions) of individual data records. There are 525,600 minutes in a year, and 31,536,000 seconds in a year.

So even a single IoT device, reporting only a single type of value, (say, pulse rate) would generate 525,600 messages per year if set to generate data every minute, and 31,536,000 messages per year if set to generate data every second! But again, it's more likely that people will wind up having multiple devices, each of which collects (and then reports in) multiple types of data values.

## Use of "The Cloud"

In order to be able to accommodate the need for lots of storage space and the need for sophisticated data analysis tools, many are recommending use of "the cloud." But another benefit of storage in the cloud is the ability to easily aggregate data from multiple people, and analyze it together, for an even bigger dataset. As discussed above, the bigger the dataset, the more likely it is to find otherwise "hidden" insights, so it's very desirable to aggregate as much data as possible. But aggregation of data from multiple people implies that someone other than you has access to all of that data. Who will that be, and what will the rules be for use of that data? How will the data be secured from prying eyes? Will the data be de-identified in some way? There are many security and privacy questions that must be addressed, the minute individual data owners relinquish control of their data to a third party. These issues will be discussed in an upcoming chapter.

## Closing Thoughts

The Internet of Things has great potential in healthcare. Huge amounts of data have the potential to be generated from wearable and non-wearable devices and sensors. Having access to this "Big Data" enables the possibility of discovering new insights and making new associations. But there are challenges which must be addressed if the IoT and Big Data are to live up to their potential in the furtherance of healthcare and health maintenance. As often happens, technologies are deployed and utilized before all of the issues are fully thought through. With the rapid adoption of IoT in healthcare, now is the time to start thinking through these issues, so that we not only get the most out of IoT and Big Data, but do so in a safe and secure manner to protects our personal privacy and keeps our personal data safe from those who should not have access to it.

# References

1. The IoT and the Humanization of Healthcare Technology, accessed at http://www.verizonenterprise.com/resources/reports/rp_iot-and-the-humanization-of-healthcaretechnology_en_xg.pdf

# *Case Study*: The IoT and Big Data in Healthcare Unleashing the Next Generation of Value Creation

-DR. ANAND K. IYER, CHIEF DATA SCIENCE OFFICER

We are increasingly living in a world dominated by two very simple things: 0s and 1s. Enter stage left the digital data era. It's everywhere that we expected. For sure. But, it's also manifesting in places we could have only dreamed of not even a decade ago. Eric Schmidt, the Executive Chairman of Google recently said "from the dawn of civilization until 2003, humankind generated five exabytes of data. Now, we generate five exabytes of data every two days, and the pace is only accelerating!" Five exabytes. That's 5 followed by 18 zeroes – equivalent to 2 raised to the 60th power! It's too large to even comprehend. It begs the logical question: Who is generating this data? In fact, not just who, but as we'll explore, what. This chapter takes a closer look at how the healthcare industry is being transformed from the inside-out because of this effect.

We begin with some basics. In what the wireless industry labels as M2M or machine-to-machine, machines or devices themselves are both providers of and subscribers to data. To better understand this concept and its tectonic effect on society, we refer to the early days in communications. Rumor has it that Alexander Graham Bell famously said "why would one ever need more than one telephone in a village?" In his mind, there was one communication point for N homes in a village. This model clearly evolved such that there were N communication points for M homes in a village or town, where N and M were initially equivalent. The number of unique communication pathways, or in modern parlance – data transactions – was therefore $N*(N-1)/2$. We recall this simple formula from high-school algebra.

But with the advent of cable, fax and high-speed internet access, N had quickly grown to 4N communication points for the same M homes. Additionally, there was typically a person – a human – at the end of each of these communication points. A person watching television. Someone sending a fax. Another making a telephone call. And in theory, any one of the four points in a home could communicate to any four points in any other home. Just substitute 4N for N in the above equation, and recognize that the growth rate is a quadratic one – proportional to the square of the number of points in question.

Today, the concept known as the "Internet of Things" – or IoT for short, takes this equation to a new realm. Think of how many N communication points there are within a home today. In most cases, the four listed above. But add to that the number of mobile phones, tablets and PCs in a home, and that number, for a typical family of four, rapidly rises to over 10 or even 15, as each of us have multiple mobile internet devices. But it's not just people who are communicating. It's our front doors, saying they've not been locked, the window or garage door that remains open, the refrigerator that is in need of a water filter change, the thermostat, or even every light bulb or electrical fixture in what we label as "smart homes." The list goes on. Washing machines. Ovens. Refrigerators. You get the point. Now, that same 10N or 15N has grown to 50N or even 100N, and just remember the quadratic growth effect!

The evolution of such communication and data pathways has been linked to the increased prevalence of what we term as local area networks, or within-the-home, personal area networks (LANs and PANs in wireless parlance). These are the highways that allow the IoT devices to communicate to one another. But now, with the advent of digital healthcare, a new kind of network – a BAN, or Body Area Network is emerging. A patient who suffers a chronic disease such as diabetes or congestive heart failure has multiple "sensors" that collect data about them or their condition – a glucose meter, a blood pressure cuff, a weight scale. Today, in some cases, such sensors may be worn directly on the body, through devices such as smart watches or patches, or in the case of continuous glucose monitoring, may even be placed sub-cutaneously inside of our bodies! We now are entering the next frontier of the IoT for healthcare – that is, one which has either the patient (or consumer) at the center of a circle, with a series of sensors or devices around them that are pertinent and unique to them. And, each of these "things" will generate different kinds of data at different data generation frequencies. We now explore the effect of these emerging IoT devices, the data that they generate, and perhaps most importantly, what can be done with that data and the value that can be unlocked for the healthcare industry.

Healthcare IoT devices can be broadly defined into two categories: active and passive. Active IoT devices are those connected devices that the patient must consciously engage with – a blood glucose meter, a blood pressure cuff, a weight scale, etc., for which they must initiate use of the device that then completes a function, and generates certain data as an output that is typically beamed to a data repository in a secure fashion. Passive IoT devices perform the same functions, in that they collect data and beam these data into a repository, but without active interaction from a patient or consumer. Examples of passive IoT devices are fitness sensors, activity monitors, other wearables and sensors that may be embedded into devices that the patient or consumer is carrying, such as embedded activity monitors in their smartphones, or with the advent of cost-effective nanotechnologies, even into the clothes they are wearing.

The advent of these IoT devices in healthcare now dramatically expands the realm of data collected. The figure below elaborates on this concept.

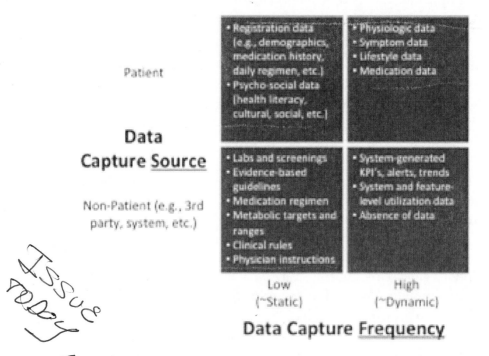

The two axes in this figure are the frequency at which data is captured (x-axis) and the sources of these data (y-axis). Today, much of the data in healthcare is generated in the lower left quadrant. That is, data that is captured quarterly, semi-annually, or even annually, that is coming typically from an electronic (or paper) health record, or healthcare payer claims processing system. Such data typically includes lab data for patients who suffer from chronic conditions, their medication regimens, the rules around the management of their condition, their cost and claims profiles and typically, their physicians' instructions. Needless to say, such data do not change frequently.

The inclusion of healthcare IoT devices effectively creates three expansion vectors in this figure. First, the patient or consumer who is now at the center of these devices has parameters that they enter or configure these devices with. This is the top-left quadrant, and includes data such as their registration information, demographic or socio-economic profile, settings, and other data such as cultural preferences, typical food and activity choices, etc. These data are important as they establish certain boundaries and criteria for how the IoT devices will function for a given patient, but such data will not change frequently. They could, however, change over time. For example, food choices evolve, activity types evolve, a patient's health literacy or knowledge of their condition evolves, but none of these are likely to change daily or even weekly.

Second, the IoT devices themselves – in this M2M world – are creators of and subscribers to data. This is the top right quadrant, where the sources of the data are now the IoT devices associated with the patient, with a frequency of capture that could be daily, or even more frequently if required. In the domain of healthcare, these data typically fall into four categories:

- **Physiologic Data:** These are measurable quantities from the IoT devices, such as a glucose reading, a blood pressure reading, a spirometer reading, etc. They are associated with specific healthcare metabolic data parameters that are specific to a certain condition or disease.

- **Symptom Data:** These are data that may be entered by the patient or consumer and are ancillary to the physiologic data captured. For example, a glucose reading can be accompanied by how the patient was feeling (sweaty, tired, nausea), where they were (in a restaurant, at home) or how their day was going (hectic, normal), etc. In diabetes, symptoms could include degree of tiredness, dizziness or thirst as it relates to a hypoglycemic experience. In oncology, it could be the level of pain, neutropenia-induced fever or nausea after a chemo therapy infusion. In some cases, IoT devices can measure these passively through wearable sensors – items such as temperature, or level of anxiety for patients who suffer from post-traumatic stress disorder, etc.

festyle: These are data related to activity, sleep, diet, smoking
us, etc. IoT devices easily capture data elements such as the
number of steps taken, distance walked, or quality of sleep.
Increasingly, these data are being captured more passively than
actively, because of the increasing prevalence of sensors that can
capture such data, and the inclusion of these sensors into the
devices we carry with us or even sleep with, such as smart phones,
smart watches, etc.

- **Medication:** A very important source of data in healthcare today,
medications – what's consumed, the dose consumed and the time
of consumption – are often left to the burden of the patient or
consumer to manage. And if left unchecked, the consequences
can be severe, both to health as well as to the costs of delivering
healthcare. The New England Journal of Medicine (NEJM)
published that improved management of drugs has the potential to
reduce hospitalizations. In the case of diabetes, misadministration
of diabetes medications account for 25% percent of all emergency
room visits related to adverse drug events, and 65% of adverse
drug events were related to unintentional overdose (in the case
of insulin dosing). Today, there are few IoT devices that can
automatically detect theconsumption of a drug. But, there are a
few solutions that are emerging that use low-power, digestible
near-field communications (NFC) technology to do just that,
where the time, dose and drug can be captured passively. This
application of NFC technology will lead to significant growth and
innovation potential as IoT devices become more prevalent.

As seen in this figure, IoT devices in healthcare have a tremendous
potential to unlock new sources of data, thereby increasing the magnitude
of N, along with the quadratic factor mentioned earlier. It now remains
to address "what can the healthcare industry do with this tsunami of data
being generated and captured?"

To answer this question, we invoke the concept of "IDEA": Inform,
Discover, Extrapolate and Adapt, as described in the following figure.

We begin with the lower left quadrant, which is where much of
healthcare analytics resides today. This is the realm of information –
presenting primary analyses to inform different constituents on either
patient-level or population-level findings. These reports assume the
presence of both data as well as the analysis intent – the "known-known"
quadrant.

**Analysis Intent**

"Don't Know What I'm Looking For"

"Know What I'm Looking For"

**Discover**
Using known data to draw insights
- Patterns
- Discriminant functions
- Behaviors

**Adapt**
Using learning techniques to provide new insights and choices for optimizing outcomes
- New product features
- New service features

**Inform**
Presenting primary analyses of the data
- Engagement or usage data
- Clinical data
- Population data

**Extrapolate**
Using existing data to model patterns and predict future occurrence of events
- Probabilistic models
- Machine learning based models

"Have Data"                    "Don't Have Data"

**Data Presence**

And, analyses can be performed either in aggregate or by filtering by common variables, such as age, gender, medication regimen, ethnicity, etc. Both the analytical engines to perform such informative analysis as well as the presentation engines exist today and are quite robust.

Once this primary analysis is done, informative analysis moves upwards to the top-left quadrant – that is, towards discovery. In this quadrant, the data exist, but the analysis intent is unknown. Is there something that can be learned from this IoT data? Discovery invokes mathematical models of statistical pattern recognition: linear or synthetic discriminant analysis and nearest neighbor clustering to name a few, which allow the discovery of trends, patterns and key relationships that can indicate correlation or even lead to the confirmation of causality between multiple variables. The realm of patterns to be discovered is rich in value, and can include insights into medication patterns, patient behavior patterns, population behavior patterns, exercise and diet patterns, etc. It is here in this quadrant that IoT plays a significant and emerging role, as it unlocks several new streams of data that heretofore were not available, but that could lead to more precise observations and conclusions for individual patients or entire populations. What the Obama administration and the National Institutes of Health are labelling as "Precision Medicine" in many ways can benefit from the multi-variate discovery offered by IoT devices.

Once discovery is established, and reference patterns of interest are identified, those patterns are then extrapolated to where the analysis intent is now known, but the data are nonexistent. This quadrant – the lower right, is the realm of predictive modeling, that invokes Bayesian, Markovian and neural network machine learning science, among other similar techniques. Through IoT data gathering, can a skipped medication and the conditions that lead to the skip be predicted? Can hypoglycemia or a pending cardiac event be predicted based on the reference patterns that are captured and evaluated during discovery3?

An example of extrapolation is the ability to create an engine to predict the state of hypoglycemia in a patient. To date, hypoglycemia remains a major cost burden in the US and globally. While the cost of an average acute healthcare utilization event (e.g., ER visit, etc.) for hypoglycemia is $1,868 per episode, the maximum can be as large as $13,716 per episode. There is implicit value in being able to detect the onset of hypoglycemia through the detection of patterns of variables that are associated with this onset. In this case, the exact blood glucose value is not of interest – that is, there's little incremental value in knowing that the blood glucose level is 68 mg/dL or 58 mg/dL. It is however important to know that it's less than 70 mg/dL or in the case of severe hypoglycemia, less than 50 mg/dL. Therefore, rather than predictive modeling (which predicts a specific value), there's merit in a classification engine that determines that the value falls into a range that is either acceptable, low or very low, thereby reducing the dimensionality of classification to just three discrete states or ranges. A random forest algorithm was used to classify – within 93% accuracy – the onset of hypoglycemia using sparse, patient self-reported data on glucose levels, medications, symptoms and activity levels6.

Such algorithms and approaches can add significant value in the determination of optimum therapies for patients across a number of conditions, making the choices for providers simpler, knowing that their recommendations will have a higher likelihood of achieving the desired outcomes. For example, if there's reasonable certainty, based on patient behavior, that exercise and diet may not be embraced by a patient, then a provider can focus on different medication therapies instead of the proverbial "you need to lose weight if you want to take control of your condition!"

Finally, once models are established in the lower right quadrant, IoT devices allow the migration to the top right, where adaptive analysis takes effect. In this quadrant, the ongoing inputs from IoT devices – either

actively or passively, make real-time changes to the algorithms that engage patients or that can provide clinical decision support to healthcare providers. It's analogous to a cruise control mechanism in a vehicle. Once the vehicle has reached the desired state, a small control system that monitors deviations from the desired speed comes into affect, and adapts the speed to be maintained within a reasonable margin of error.

*When putting all four quadrants together, the IoT devices therefore:*

1. *Create a basis for informing different stakeholders on what might be relevant trends or patterns of interest*
2. *Allow the discovery of reference patterns of interest*
3. *Enable the mathematical modeling of such patterns*
4. *Deliver "smart" or "adaptable" features that adjust over time, but in a manner that is specific to a given patient or consumer*

*Where does one take IoT and healthcare data in the future? Imagine the inclusion of new streams of data. Genomic data is increasingly becoming available and affordable to patients, and such data can greatly assist in the delivery of precision therapies. Social data that are captured from different devices that are used by the patient or consumer, that deliver further insight into the patient. Akin to a Fourier Transform series, where the higher-order terms provide finer or nuanced input into a mathematical signal, the IoT devices give us a higher resolution, "Hubbell-like" view into patients and consumers in ways we could not have imagined in the past.*

*Anand K. Iyer, PhD, MBA, is Chief Data Science Officer of WellDoc Inc. With a doctorate in image pattern recognition from Carnegie Mellon University, he leads the company's data science efforts in the domains of informative, predictive and adaptive modeling to further improve patient outcomes and reduce healthcare costs through real-time data from WellDoc's clinical and behavioral science-driven mHealth platforms. He is co-author of a chapter on mobile prescription therapy in mHealth Innovation: Best Practice from the Mobile Frontier (HIMSS Books, 2014), available in print, eBook and Kindle editions.*

# References

1.  Daniel S. Budnitz, M.D., M.P.H., Maribeth C. Lovegrove, M.P.H., Nadine Shehab, Pharm.D., M.P.H., and Chesley L.
2.  www.whitehouse.gov, January 20, 2015
3.  "Can AliveCor's Heart Monitor Predict Your Stroke Before It Strikes?", Fast-Co, September 5, 2014
4.  The Milliman Healthcare Analytics Blog, "Analytic Basics – Completeness and Outlier Episode Flags. 17 July 2014
5.  www.diabetes.org, September 2015
6.  Hypoglycemia Prediction Using Machine Learning Models for Patients With Type 2 Diabetes, Bharath Sudharsan, Malinda Peeples and Mansur Shomali, Journal of Diabetes Science and Technology, 14 October 2014
7.  https://en.wikipedia.org/wiki/Fourier_analysis, October 2015

# Chapter 11
# Analytics

**Movie 5: Analytics by Alisa Niksch**
https://vimeo.com/156575176

# Editor's Note

Analytics and specifically big data analytics are the product of any and all of the following sources: EHR, HIE, ACO, and PHR, but also patient-generated data generated by many types of medical devices including wearables, smartphones, and bedside monitors.In addition to the benefits of "actionable" self -awareness and clinical convergence, wearable health care technologies deliver a rich source of information, and not only to measure various aspects of an individual's health. Looking ahead, enterprise data repositories and patient-generated health data from IoT devices will be the key to population health management, to gleaning reimbursement in a value based world, and to producing measurable gains in outcomes and patient satisfaction. Big Data derived from wearables mated with contextual analytics will be leveraged to extract value, identify long term patterns and risk factors for clinicians and researchers. Analytics will complete the chain of healthcare information and care management, delivered more intuitively and proactively.

-Rick Krohn

# Analytics

-SKIP SNOW

**Movie 6: Introduction to Analytics by Rick Khron**
https://vimeo.com/156575353

## Connected devices, predictive analytics, and a certain future

There is no doubt that connected devices will change the face of medicine. And the way that they will do so will be through the predictive power of the data they yield, and the direct coaching power of the tools powered by that predictive data.

Many experts claimed that core changes in research methodology and population health management will occur over the next two decades. Unregulated consumer devices data will satiate a thirst for everyday environmental information from all corners of the healthcare ecosystem. Taking in this data and being able to predict risk and change a consumer's health journey, ameliorating pain and reducing cost, is imperative. Consumers and patients are increasingly storing activity and physiological data in vast could repositories. Smart environments are increasingly becoming key tools in research laboratories. Environmental and demographic data are defining a new world of evidence for consumer-driven health.

Already, the oceans of data from wearables allow the everyday environment to predict the presence of Parkinson's disease or the propensity of an elderly person falling or how successfully a stroke victim will transition into a home setting. Some studies indicate that algorithms exist for identifying what physical activity a person is doing.

Jamie looked to see where things were operating at scale. Up to now, findings have been constrained. Though many inventions, processes, and tools exist, they are not deployed at scale within any healthcare context. While ambitious programs driven by healthcare systems are scaling up, we find them highly reliant on regulated devices. Few solutions use mass-produced consumer devices. This would drive down cost and drive usability up at scale. Some stellar institutions are rolling out connected solutions, but they are primitive. Banner Health's forward-thinking ones embracing the future of the connected home cannot scale beyond protecting a thin slice of the most risky patients in the system.

Many social, legal, business, and technical obstacles will be resolved before the evidence from wearables begins to realize even a fraction of its potential value. This chapter informs you of the state of the art, provides predictions on where this segment of predictive analytics is going, and offers prescriptive advice to end users and vendors wishing to participate in these radical transformations.

## Overview and thesis: The promise

Wearables, connected devices, the myriad signals from our bodies drive evidence-based medicine to the everyday environment. But Jamie wondered when all of these tools will be part of the everyday delivery of healthcare. We predict that by 2035, our bodies' signals will supply data integrating with other evidence as part of everyday care and wellness. The source of evidence will be the wired body, the wired home, the wired ethnographic digital signature of our lives via social media and other published and private sources. In commercial, research, and clinical settings, we see strides being made in creating devices, protocols, algorithms, and accumulating data repositories with countless biological signals being present. Data coming from connected devices in the everyday environment will be used at scale in order to predict outcomes and risks, or suggest changes of behavior, but not for 20 years.

This chapter narrates Jamie's journey as she observes a transition taking place in healthcare analytics and predictive analytics. The wearables and connected devices market is producing mountains of data, and this data can be of great use in predicting things about people's health, well-being, and disease state. We're in early days of collecting evidence via the data, and it is too early to say we understand what it means. In the next two decades, we will see data from connected devices in the consumers' everyday environments. The information from these data streams will play a pervasive role, helping people understand how to become healthier and avoid significant care risk.

The maturing of sensor technologies and creation of physical smart environment testbeds provides convincing evidence that we can effectively create such smart environments and use them to aid with clinical assessment and understanding of behavioral differences between healthy older adults and older adults with cognitive and physical impairments.

This most affects the elderly, whose health surely will be managed with help from signals from their everyday environments. In an informal survey of the published work on the power of wearable data for predictive analytics, the papers that seemed most authentic often addressed the departments concerned with gerontology.

This chapter is presented in the following form:
- Review where we are in the marketplace
- Home in on a couple of important scenarios
- Give prescriptive advice
- Sum it all up

# Review of our current state

What we see is great promise from the data provided by wearables to the future of predictive analytics for healthcare. In a fractured landscape of complexity, the leaders from a clinical, manufacturing, and technology perspective are coming into focus. Wearables and sensors in the everyday environment at best amount to primitive coaches hosted on our phones. These phones are the front end of voracious appetites from companies that consume this data. To the extent possible, they semantically link the signals to other ethnographic information about the consumer, creating large repositories of insight from our everyday world.

# In the marketplace, wearables are primitive coaches, not predictors of health risk

The consumer tools in the wearable market are still primitive coaches at this point. They are not useful as predictors of significant and immediately actionable health risk. While a great deal of work is being done, this work is preliminary and not at scale. Below we enumerate some of the reasons constraining this data is useful at scale.

- The use of sensor devices at scale in everyday settings is still relatively new, and the raw data from these devices is for the most part not available; it is the property of the companies that collect it. This means that the data is often inaccessible and trapped within silos.

- The signal data is wildly different in terms of what is collected, how often it is collected, what is stored, and the fidelity of the instruments. This makes the data hard to work with as there is often an impedimental mismatch between data sets, and quality is inconsistent across sources.

- The data from consumer devices is hard to access. Consumer wearable firms "are difficult to work with from a university perspective," said Diane Cook, Ph.D., head of the Center for Advanced Studies in Adaptive Systems at the University of Washington. This is because there is a perception that they work in a closed, disinterested system. This barrier will break down of its own accord as these companies seek collaboration with those who can make sense of the evidence that is being collected.

- Not enough is known about what the signals from these devices mean. The most rigorous work takes place not in the everyday environment, but in simulated environments that are hypercontrolled. The intensity of control over this research means that small samples of data are available but that the data is very pure and good. These efforts must set the benchmarks for a more casual form of work that will take place in the real world of the everyday devices; to integrate these two approaches is both necessary and a great risk.

# Three types of hardware drive the current market and affect analytical evidence

Jaimie observed three types of devices driving the market. Pure consumer devices like Apple's new watch are easy to use and well-integrated with our communication networks. Regulated medical devices are secure and reliable and provide medical-grade data, but they are hard to use and often are not well integrated with the consumer's digital life. In the lab, proprietary solutions are often cobbled together with
kits because that is the easiest to do with the demands to
integrate with existing information systems. What she thought
was needed was a consumer device that could, if necessary,
collect raw data, but had a good price point and was easy to
use out of the box.

- Consumer device companies have wearables with great human factors, usable interfaces, actionable information, and aesthetic appeal. They present mostly incomplete access to their data, and even when they do present access to the data, it is often hard to correlate the time stamps of the data with time of other synchronous events. An interesting alternative to this is Apple, which offers low-level APIs to access all the sensor devices empowered by its devices, a research framework, and of course great formfactor appeal. The price point is very high, and so Jamie did not see this solution as operable at scale for her populationconsisting of many lower income people.

- Regulated devices, meaning devices approved by the U.S. Food and Drug Administration, are the most reliable, often very expensive, and with unsatisfactory human interfaces. However, these devices are trussed clinically, and thus we will probably see them at the forefront of the rollout of predictive analytics from everyday environmental signals. We heard active resistance to these devices in the field with managed care workers. They cried for a consumer device that could get this information. They said their patients felt stigmatized by the awkward medical devices.

- Building systems from kits and proprietary hardware is the third mechanism. Labs buy kits customizing them to fit particular use cases. Often kits combine sensors for environments with sensors for the body. For sophisticated research, this is probably the most efficient of the current approaches. However, look for the consumer companies to quickly eliminate most of these vendors as their relationships with the research industry improve. These kits can customize how often samples are taken, allow you to operate on the raw data, and often expose hardware at a primitive level. The Shimmer platform offers a robust API and even access to its source code, allowing products to be radically modified.

## Consumer-facing companies struggle to understand physiological and activity data

Jamie sees major consumer producers such as Fitbit, Jawbone, Apple, and Samsung acquiring teams of scientists working to make sense of the oceans of data their products generate. She notices two streams of analysis being defined: Tools are being deployed in rigorous research settings in clinically supervised environments. The manufacturers work with consumer data in order to do the predictive analytics outside of a clinical scope. This work serves the healthy and assists to coach the well. These two streams bifurcate the market for wearable analytics into two segments: the

Figure 1: Jawbone proposes a heart coach with sophisticated predictive analytics under the cover that would parse activity patterns and map them to clinical risk. The app would then coach the user to a better relationship to health and activity.

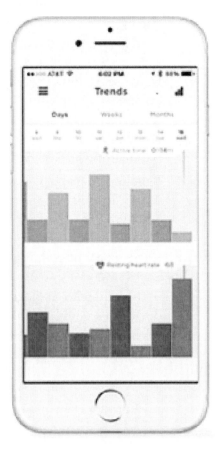

FIGURE 1

# What the consumer companies are doing

It is a mad race in the wearable market. Seemingly every week we see one company gobble up another, we see innovations come to market, and more importantly we see month by month the consumer companies making announcements about the insight gained from their data. This incrementally is adding to a new body of evidence. Jamie saw two examples of how industry serves this bifurcated market.

- Jawbone's virtual coach helps a user achieve a healthier heart by using its power of observation and predictive analytics to give consumers advice. By examining the relationship with activities and physiological signals including the pulse, Jawbone is able to calculate the resting heart rate of all of its users and map that rate to other signals. It has published its ability to predict primitive relationships between resting heart rates and activities of users. This early finding is important because it demonstrates that these consumer firms creating wearables are executing and becoming electronic health coaches that use their vast data resources to understand a population's everyday activities.

 Developer Program

## Core Motion Framework

Classes

The Core Motion framework lets your
application receive motion data

Classes

NSObject

    CMLogItem

    CMAccelerometerData

    CMAltitudeData

    CMDeviceMotion

    CMGyroData

    CMMagnetometerData

    CMMotionActivity

    CMMotionActivityManager

    CMMotionManager

    CMPedometer

    CMPedometerData

    CMStepCounter

The Apple developer's documentation for the Core Motion framework available on compliant i devices allows for a researcher to access very precise hardware-driven measurements. This, coupled with the HealthKit, ResearchKit, and all the other Apple development libraries, makes Apple's devices attractive to anybody who develops at scale.

FIGURE 2

- Apple offers significantly low-level access to user-generated biometric data via its many application programming interfaces (APIs). This, coupled with its robust user interface capabilities, makes it an ideal platform to work with if a project has sufficient resources to develop proprietary applications, and then can fund participants' use of Apple equipment.

# Chief medical information officer challenges big consumer companies

As Jamie searched for a strategy to innovate in this space, she noticed Dr. John Showalter, chief health information officer at the University of Mississippi, make the point that consumer companies must accelerate the process. He says that if we wait for the medical community to act, we will wait too long.

Healthcare innovation moves very slowly. Studies indicate it can take 17 years for an effective intervention to be adopted. Avoiding risk and the need for strong causal evidence are major factors contributing to slow adoption. Population health offers the chance to accelerate technology adoption by implementing low-risk interventions based on strong associations; however, healthcare doesn't have that in its DNA. We need to look at outside for ways to make advancement, such as crowdsourcing of algorithms for Netflix in 2009. That kind of approach could create powerful and accurate algorithms very quickly. The efficacy of those algorithms could then be studied in more traditional ways like clinical trials.

Realistically, the risk of clicking on a movie, while important to Netflix, is not a life and death matter, and the types of efficacy that can be gained from creating the right interventions based on predictions emanating from wearable data can actually be life critical.

In fact, such a contest does exist (http://tricorder.xprize.org/). Qualcomm has offered a $10 million prize. It is offering this prize to the person or organization that delivers a device capable of capturing key health metrics and diagnosing a set of 15 diseases. The contest envisions a device similar to the handheld tricorder device from Star Trek. Those offering the prize understand that even if such a tool could be invented, rolling it out at scale would be a slow journey.

# Big insights are fueled by small signals

In general, what we see in the peer-reviewed medical research is small amounts of data being applied to large problems and tentative conclusions that lead to more research. Time and again we learned that picking the algorithm to create insight is more of an art than a science, and is largely domain-specific. This is the kind of truth that you will not hear from vendors who want you to think of their predictive powers as black science. Time and again we heard about how the small sets of populations studied can easily lead to skewed results, and we rarely have seen any studies rise to the true level of a clinical trial in which a control group is compared to those who use the wearables and get interventions based on predictions. These studies will take place over time, and we will gather the proper empirical evidence from these everyday signals so that we can use them to predict health risk and change the risk curve. In this section, let's speak to some of the more important use cases we see, and then let's deep dive into to compelling ones:

- University of California, San Francisco, extends care in managing cardiovascular disease to the home. It uses a strategy of coaching and home monitoring to predict risk. (http://www.pcori.org/research-results/2015/health-eheartalliance-phase-ii )

- Over the next five years, the Michael J. Fox Foundation for Parkinson's Research will use home monitoring devices coupled with an Android app and the Pebble watch to collect data from 10% of the Parkinson's population. In this phase of the research, the data will be gathered and examined. This project aims to establish the infrastructure for a reservoir of data around the everyday physiology and activity of a broad Parkinson's population. (http://www.pcori.org/research-results/2015/fox-insight-network )

- The Health eHeart Alliance promised to collect and be a repository for heart disease data from the everyday world. With a grant from PCORI and sponsorship from Fitbit, this looks like an interesting place where medical and consumer data might come together. (http://www.pcori.org/researchresults/2013/health-eheart-alliance)

- At the University of Colorado Denver, Dr. Michael Kahn and his research team intend to recommend standardized mechanisms for understanding information coming from "personal health records, Internet blog postings, social media sites, and wearable electronic sensors." This seedling project is once again an attempt to first collect and then make sense of the myriad data coming from the Internet of Things and consumer-generated content in order to harness its predictive power. Because there is no standard for data that ends up in a personal health record, keeping an eye on this work and seeing how it can contribute to an eventual standard at HL7 (http://www.hl7.org/index.cfm) or elsewhere is of interest. (http://www.pcori.org/research-results/2013/building-pcor-value-and-integrity-data-quality-andtransparency-standards )

- The University of Washington is predicting the functional independence measure (FIM) for stroke victims based on  data from wearables and motion detectors in a controlled environment. FIM is a well-validated assessment measuring functional status on a 0-7 scale. The work established that by using FIM, a human-measured assessment, as a benchmark, the score could be predicted based on machine data from the experiment and some minimal social and chart data to supplement. (http://www.eecs.wsu.edu/~cook/pubs/ia15.pdf )

- Significant work along several dimensions is taking place at Professor Cook's University of Washington lab, and this resource should be considered an important asset to the wearable community. This link lists Cook's published research: http://www.eecs.wsu.edu/~cook/pubs.html.

- The University of Arizona demonstrated a capability to predict which elderly people are at risk of falling at home by understanding how they move about their homes. The study monitored the activity of elderly ambulatory patients by using wearable equipment and motion detectors. The most significant results came from wearables and demonstrated that how a person walks determines the risk of falling. (Gerontology 2014;60;483-492, DOI 10.1159/000363136)

- A study at the College of Computer and Information Systems, Umm al-Qura University, in Mecca, Saudi Arabia, focused on identifying activities in a healthy population based on the motions of the body. The activities of individuals were assessed in detail and mapped to lying down, sitting, standing, walking, running, cycling, Nordic walking, ascending stairs, descending stairs, vacuum cleaning, ironing clothes, and jumping rope. Wearables were strategically placed on subjects' bodies to supply the data to determine what sequences of movements predicted which exercises. Classification results demonstrated a high validity

FIGURE 3

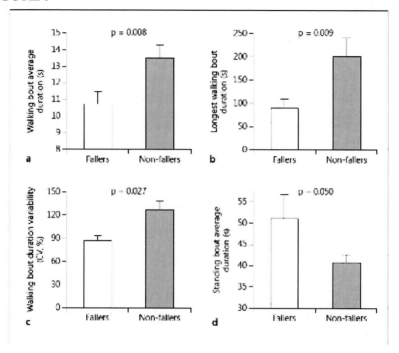

The diagram above shows how people's gait and how long they stand are predictive of whether they will fall. The data shows that simply understanding if a person walks a lot is not sufficient to predict falls; it is necessary to understand how the person walks to predict falls.

validity showing precision (a positive predictive value) and recall (sensitivity) of more than 95% for all physical activities. This yields evidence for appropriate rules to determine what a person is doing rather than relying on that person to tell the device what he or she is doing. The drawback in this research is that a person had to wear several sensors in order to gain the fidelity of these results. (http://www.ncbi.nlm.nih.gov/pmc/articles/PMC4512690/)

- Jawbone Inc. has correlated resting heart rate with body mass index, activity as measured by steps per day, activity type (self-reported), and bedtime. While the result is fairly primitive, the correlations in a large population help us tie back to other factors, and because the sample of users is so large, this data should be considered a source of reference data, if available. At the time of publication, Jawbone had not responded to inquiries about the availability of the source data for research. (http://jawbone.com/blog/hearthealth-what-really-makes-a-heart-healthy/ )

# Banner Health System stalks the future with Philips

Jamie observed Banner Health extending care to the riskiest patient population after discharge from its flagship hospital. The core enabling technology contains an analytics engine that predicts from physiological symbols which patients are in need of care.

In May 2014, Banner released a study that followed 135 risky post-acute patients for more than a year. All participants had significant co-morbidities with complex cases. The results were impressive from a financial perspective. Overall cost savings of 27% was realized because of a significant reduction in hospitalizations for the population. There was a 45% reduction in hospitalizations per capita for the population. The number of hospitalizations per capita was down from 11.5 visits per 100 patients per month to 6.3. The average number of days in the hospital for this population per month trended down from 90.2 days to 65.8. Implicitly, this reduction in cost to the system also means that consumers staying home so much more enjoyed both better health and a significantly better quality of life.

The partnership between Banner and Philips is one we see time and again in industry. Philips uses the clinical environment of a major regional hospital to tune its algorithms, enhance its computer software's user experience, and respond to real-life clinical practice by enhancing the software according to what it finds in customer sites like Banner. In the meantime, more data flows into the Philips repository, building a base of evidence that is astounding.

Today Banner is managing a population of more than 500 using the evolved platform. It plans to increase the population to around 1,000 within a year. These sweeping changes are part of the overall shift to value-based care we see all around us. According to Hargobind Khurana, M.D., senior medical director of health management at Banner Health, Banner bears at least partial financial risk for more than 400,000 people representing over 27% of the population it serves. This movement to a risk-bearing model is taking place throughout the industry and is shaping the future of healthcare and the software that drives it. The partnership between Philips and Banner is mutually beneficial because Philips can use Banner as a clinical lab to enhance its product, and Banner can call on Philips to customize the solution to its needs because Philips views Banner's needs as being mostly generic.

FIGURE 4

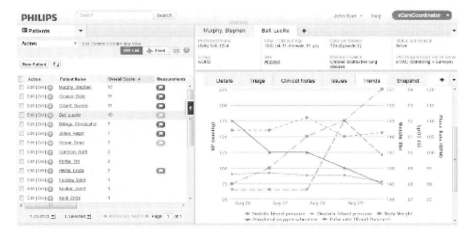

The Philips eCareCoordinator clinician's interface shows a panel of patients on the left, with red flags indicating the patients at high risk, and a detailed trend analysis of a four-day period for a male suffering from chronic obstructive lung disease. Notice the home-based observations from connected devices allowing weight and oxygen saturation trends to become visible and allowing a clinical intervention to be planned.

## Predictive analytics from home-based signals are at the core of the solution

The system triages all signals coming from the population and creates a set of alarms by predicting which signals are of significant risk. Then each morning a team of clinical folks—in the case of Banner, registered nurses—triages that list, either clearing the signals upon consultation with the patients and understanding their condition, or escalating to a medical doctor who can order interventions. According to Chong Jacobs, M.D., a physician on the home care team at Banner Health, while she misses touching patients and having the nuanced physical presence of an in-person visit, the video and enhanced data from the IoT devices more than make up for that gap. "I get to prioritize my workday based on my sense of the acuity of my patients," she says. This is in sharp contrast to her experience in traditional clinical settings where the workday is guided by the cadence of physical appointments, not on the acuity of patients. This benefit often not considered in a predictive-based care environment is the fundamental assumption of population health management. That said, the workflow itself is still quite primitive at Banner when it comes to making predictions actionable.

In a site visit, it became clear that using the signals from the connected devices was urgent. Furthermore, patients are asked to self-report how they feel about their health each day, using a graphical scale that goes from a sad face to a happy face. The clinical staff members thought this self-report was in fact one of the most important assays that they get. This, they say, is especially important if and when they are responding to a physiological signal.

What becomes clear is that the program Banner is running without tool enhancement would not scale without significantly more staff. There were just too many human components to the workflow to really fan this work out to a broader population, and therefore programs like this can only scale to the most sick—those who it is worth spending a great deal of money on because the difference in quality of life and cost would be radica l. This is a fact that the folks at Philips own and acknowledge.

Our solutions are more than technology. They are a system built around technology. And this solution is significantly better today than it was a year ago, and will be significantly better a year from now because we are optimizing and improving it every day with the help of our clinical partners.

FIGURE 5

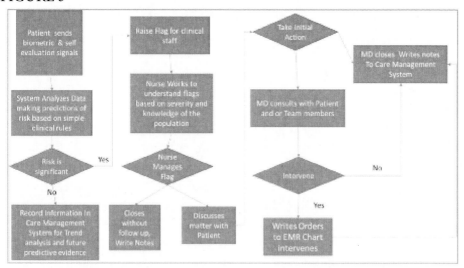

At Banner Health, the Hospital @ Home Program workflow is labor intensive but very effective. Scaling this workflow would require more sophisticated algorithms, which Philips and Banner are working on together.

# Controlled environments in academia give us important evidence

The Center for Advanced Studies in Adaptive Systems at Washington State University's School of Electrical Engineering and Computer Science is an advanced research lab led by Professor Cook, who is also one of the directors of the artificial intelligence laboratory at the university, as well as serving as an editor for several peer-reviewed journals. The lab hosts a two-story smart home and conducts a number of studies focused on predicting disease states and helping mine the core information about what movement via connected devices might mean. The lab shares data sets with the public and thus does contain a great deal of reference data for scrutiny.

FIGURE 6

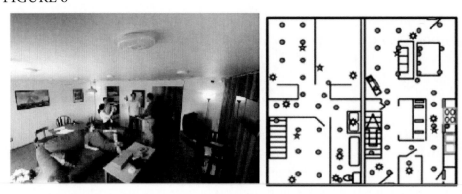

The smart home lab at the CASAS Project, Washington State University, is a two-story home with sensors located throughout, and which is increasingly integrating wearables into studies that examine human pathology and the ability to predict aspects of disease, even including a preliminary diagnosis, and the development of risk-based interventions based on predictive algorithms.

In a discussion, Cook spoke to the need to first understand normative activity of healthy people across a variety of environments. Once we accomplish this difficult task, we can discover the exact shape of particular pathologist like Parkinson's disease or dementia based on people's behavior in the everyday environment. In response to a question as to whether her study, "Analyzing Activity Behavior and Movement in a Naturalistic Environment using Smart Home Techniques" was actually able to diagnose disease, she enthusiastically responded to a future capability but was hesitant to say that her team of scientists had in any definitive way accomplished that. Responding to the question of whether the study was capable of rendering a preliminary diagnosis, she said:

> It is a step in that direction, but it's certainly not the whole thing. These are scripted activities performed in a very controlled setting. Ultimately we will want to be able to do this in people's own homes. That raises the complexity to a level we are not yet at.

The study took 32% of 260 elderly individuals as subjects.
The population consisted of people with:
- Just Parkinson's disease (PD)
- Just mild cognitive impairment (MCI)
- Both PD and MCI (PD MCI)
- Neither PD nor MCI (N)

Then, using smart environmental sensors and crude wearables (i.e., Android phones strapped to the body), they found that they could predict if a person was N, PD MCI, MCI, or PD with a fair amount of certainty. They could only do so by examining a broad set of inputs together, finding patterns in how these entities are interconnected via algorithmic regression. The team iterated around the rules for preprocessing data and the algorithms used to use in order to find patterns in the data. This process is the essence of any requirement for predictive analytical capability. To be able to look at raw data, find preliminary results, tune, and then go deeper in a methodological manner is core to the state of the art when it comes to healthcare analytics at the edge of artificial intelligence. Tuning those processes so that teams with less expertise than Cook's can execute on them will be necessary if the industry is to mature to an operational state. One possible path of execution will be to follow the cloudbased artificial intelligence players like IBM's Watson and piggyback off the learnings that their systems and engineers make as other core healthcare use cases are presented to the team.

## Conclusions

Home is where people live. Home is where healthcare is happening. Home is where healthcare is shifting. The human factors, and how people interact with these devices, how people feel about themselves, how they describe it—these are key determining factors. These are things you miss when you are not doing this in an ethnographic way in the environment where health is actually happening. (Greg Gordon VP &, Head of Strategy, Home Monitoring, Philips.)

Jamie realized signals from the everyday environment will clarify the relationship of our activities to our bodies and health. She realized her institution was to play a vital role producing the evidence that these signals yield. She understood the complexity and difficulty in finding and linking the signal data with the context of our lives and our medical records. She thought of the differences and commonalities in the various requests she got from the medical staff to do pilots or studies in remote care.

While in an overall sense it will take at least two decades for he data and algorithms to become a part of our standards of care, there will be incremental work at scale along the way. Within certain departments of medicine, such as gerontology, we will see quicker adaption. In departments where risk is high, in a value-based world, return on investment for wiring a cohort of high-risk patients clearly serves institutional goals. We are seeing this as an increasingly adapted program across most fair-sized hospital systems that bear risk. Also, look to the consumer companies to more closely couple with major medical institutions and look for consumer devices to play an important part of this ecosystem. The trick is going to be to move the data from a consumer context to a medical context in a sufficiently rigorous and standardized manner so that the medical community can easily integrate it and do the necessary science to make the information sufficiently actionable.

# Recommendations

1. Count on the consumer to demand a user experience that gives the most value.

2. The consumer wearable vendor community must work with the scientific community in order to find funding and do research into what the data actually means. This presents a major potential source of revenue for these companies, as they can fund significant research in clinical settings.

3. When approaching a new predictive problem area, it is best to start shallow and then dig deep. Start shallow to figure out if the data even contains something that is learnable. Then dig deep, tuning algorithms and preprocessing steps in order to eek the maximum amount of performance from the data set and future data sets.

4. But the process is largely one of trial and failure; there is no best practice algorithm or preprocessing steps guarantying results.

Do not go it alone financially. We are in a period of research.

5. Funding is available for well-conceived studies, and gathering the correct team to chase that money and execute is an important part of executing on any program to drive the value of the data from wearables forward. In particular, look at PCORI, which is discussed above and in footnote vii.

# References

1. The Patient-Centered Outcomes Research Institute (http://www.pcori.org/ ) was created as part of the Affordable Care Act in 2010. Its mandate is to "assist patients, clinicians, purchasers, and policy-makers in making informed health decisions by advancing the quality and relevance of evidence concerning the manner in which diseases, disorders, and other health conditions can effectively and appropriately be prevented, diagnosed, treated, monitored, and managed through research and evidence synthesis" (2014 annual report). In 2014, the institute distributed $671 million in grants for projects. Clearly, investigating the predictive power of the signals from the everyday environment is 100% in the charter of this institute.

2. Diane Cook, Maureen Schmitter-Edgecombe, and Prafulla Dawadi, "Analyzing Activity Behavior and Movement in a Naturalistic Environment using Smart Home Techniques," http://www.eecs.wsu.edu/~cook/pubs/bhi15.pdf, IEEE Journal of Biomedical and Health Informatics, August 2015.

3. Diane Cook, Douglas Weeks, and Vladimir Borisov, "Predicting Functional Independence Measure Scores During Rehabilitation with Wearable Inertial Sensors," http://www.eecs.wsu.edu/~cook/pubs.html, 2015.

4. Diane Cook, Maureen Schmitter-Edgecombe, and Prafulla Dawadi, "Analyzing Activity Behavior and Movement in a Naturalistic Environment using Smart Home Techniques," http://www.eecs.wsu.edu/~cook/pubs/bhi15.pdf, IEEE Journal of Biomedical and Health Informatics, August 2015.

5. In an interview on 8/25/15 Ph.D. candidate at the University of Washington Vladimir Borisov discussed the fact that vendor Shimmer allowed his team to download the product's C++ source code in order to modify it and modify its capabilities at the lowest possible layer.

6. Captured in an interview and subsequent email exchange with Dr. Showalter.

7.  This quote was captured in an onsite interview with Vicki Buchda on 8/4/15.

8.  From an email correspondence with Manu Varma, head of marketing and strategy, Philips Hospital to Home.

9.  "The CASAS project treats environments as intelligent agents, where the status of the residents and their physical surroundings are perceived using sensors and the environment is acted upon using controllers in a way that improves the comfort, safety, and/or productivity of the residents. Research groups utilize CASAS datasets for use in their own research, creating a collaborate approach and improving technology evolution." http://ailab.wsu.edu/casas/about.html

10  Diane Cook, Maureen Schmitter-Edgecombe, and Prafulla Dawadi, "Analyzing Activity Behavior and Movement in a Naturalistic Environment using Smart Home Techniques," http://www.eecs.wsu.edu/~cook/pubs/bhi15.pdf, IEEE Journal of Biomedical and Health Informatics, August 2015.

11. Diane Cook, Maureen Schmitter- Edgecombe, and Pratfulla Dawadi, "Analyzing Activity Behavior and Movement in a Naturalistic Environment using Smart Home Techniques". 2015, http://www.eecs.wsu.edu/~cook/pubs/bhi15.pdf, IEEE journal ofbiomedical and health informatics, August 2015

## *Case Study*: DaVincian Healthcare and HelloDoctor24x7 Bring Lifesaving Healthcare to Remote Reaches of India

Odisha, India – Deva Khatua was orphaned when his mother died shortly after childbirth and his father abandoned the family. At just 4 months of age, living in an area with inadequate sanitation, Deva began suffering from gastroenteritis and soon became severely dehydrated. Without any hospitals or even clinics nearby, his worried grandmother

brought Deva to the HelloDoctor24x7 kiosk located in their village's Com-mon Service Center. Deva's grandmother had reason to worry. Gastroenteritis is the second leading cause of death worldwide among children younger than five. Our HelloDoctor24x7 technician at the kiosk recognized Deva's life-threatening symptoms and immediately started oral rehydration therapy and referred him to the closest hospital for more comprehensive treatment. As a result, Deva fully recovered from his illness. His grandmother is grateful and comforted knowing that HelloDoctor24x7 is available to the community.

DaVincian Healthcare is proud to partner with HelloDoctor24x7. Founded in 2009 by a team of physicians and engineers, HelloDoctor24x7 uses a mobile telemedicine platform to bring acute, chronic and preventative healthcare to remote regions in India where those services are scarce. Today, HelloDoctor24x7 operates in 222 Common Service Centers in the State of Odisha, one of the most economically disadvantaged regions in India. Common Service Centers are an important part of Indian life where villagers are able to obtain basic necessities, pay bills, shop and now - with HelloDoctor24x7 - access vital healthcare services. To date, more than 7,000 physicians have served over 100,000 patients.

DaVincian Healthcare is inspired by and shares the vision of HelloDoctor24x7. DaVincian's telemedicine platform and analytic capabilities are now part of the HelloDoctor24x7 kiosks, broadening the scope and quality of healthcare services available to underserved Indian communities. In 2016, we expect to dramatically expand our presence throughout Odisha from the 222 kiosks in use today to 4000, impacting more than 1 million lives annually.

Join us in spreading healthcare to the world. Together, we can save more children like Deva.

# Chapter 12

# The Future of Wearables and the IoT in Healthcare

**Movie 7: The Future of Wearables and IoT in Healthcare by Aenor Sawyer**

https://vimeo.com/156575723

# Editor's Note

In these pages we have championed Wearables and the IoT as headliners of Health e-Everything. But it's impossible at this early stage to know how these technologies will unfold, or what will be there ultimate impact on the industry. And there are concerns. As the capabilities and numbers of IoT devices continue to grow, will we be over-measured and burdened by our quantified self? And can wearables truly effect behavior change across the range of healthcare issues and constituents? Will we be overwhelmed by Big Data? As the volume and complexity of wearable data grows, the technology creates challenges for service providers that are transporting the data and the firms that are collecting and analyzing that data. One the great challenges will be to curate, manage and process data, at or near real-time.

There is also an economic dimension to the growth of wearables which may bend the cost curve and usher in the personalization of healthcare. Business models based on today's largely static information architectures will face challenges as new ways of creating value arise. When a customer's buying preferences are sensed in real time at a specific location, dynamic pricing may increase the odds of a purchase. Wearables will likely impact our buying habits and the structure of the retail sale. From a commercial perspective, adoption of innovative wearable technology presents several challenges. The health care industry will need to find a way to successfully monetize these solutions, address consumers' information and security concerns, recognize and respond to the fact that as mobile applications mature, they could face the scrutiny of a variety of organizations such as the Food and Drug Administration (FDA), Federal Communications Commission (FCC), Federal Trade Commission (FTC) and others.

With entrepreneurial and innovative spirit the IoT is inserting itself into healthcare in unexpected ways, and its ultimate speed and trajectory are at this point unclear. Will IoT-enabled wearables and nearables supplant traditional care delivery? Will activated health consumers alter the calculus of population health? Can the IoT truly crack the code of patient privacy and data security?

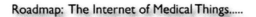

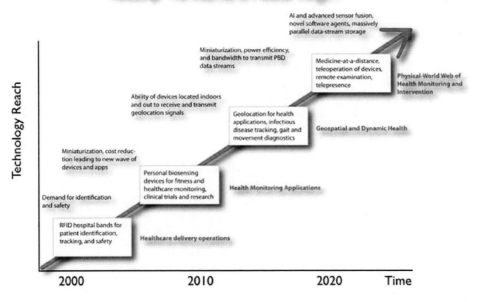

What we can expect is an increasing range of innovations and interventions that leverage the convenience, efficiency, and clinical effectiveness of wearables and the IoT. This much we can predict – an infinite array of smart connected solutions designed to improve our health, environment and productivity through intelligent use of data. Whether that means empowering us to monitor and control our domestic air quality, or equipping medics with cloud-based tools that allow them to 'consult' with patients who aren't even in the same room, or even the same city.

-Rick Krohn

# From Wearable Sensors to Smart Implants

-J. ANDREU-PEREZ, D.R. LEFF, H.M. IP, G.Z.-. YANG

Increasing health costs and incidence of chronic diseases such as cardiovascular and cancer, senescence-related dependence and sedentary lifestyles (e.g. obesity) are major healthcare challenges. The future of healthcare delivery depends on new technological advances with emphasis on prevention, early detection and minimally invasive management of diseases. Wearable devices are common nowadays for monitoring physiological indices such as ECG, heart rate, blood pressure, blood oxygen saturation (SpO2), body temperature, posture and physical activities. This single sensing modality is defined here as "first generation" monitoring devices. Better networking capabilities of these sensors have made smart context-aware monitoring possible by fusing the information obtained from these sensors with others embedded in the environment. These developments in sensors' electronics and embodiment have given rise to a new, "second generation" of sensing technologies featured with continuous monitoring. This continuous monitoring can be essential to capture critical events such as myocardial infraction, arrhythmias and strokes.

Advances in sensor technologies have been driven by innovation in low-powered micro-electronics, micro/nano fabrication and miniaturization. These developments have been accompanied by improved bio-compatibility of materials thereby minimizing foreign body reactions and facilitating smart implantable devices and prostheses. Implantable sensors have propelled the number of benefits that sensing provides to patients. For example, a fully non-invasive blood test glucose can be implemented as a smart implant,which may sense blood glucose levels or signs of neutropenia without the need for performing a capillary test.

An important consideration is the enormous volume of data collected by continuous sensing. Extensive sensor deployments over a patient population, produce a new source of Big Data which underpins the creation of health Biobanks of longitudinal plus high frequency pervasive data.

This new informational source can be connected, processed and examined in the cloud in combination with other Big Data sources (patient health records, - omics data etc.). A timeline of technological platforms that have triggered this technological evolution is presented in Figure 1.

In the last decade, the field has evolved through progressive advancement in sensing and intelligence for pervasive health applications. More recent advances have focused on wearable/implantable devices equipped with continuous multimodal sensing capabilities, and support for data fusion deployed in a wide range of clinical applications. Advances in sensing hardware can be attributed to parallel developments in sensor embodiment technology, micro-electronics and fabrication processes, and the availability of wireless power delivery leading towards miniaturized implantable sensors.

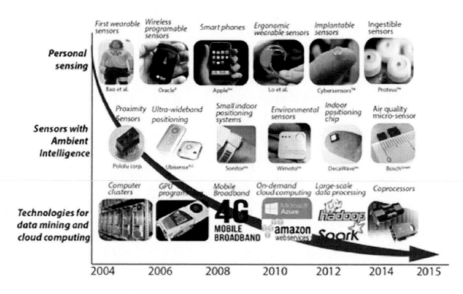

Fig. 1 Evolution of the allied technologies for pervasive healthcare in recent years.

From a clinical perspective, the evolution of each generation of pervasive health has been enabled by a sequence of technological steps towards integrated care, bridging the gap between health and disease management. From a technical standpoint, there is still a need for horizontal advances within each generation with the finality of improving device quality. However, vertical developments may bring an entirely new generation of low-powered wearable sensing devices and smart implants that are low drift, resistant to biofouling, and can be effortlessly implanted and extracted when no longer necessary.

Unique challenges towards personalized healthcare include long-term continuous sensing, intelligent interpretation and timely intervention, which in turn presents a myriad of opportunities for sensor informatics. Future research will also need to focus on integrating large data sets from heterogeneous sources including pervasive health data. If overcome, these technical challenges are set to transform our understanding of healthcare delivery. Big data mining and social network analysis provide new ways of managing global epidemics such as Ebola, accelerate warning systems, incorporating geographic location systems to track cases and systematize outbreak response. All of this can be translated into a new era for medicine, moving from a reactive to a proactive discipline.

# References

1. J. Andreu-Perez, D.R. Leff, H.M. Ip, G.Z-. Yang, "From Wearable Sensors to Smart Implants – Towards Pervasive and Personalised Healthcare", IEEE Transactions in Biomedical Engineering, [In press], 2015.
2. G.Z-. Yang, "Body Sensor Networks", 2nd ed., Springer, Germany, 2014. For the full version of this article, please see: J. Andreu-Perez, D.R. Leff, H.M. Ip, G.Z-. Yang, "From Wearable Sensors to Smart Implants – Towards Pervasive and Personalised Healthcare", IEEE Transactions in Biomedical Engineering, 2015.

# Connecting Implantable Devices - The Next Iteration of Wearables?

-ALISA NIKSCH

Wearable technology has highlighted the potential for medical devices to be both connected and personal. Patient generated data now plays a role in transforming disease management. However, the market has shown mixed signals for the long term adherence and success of fitness wearables. Despite a Pew research survey showing that 62% of individuals with 2 or more chronic conditions will track symptoms, a high rate of attrition in usage of fitness wearables has become a significant concern for the advancement of this model for remote patient monitoring. (http://www.pewinternet.org/files/old-media//Files/Reports/ 2013/PIP_TrackingforHealth%20with%20appendix.pdf)

Wearable devices focused on medical needs, on connecting patients to clinicians and caregiver support to optimize management strategies, are just being explored. Needs for continuous data trending and optimal compliance from the user has prompted further exploration on the form and function of wearables, including making them a permanent or semi-permanent implanted device.

## Why Implantables?

Implantables are probably the extreme iteration of what we know as wearable technology today. Implantables have the potential to extract a continuous stream of data without any action required on the part of the user. As voiced by David Lee Scher, MD, Associate Professor of Medicine at Penn State College of Medicine and Director, DLS Healthcare Consulting, "The advantage of implantables addresses a fundamental desire of the user for convenience, and provides multiple accurate, real time data points for providers."

Platforms utilizing the power of smartphones, cloud-based data storage, and machine learning can enable earlier detection of clinical changes in patients battling chronic disease states. With digitally connected implantable devices, the challenge of active compliance is obviated, and there is no requirement to incorporate a reward-for-behavior change feedback loop into a mostly passive system. However, there is debate whether taking away a feedback loop with passive data feeds erodes patient engagement in other ways. In addition to the Pew Research data from 2013, there is evidence from research done through IMS Health (IIHI_Patient_Adoption_of_mHealth.pdf) that having a physician involved in the prescription and follow up of a mobile health tool can vastly improve retention above and beyond industry averages (Figure 1). However, there clearly remains significant uncertainty whether digital health platforms, including wearables, will have the long term stickiness needed to effect better health behaviors.

## Top Apps Average Fill Rate and Average Sustain Rate

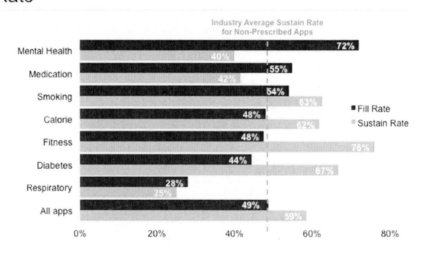

Source: IMS Health, AppScript, July 2015; IMS Institute for Healthcare Informatics, August 2015

IMS INSTITUTE
FOR
HEALTHCARE INFORMATICS

It goes without saying that implantation of a device into a human subject for biometric tracking would imply a compelling medical indication. Implantable medical devices which deliver therapy in response to sensory data have a rich history and well established precedents, most of which have not leveraged IoT-based transmission of health data. For instance, the cochlear implant was the model of neuromodulation in its earliest implanted form. Neuromodulation has expanded its use to include chronic pain management, migraine therapy, GI motility and bladder neurostimulation. Implantables are under investigation for other clinical challenges such as diabetes control, Parkinson's Disease symptom control (http://www.ninds.nih.gov/disorders/deep_brain_stimulation/deep_brain_stimulation.htm), and elevations in intracranial pressure after traumatic brain injury. Medtronic formed a partnership with Samsung in 2015 to integrate digital health solutions into their insulin pumps and expanding to their battery of neuromodulation devices (http://www.fiercemedicaldevices.com/story/medtronic-samsungpartner-develop-neuromodulation-implants-apps-smart-devic/2015-12-11). DARPA has even invested in this space, recently receiving $78.9 million to develop a microimplant series called "ElectRx" for neuromodulation of biological functions (http://www.extremetech.com/extreme/188908-darpas-tiny-implantswill-hook-directly-into-your-nervous-system-treat-diseasesand-depression-without-medication).

Implantable devices with diagnostic and therapeutic capabilities have matured in certain fields like cardiology and neurology more rapidly than others. Areas such as orthopedics, with vast numbers of joint replacement procedures annually, are ripe for leveraging available biosensors to maximize the value of the implant to the recipient. With over 7 million Americans living with a hip or knee replacement (http://www.ncbi.nlm.nih.gov/pubmed/26333733), the prospect for making these devices digitally active is incredibly enticing.

# History Of Implantable Technology For Remote Patient Monitoring

The most relevant discussion of the history of remote patient monitoring through implantable technology centers on the remote monitoring systems connected to implantable cardiac devices, including pacemakers and cardiac defibrillators. These systems, now adopted around 15 years ago by all four major cardiac device manufacturers, have produced significant changes in healthcare utilization within their patient populations. Using manufacturer specific mobile units, active or passive transmission of detailed device data can occur (Crossely GH, et al. Clinical benefits of remote versus transtelephonic monitoring of implanted pacemakers. J Am Coll Cardiol 2009; 54:2012–9). Confirming earlier studies, in 2010 the CONNECT (Clinical Evaluation of Remote Notification to Reduce Time to Clinical Decision, J Am Coll Cardiol 2011;57:1181–9) trial demonstrated that wireless remote monitoring allowed clinicians to make treatment decisions 17.4 days sooner than with in-office visits alone. There was also a statistically significant decrease in mean length of stay for cardiac related diagnoses from 4 days in the in-office group to 3.3 days in the remote monitoring group. Also in 2010, the ALTITUDE Trial was published, examining the survival rates for wirelessly connected patients with implanted devices vs. those only seen in a clinician office. For the 69,556 implantable defibrillator (ICD) patients receiving remote follow up on the network, 1 and 5 year survival rates were higher compared with those in the 116,222 patients who received device follow-up in clinics only (Saxon LA, et al. Long-term outcome after ICD and CRT implantation and influence of remote device follow-up: the ALTITUDE survival study. Circulation 2010;122:2359–67). Potentially the most important factor to physicians, in 2006 the Centers for Medicare and Medicaid Services (CMS) approved structured billing codes for these procedures, incentivizing broader adoption of wireless remote monitoring (Kalahasty G, et al. A brief history of remote cardiac monitoring. Card Electrophysiol Clin. Sept 2013; 5 (3): 275-282).

This prototypical model of remote monitoring associated with implantable device systems has vast implications for developers of other mobile health technologies, as examples of digital recording, storage, transmission, and data analysis. Simply the burden of the number of study subjects involved in validating the wirelessly connected model should give pause to developers of digital platforms. However, passive data acquisition, with evolution of continuous wireless data transmission from device to database, mitigates much of the compliance issue. Automation of alerts built around preprogrammed algorithms rounded out this system to improve provider response to patient needs. Perhaps most importantly, all of this concluded with a reimbursement strategy. What has been lacking, however, is patient access to data from implantable cardiac devices. This has been contested by patient advocates such has Hugo Campos, who recently shared his story with Slate.com (http://www.slate.com/articles/

technology/future_tense/2015/03/patients_should_be_allowed_to_access_
data_generated_by_implanted_devices.html). Future implantable devices,
while drawing on the precedent of cardiac devices, likely have  consumer
pressure to connect the user to data obtained by the device. However, the
path towards this conclusion will require some intelligent and discerning
steps geared towards the interests of several invested parties.

## Device and Accessory Regulation

Regulation of medical devices, especially when implanted in a human
subject, is a complex process which has been fully elaborated in texts
outside of this one. However, wirelessly connected implantable devices
have only been recently explored by the FDA in a systematic way. The FDA
has approved wireless services associated with medical devices in the past,
mostly developed by large manufacturers such as Medtronic (http://www.
medscape.com/viewarticle/783361; http://www.diabetesincontrol.com/
new-product-medtronicscarelink-pro-30/). However, the universe of IoT
connectivity and mobile device has expanded much more quickly than
regulatory agencies have had to evaluate their safety. Finally, in January
2015, FDA issued draft guidance that would permit device accessories
(including linked software platforms) to be classified at a lower risk
than their associated hardware devices. Accessories are defined in two
categories: (i) one in which the article is labeled and branded to indicate
use with the parent medical device; or, (ii) the article is intended for
support, supplement, or augment the function of a parent medical device.
(http://www.fda.gov/downloads/medicaldevices/
deviceregulationandguidance/guidancedocuments/ ucm429672.pdf)

In the universe of digital health, the development of software platforms
associated with wearable devices meant for diagnostic purposes or which
provide treatment algorithms would mostly fall into the first category. It
is acknowledged by the FDA that the risk profile of the device accessory
may have a very different risk profile, and would undergo a different
pathway for review. It can be expected that the targeted patient population,
and the complexity of the data analysis and automation will influence
the requirements for regulatory process. As is increasingly recognized,
proving validity of a connected device platform will require demonstration
of selected outcomes in real-world user cohorts. Without these, certain
functionalities of the software may be restricted for clinical use. Deborah
Kilpatrick, PhD, CEO of Evidation Health, anticipates this development.

She states, "We use linked medical, behavioral and contextual datasets to define "digitally-enabled" health outcomes in a patient population. That approach theoretically holds for any connected device. One the other hand, it could depend on how the connected, behavioral data feed is used. If its source is a clinical-grade wearable being used by a physician to manage care, there could be differentiating regulatory drivers of how such data feeds would be handled to measure patient benefit."

As a final point, it is important to mention that the FDA has not made demonstration of data security a prerequisite for digital health IT platforms; it has up to this point laid the responsibility for implementing security measures for a medical device on the manufacturer itself. One may argue that given the growing impact of IoT in medical device and wearable platforms, a greater oversight of this aspect of product development may emerge in the near future.

## Security Issues

"The biggest vulnerability was the perception of IT health care professionals' beliefs that their current perimeter defenses and compliance strategies were working when clearly the data state otherwise."

FBI Advisory, April 8th, 2014—PIN# 140408-009

The security of connected implantable devices is a potentially devastating concern (Blake, A. Medical devices too prone to hackers, researchers say. Washington Times, August 6, 2015).

While most of the hardware and software pairings may not contain security flaws leading to adverse health effects on the user, there are often links to protected health information (PHI) which can be lucrative to the opportunistic hacker. Neither the FDA nor HIPAA policy focuses on IT security. Names, dates of birth, home or email addresses and even social security numbers can be extracted from hacked medical records. It has been reported that private medical information is 10 times more valuable than a credit card number (http://www.reuters.com/article/us-cybersecurityhospitals-idUSKCN0HJ21I20140924), the temptation to sell private information found in health records is real and is growing.

When former U.S. Vice President Dick Cheney had the battery of his implantable cardiac defibrillator replaced in 2007, physicians made the decision to disable the wireless capabilities of his device because of of his device because of plausible security threats (http://www.cnn.com/2013/10/20/us/dick-cheney-guptainterview/). The possibility of a terrorist breach of implantable cardiac devices was then resurrected in a 2014 episode of the Showtime series Homeland (https://www.newscientist.com/article/mg22429942-600-murder-by-hackable-implants-nolonger-a-perfect-crime/). According to medical device and healthcare security experts Scott Erven and Shawn Merdinger speaking at DefCon, the world's largest hacking conference in August 2014, the digitalization of medical devices has exposed hospitals and patients to increasing rates of security breaches and interference with medical device function. Using open source reconnaissance tools, the pair was able to gain swift access to over 100 credentials used to manipulate the function of common medical devices manufactured at GE Healthcare and Phillips, just to name a few. They disclosed their successful breaches to ICS-CERT, a unit operating under the U.S. Homeland Security Department to coordinate government, law enforcement, and industry entities to mitigate cyber security emergencies. While many of these breaches did not directly endanger patient well-being, the impact on future risk assessment of any digitally connected implantable medical device was not lost on these experts.

Security breaches in the software component of medical devices may be due to fixed manufacturer-created passwords, patient data transmitted across improperly secured networks, and software security flaws which are replicated faster than they can be repaired (https://ics-cert.uscert. gov/sites/default/files/Monitors/ICS-CERT_Monitor_%20Jan-April2014.pdf). Many security vulnerabilities are notoriously found in the linkage of new health IT software to legacy systems within medical centers and other healthcare enterprises. While hackers looking at connected implantables may only have the intention of pilfering demographic information for a quick payoff, the potential is clearly there for more nefarious activity.

## The Design Challenge

The design cycle for implantable medical devices has proven to be a lengthy and challenging one. Hardware design protocols have focused on absolute size, battery life, incorporation of wireless capabilities, and reduction in risk of the implant process. However, the addition of wireless connectivity and the IoT revolution have created another design challenge—one that puts the patient in the center of the healthcare data matrix. Software platforms which communicate with implanted hardware will be increasingly operated by the patient. What is seen, what response is provoked, and how the system finds value in a person's lifestyle are items which cannot be assumed by digital health companies.

Enter a new outlook from design experts now exploring the ecosystem surrounding digital health technologies. Karten Design, a product design consultancy in Marina Del Rey, CA, has taken the plunge to make connected implantable devices seamless for patients and clinicians, and ultimately successful for manufacturers. Stuart Karten, Principal at Karten Design, has made it the company's priority to support patient experience and address the needs of in-home caregivers, a group he feels is an underserved population within healthcare. "Our goal is to make the product blend invisibly with the lifestyle patients have. We want to transform data into information—information implies a value to the user", Karten explains.

Companies like Endotronix, which has developed an implantable sensor to track pulmonary artery pressure as a marker for congestive heart failure management, have leveraged this kind of expertise to develop their digital platforms. In the case of Endotronix, a portable handheld reader and a streamlined user interface was developed to make acquisition and utilization of patient generated data easy and effective.

Design of the interface with connected implantable devices is an enormous key to adoption. Patients must find these platforms simple and convenient to operate. The design of the hardware and software needs to account for the lifestyle and limitations of the likely end user demographic. Even though most noninvasive wearable technologies are marketed towards consumers in their 20's and 30's, 53% of study subjects involved in research of mHealth tools were seniors (Figure 2). The time and effort required for remote monitoring, data review and communication on the part of the patient must outweigh time and effort for traditional calls and visits with caregivers and clinicians. The data presented must be valuable and unobscured by extraneous features to both patient and clinician, essential to usability. As Karten expressed, "The biggest false assumption is that physicians will be looking at this information all the time—there is a lack of understanding of where this technology fits into a clinical workflow." Finally, while implantable devices partly remove the need for a patient feedback loop for participation in health management, an effective digital interface can further engage patients in their treatment plan. In the future, if digital health devices evolve in a more implantable direction, smart design will make these tools not just an optional accessory, but an integral part of the user's health, even part of their identity.

# The Road to Commercialization

Commercialization of implantable devices as an extension of the wearables market must address all of these rapidly evolving topics. In addition to this, how a wearable digital health product achieves adoption by multiple parties in the healthcare ecosystem must be seen strategically and thoughtfully. While wearable technology has been made feasible by the incredible advancement of biosensors and wireless communication, a successful product cannot thrive on the sophistication of the tech alone.

Virtually no one disagrees that the patient is the focal point in the development of a diagnostic or therapeutic device. Even more consideration for safety and risk is deserved when the device is invasive. The invasive nature of any device requires that both patient and physician must be persuaded that the implantation of the device garners more benefit than risk to the patient. As physicians are inextricably linked to the process of implantation, as well as the fallout from any complications, they will naturally voice the most skepticism toward these technologies. Questions will arise as to what training and quality assurance is needed for clinicians to safely implant and manage a device.

## Makeup of Patients Enrolled in mHealth App Clinical Trials

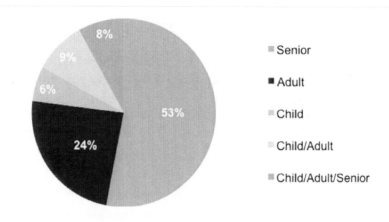

Source: Clinicaltrials.gov, June 2015; IMS Institute for Healthcare Informatics, August 2015

IMS INSTITUTE
HEALTHCARE INFORMATICS

Clinical trials using wearable technology, with questions directed at what benefit is gained from an implantable model, will need to be conducted with likely significant investment of time and finances. It is worth reiterating that the ALTITUDE implantable defibrillator trial, conducted simply to demonstrate the benefit of wireless data transmission, enrolled 185,778 subjects to support the final outcome. The scale of what may be needed to support manufacturer claims should not be underestimated.

The value of the digital platforms connected to these devices will also be a challenge for some physicians to accept. Physicians are already overwhelmed with data from EHRs and various other databases, and don't feel that more data equals useful data (http://www.npr.org/sections/health-shots/2015/01/19/377486437/sure-you-can-track-your-health-databut-can-your-doctor-use-it). Data as presented to medical personnel has made a poor first impression. The power of data for examining population health and providing preemptive treatment based on clinical markers has not diffused extensively into the wider medical community. Dr.Joseph Kvedar, Vice President of Connected Health, Partners Healthcare and Associate Professor at Harvard Medical School, agrees that physicians will be the most difficult to win over. But this is not always the fault of the developers. While data supporting the use of a connected device or software platform is important, Kvedar states, "Sometimes physicians don't think creatively, and resist the insights that data analytics could provide." This being said, the ability to sell to physicians and medical enterprises will often require an appeal to the hardware's ability to intervene and the software's capability of averting the intervention through intelligent data interpretation.

Device development often has a prolonged cycle, whether from an investigational or regulatory standpoint. With the complexities involved in an implanted medical device, the resources needed to conduct adequate studies on the technology and design concept, as well as the capital needed for the regulatory process, often weeds out the smaller scale entrepreneur. There are certainly notable exceptions which have thus far overcome these obstacles, notably Endotronix (heart failure management), Axonics, Inc. (neuromodulation for urinary incontinence), Dexcom, Inc. (connected continuous glucose monitor for diabetes) and the Pulsante SPG Microstimulator (migraine and cluster headaches). However, the larger device companies (e.g., Medtronic, St. Jude Medical, Boston Scientific) continue to dominate the cardiovascular, neuromodulation, and diabetes implant market, with progressive adoption of wireless connectivity and mobile health tools to improve convenience and accessibility of data for patients and clinicians. They have also been able to successfully lobby the Center for Medicare and Medicaid Services (CMS) for new procedure codes to gain reimbursement, a big obstacle in the commercialization of digital health tools. The chronic care management reimbursement code allowing for remote encounters implemented in January 2015 has also been an encouraging measure. There are still, however, large gaps in payment for even the most standard device monitoring, both in the U.S. and Europe (http://europace.oxfordjournals.org/content/17/5/814).

This being said, there is a question whether creating a de novo implantable product is always the best pathway to creating disruption in the wearable market. It already has been mentioned that the orthopedic surgery field would be a growth market for biosensors. Already, small populations have been studied with gyroscopes and accelerometers for gait analysis and assessment of recovery after knee replacement in the UK (Kwasnicki, RM, et al. Int J Surg. 2015 Jun; 18: 14-20). The potential to scale these technologies in existing implanted devices is certainly worth exploring, and may be a wise next step in mitigating risk.

# The Future of Implantables

The technology at the foundation of wearable health devices has been a source of hope for transforming the way we manage the most challenging and costly medical conditions people experience. The union of medical devices, digital connectivity, and IoT access can provide more value, more directly, to people suffering from chronic disease. Implantable devices have gravitated initially towards the cardiovascular and neuromodulation spaces, with some more recent advances in diabetes management. With increasing investigation into the benefits of digital connectivity of such devices, findings of decreased rates of hospitalization, decreased time to clinical interventions, and increased patient satisfaction are supporting further deployment of wirelessly enabled devices.

There continue to be obstacles to building, developing, researching, securing and selling the value of new connected implantable devices. The invasiveness issue is certainly the elephant in the room when it comes to discussing these technologies, especially if similar or equivalent data can be acquired using less invasive (and cheaper) methods. Another alternative is to examine existing devices which could be fit with specific biosensor technology, which is a strategy supported by Dr. Joseph Kvedar, "Sensors are getting better and more versatile...I would support more of an augmented version of devices which would already be implanted in patients."

The future of connected implantable device technology is complex. Implanted devices naturally lend themselves to certain medical specialties, and the extraction of granular, real time data using digital connectivity increases their value proposition. Other tracking of clinical data may not justify an implant due to a risk-benefit imbalance. However, the potential of digital technology and smart data analytics to provide better health outcomes and contain costs is impressive, and is being demonstrated in health care systems every day. As stated by Deborah Kilpatrick, "I do believe it is a question of "when", not "if", when it comes to new, digitallyenabled outcomes---and they will impact our understanding of how therapeutic devices work in the real world."

**Chapter 13**

# Roundtable Discussion: The Outlook for Wearables and the IoT in Healthcare

# Editor's Note

**Movie 8: Continuing the Conversation**
https://vimeo.com/156578369

Looking ahead, the Implantables and the IoT hold great promise, yet business, policy, and technical challenges must be tackled before these devices and systems are fully embraced. Early adopters will need to prove that the new sensor-driven business models deliver value and efficiency. Industry groups and government regulators must architect rules on data privacy and data security that span multiple information infrastructures, ranging from the individual to the networked enterprise. On the technology side, the cost of sensors and actuators must fall to levels that will spark widespread use. Networking technologies and the standards that support them must evolve to the point where data can flow freely among sensors, computers, and actuators. Software to aggregate and analyze data, as well as graphic display techniques, must improve to the point where huge volumes of data can be absorbed by human decision makers or synthesized to guide automated systems more appropriately.

In the following pages we complete our discussion with our roundtable of wearable and IoT thought leaders, who share their perspectives on the opportunities, obstacles, and trajectory of these hyper fueled technologies.

-Rick Krohn

# Video Interviews

https://vimeo.com/157308924

Daniel Kraft

**Question 1: What kind of wearables have you used and if you don't use them what's your best use case for wearables?**

https://vimeo.com/157308924

Matthew Holt

**Question 2: Has the Internet of Things and wearables changed your work or if not how is the Internet of Things (IoT) been implemented in your work settings?**

https://vimeo.com/157308924

Lisa Suennen

**Question 3: A lot of investment is being funneled into the wearables market and a lot of product failures are going to take place. What are the key ingredients for success of a wearables product or service?**

https://vimeo.com/157308924

Donald Jones

**Question 4: What are the main obstacles facing the clinical adoption of wearables, integration with existing systems, regulations including the FDA, economics such as value based payments or utility-issues like user fatigue and what about standards? And as for the Internet of Things, what about regulation, the FTC or security, HIPAA and high tech?**

https://vimeo.com/157308924

**Question 5: Looking ahead, how do you see the wearables Internet of Things and market evolving?**

# Contributors

# Bill Ash
## IEEE-SA Strategic Technology Program Manager

Bill Ash is the Strategic Technology Program Director for IEEE-SA. He received his BSEE from Rutgers University School of the Engineering. His background is in the RFindustry as he worked as applications engineer on wireless communications systems. Bill has been with the IEEE Standards Association (IEEE-SA) for over 12 years working with standards development groups covering technologies such as RF emissions, distributive generation and the National Electrical Safety Code®. He is currently leading the eHealth, smart grid , and smart cities, for the IEEE-SA.

# Jeff Brandt

Jeff is background encompasses a unique combination of disciplines in healthcare, security and Computer Science. He's developed multiple healthcare products. His passion is secure connectivity and healthcare. Jeff participated in the development of multiple mHealth platforms and Apps. Susannah Fox, CTO of HHS once introduced Jeff as one of the pioneers in mHealth.

Jeff is a Manager, of Healthcare IoT and Security at Accenture. His undergrad degree is in Computer Scientist and his post-graduate work in Bio-medical Informatist at Oregon Health Science University, School of Medicine.

His career has been focused around secure communication in both mobile and data. He developed one of the very first secure Personal Health Records (PHR) for the iPhone and Android. He started his security work in online payments for retail and music industry. He also co-wrote multiple books and publications on mHealth and security.

Jeff states that he is a calculated risk taker and adventurer, he has traveled extensively and worked in other countries and once quit his job to go Jeff Brandt sailing with my wife.

# Lynne A. Dunbrack
### Research Vice President

Lynne Dunbrack is Research Vice President for IDC Health Insights responsible for the research operations for IDC Health Insights. She manages a group of analysts who provide research-based advisory and consulting services for payers, providers, accountable care organizations, IT service providers, and the IT suppliers that serve those markets. Lynne also leads the IDC Health Insights' Connected Health IT Strategies program. Specific areas of Lynne's in-depth coverage include mobile, constituency engagement, interoperability, health information exchange, Internet of Things (IoT), telehealth and virtual care, cybersecurity, privacy and security.

Lynne has been quoted by national media outlets such as The Wall Street Journal, Investor's Business Daily, The New York Times, Forbes, and San Jose Business Journal. She also speaks regularly at industry conferences.

Lynne holds a B.A. from the College of the Holy Cross, and an M.B.A. with a concentration in healthcare management and an M.S. in Management Information Systems from Boston University's Graduate Lynne A. Dunbrack School of Management.

# Anand K. Iyer, Ph.D., MBA
## Chief Data Science Officer

As Chief Data Scientist for WellDoc, Anand leads complex analyses from WellDoc's mobile diabetes platform, BlueStar®, to inform, discover, and extrapolate patterns that help adapt the product to enhance patient engagement and outcomes.

Earlier, as President and COO, he oversaw the creation of WellDoc's mobile- and web- based chronic disease platforms and managed the regulatory submissions to the FDA. He is also leading WellDoc's globalization efforts and programs.

A Type-2 diabetic, Iyer is a respected veteran and visionary in the digital health and wireless industries. He was founder of the In-Building Wireless Alliance, was honored as a "Global Top 35" executive in wireless in 2007, and Maryland Healthcare Innovator of the Year, 2013.

He earned an MS and PhD in Electrical and Computer Engineering, and an MBA from Carnegie Mellon University. He is also guest faculty at the Institute for Defense and Business, where he lectures on advanced wireless with Flag Officers across the US Armed Forces. He participated with the NIH on the President's Precision Medicine Initiative, and actively supported the FDA in their role with the International Medical Device Regulators Forum (IMDRF) to create a singular, global perspective on how to develop SaMD, software as a medical device.

# Steve Kastin

Steve Kastin, MD trained as a Nuclear Medicine physician at the Albert Einstein College of Medicine/Montefiore Medical Center in New York City. After joining the Department of Veterans Affairs after residency, Dr. Kastin quickly rose through the ranks to become Director of Diagnostic Services and Director of Clinical Informatics at the Bronx VA Medical Center. Dr. Kastin then went on to become Chief Health Informatics Officer for the VA hospitals in the New York City metro area, then CIO for that group of hospitals. He was then recruited by VA's National Office of Information and Technology, reporting to the Associate Deputy Assistant Secretary for Enterprise Engineering. Dr. Kastin chaired the VA's national Radiology Informatics Committee for many years, and chaired or served on a number of other national clinical and IT-related committees in VA, including the Radiology Field Advisory Group, the Technology Assessment Group, and the Informatics and Data Management Committee. Dr. Kastin most recently headed up all IT and informatics aspects of the VA's $543-million national Real Time Location System (RTLS) program. Dr. Kastin has lectured extensively on Informatics and Health IT-related topics, including health IT security, Electronic Medical Records, RTLS, big data, and the Internet of Things.

# Trey Lauderdale

Trey began his career in the Transmissions and Distribution Business Unit at Florida Power & Light, where he led a team to create a new statistical method for tracking power outages and their correlation with weather patterns in the state of Florida.

In 2005, Trey joined the Sales Leadership and Development Program at Siemens, where he rotated through the inside sales support, product marketing and distribution management teams. At Siemens, Trey was involved in numerous business development projects and helped create a new premier channel program for industrial automation distributors.

Trey joined Emergin in 2007 as Florida Area Sales Manager. He made an immediate impact, and was promoted within six months to Southeast Regional Sales Manager. He was one of the company's top business development employees and the top revenue producer in the first and second quarters of 2008, before he left Emergin to form Voalte.

Trey graduated from the University of Florida with a Bachelor's degree in Industrial Engineering and Minors in Engineering Sales and Electrical Engineering. He earned his Master's degree in Entrepreneurship from the University of Florida Warrington College of Business, where he, along with Oscar Callejas, won the top prize in the school's Business Plan Competition.

While his most gratifying success to date has been as the founder of Voalte, helping grow the company and deploying thousands of iPhone solutions in some of the country's top hospitals, Trey has also been honored with the following awards:

- April 2013: Outstanding Young Alumni, University of Florida Alumni Association
- December 2012: Florida Governor's Innovators in Business Award
- 2010: Gulf Coast Business Review's 40 Under 40

# Thomas Martin

Thomas R. Martin, PhD, MBA, is Director with HIMSS, a global, cause-based, not-for-profit organization focused on better health through information technology (IT) supporting the mHealth Community. Martin also provides support for the HIMSS Health IT Value Suite.

With more than 10 years of experience in healthcare, Martin joins HIMSS from the telecommunications and healthcare IT industries. He has lived and worked overseas in Australia, traveling extensively in Asia Pacific for business. Martin began his journey in healthcare working at the Cleveland Clinic Foundation. He has served as project lead for numerous IT implementations and mobile app developments.

Martin is the author of numerous articles and book chapters on the role of mHealth and the use of Cost Benefit Analysis in healthcare. He completed his dissertation titled Applications of Contingent Valuation and Conjoint Analysis in mHealth: Understanding the Willingness to Pay for Healthcare Smartphone Applications at the University of Delaware. He also holds a Master's degree in Business Administration from the University of Delaware. Dr. Martin's research interests include the application of cost benefit analysis, comparative effectiveness, and other economic valuations within the healthcare setting. He holds academic appointments at Georgetown University and St. Joseph's University.

# Alisa Niksch

Dr. Alisa Niksch is a practicing pediatric cardiologist and Director of Pediatric Electrophysiology at Tufts Medical Center in Boston, MA. During the course of her career, she realized the power of connected medical devices in bringing about better outcomes for her patients. This led to an affinity for digital health and new iterations of medical device design and functionality. She has now performed research or served on the advisory boards of several groundbreaking digital health and medical device startups, contributing ideas for content, algorithm workflow, and hardware design concepts to companies like VerbalCare, Sproutling, AliveCor, and Genetesis. Dr. Niksch has also been an author of manuscripts on digital health published in peer-reviewed journals, and has been lead author on executive briefs on digital health as a member of the Physician Task Force on mHealth at HIMSS. As a part of the physician entrepreneur community in Boston, she has enjoyed being part of the mentorship and organizational team at the Tufts MedStart hackathon and Hacking Pediatrics innovation competitions in Boston, MA.

She is a proud graduate of the University of Virginia School of Medicine. Her training in pediatric cardiology was completed at Morgan Stanley Children's Hospital of New York at Columbia University Medical Center, and she continued her electrophysiology training at Stanford University and UCSF Medical Centers.

# Sally Gallot-Reeves, MSM, CPM, CCM, RM
## Healthcare Project Director Frisbie Memorial Hospital

Sally manages and facilitates complex system installations, electronic documentation, space design and move planning, and process and workflow improvements. She is a Registered Nurse who holds a Master's Degree in Management, a Bachelor's Degree in Behavior, and Certifications in Project Management and Change Management. She is the former Director of Critical Care and Cardiovascular Services. Sally is also Executive Director and owner of Connect the Dots (www.ctdnow. com), a consulting firm that provides solution resources for healthcare professionals. She recently published a book, Between Shifts, a series of vignettes in poetry depicting a camera's-eye view into the healthcare worlds of conflicts and compassion, love, life and death, growth and understanding.

# Pouya Shoolizadeh

Pouya Shoolizadeh received his Doctorate of Medicine (M.D.) from the University of Central Florida College of Medicine in 2016 during which he was the co-founder and Chief Technology Officer of the student run organization Healthcare Innovations. He received his Master's degree in singlemolecule nanotechnology from University of Oxford in 2011, and before that his Bachelor's degree in Molecular and Cellular Biochemistry from University of Oxford in 2010, during which he was an executive board member of the Oxford University Scientific Society. In the near future he will be starting his residency position as a physician specializing in Neurology.

# Skip Snow

The business models fundamental to healthcare are under transformation, and software is a key differentiator determining which healthcare businesses succeed in the 21st century. Skip has spent the bulk of his career in the trenches making them happen.

With over 20 years of professional technology experience and 15 years of increasing management responsibility, he brings risk management skills and plenty of enthusiasm to the table. Experienced in working with and managing global teams delivering complex solutions on time and within budget he currently works as an industry analyst thinking writing and advising others how to get this done.

In the last four years, he delivered multiple consumer-facing solutions to companies such as Johnson & Johnson and Zappos, IMS Health and LexisNexis, and architected and managed the building of major back-end systems.

As the vice president for information and technology architecture at Kaiser Permanente, he was the steward for the technology project components for major innovations. Called on to solve the difficult problems associated with enhancing the information systems of the largest nonprofit healthcare provider in the U.S.

# Paul P. Szotek, Jr., M.D.

Dr. Szotek holds degrees from the Indiana University, Bloomington and the Indiana University School of Medicine. He completed his General Surgery residency at the Indiana University School of Medicine in Indianapolis, Indian. Dr. Szotek is board certified in General Surgery by the American Board of Surgery.

Dr. Szotek completed a Research Fellowship at the Pediatric Surgical Research Laboratories at Harvard/Massachusetts General Hospital, Boston, MA. During his time in Boston under the mentorship of Patricia Donahoe, MD, he performed stem cell research and had the privilege of performing and authoring the first peer reviewed publication describing and identifying ovarian cancer stem cells.

Since his return to Indiana University Health in 2012, Dr. Szotek has been an active member of the Trauma and Acute care surgery program and is developing the abdominal wall reconstruction program. He is an active member of the American Hernia Society and is a frequent speaker of the uses of fluorescence angiography in acute care surgery. In February 2014, Dr. Szotek performed the first surgery in Indiana utilizing Google Glass technology and is developing wearable technology for use in all aspects of medicine. Dr.Szotek is a co-founder and the immediate past-present of the Wearable Technology in Healthcare (WATCH) Society. He is currently developing telementoring applications for wearable technology in training for both students and professionals alike.

# Contact Us

**Movie 9: Continuing the Conversation**
https://vimeo.com/156578369

We hope you enjoyed Connected Health: Improving Care, Safety, and Efficiency with Wearables and IoT

For more information please contact:

**Rick Krohn**
rkrohn@healthsen.com
(912)220-6563

**David Metcalf, UCF**
dmetcalf@ist.ucf.edu
(407)882-1496
Twitter: @dmetcalf

# Index